T

10.99.

OXFORD REVISION GUIDES

AS & A Level

GOVERNMENT & POLITICS
through diagrams

Paul Fairclough

OXFORD
UNIVERSITY PRESS

OXFORD
UNIVERSITY PRESS

Great Clarendon Street, Oxford OX2 6DP

Oxford University Press is a department of the University of Oxford.
It furthers the University's objective of excellence in research,
scholarship, and education by publishing worldwide in

Oxford New York

Auckland Bangkok Buenos Aires Cape Town Chennai
Dar es Salaam Delhi Hong Kong Istanbul Karachi Kolkata
Kuala Lumpur Madrid Melbourne Mexico City Mumbai Nairobi
São Paulo Shanghai Singapore Taipei Tokyo Toronto

with an associated company in Berlin

Oxford is a registered trade mark of Oxford University Press
in the UK and in certain other countries

British Library Cataloguing in Publication Data

Data available

ISBN 0 19 913434 0

10 9 8 7 6 5 4 3 2 1

For Clare, Adele and Felicity

Typeset by Fakenham Photosetting Limited, Fakenham, Norfolk

Printed in Great Britain ·

Acknowledgements

p 24 Press Association (top), Associated Press (centre and bottom);
p 25 Press Association (top), NI Syndication/Peter Brookes/The Times,
London 26 Oct 2001 (bottom); p 27 BBC Picture Archives; p 40 Press
Association; p 43 Press Association; p 44 Press Association; p 45 Press
Association; p 63 Museum of City of New York/Corbis (top),
Bettmann/Corbis (bottom); p 70 Corbis; p 73 Wally McNamee/Corbis (left),
Nailah Feanny-Hicks/Corbis/SABA (right).

Artwork by Angela Lumley

Cover photo by FPG International/Getty Images

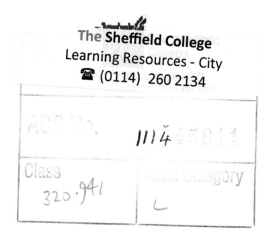

Contents

Contents (cont.)

How to revise

'I have so many notes. Where should I start with my revision?'

The first thing that you need to do is to get hold of the **subject specification** (this is what used to be called the syllabus). Your teacher might have given you this at the start of the course and it is important that you have a look at it because it tells you what the examiners expect you to know. If you cannot get this information from your teacher, look on the Examination Board websites. AQA, OCR and EdExcel all have websites containing **downloadable versions of their specifications**. Some boards also produce a **Teacher's Guide**. This gives more detailed information about the areas which teachers need and do not need to cover. You could talk to your teacher about this; they may be able to give you some useful tips. You will also need copies of **past papers** so that you can familiarise yourself with the type of questions that you will be facing. You will also need to work out a **revision timetable**. This should incorporate all of your subjects and be broken down into focused sessions of around 45 minutes divided by breaks. These breaks are important. If you leave no time for relaxation you will be less likely to keep to the timetable and your revision will be less effective.

'I have the specification and the past papers and a revision timetable that is *do-able*. What next?'

Using the information from the Politics specification for the modules that you have studied, go through your folder and divide up your notes between the different modules. It might help you to photocopy the page(s) which give the content for each module and then put the relevant photocopy on the top of each pile of notes. When this is done you should have several piles of notes, each one relating to a single module, each with a photocopy showing what you should have covered on the top of the pile. The next task is to check your notes to make sure that you have covered all of the things on the specification. Are there big gaps? It may be that you have 'mislaid' some notes, or that you missed some lessons and failed to catch up. Alternatively, your teacher might have left out certain sections with good reason. Check it out. Make sure that you are not missing something vital.

'What about actual revision?'

Look at the specification content and the past examination papers for each module. Which questions do you feel fairly confident about tackling? Which make you want to retreat to your bed with a packet of biscuits? However tempting it is to start your revision with the topics you feel happy with, it really is better to grasp the nettle and address your weaknesses first. Once you have identified these weaker areas, you need to go through making summary notes. Try – if you can – to get each small topic onto a single page. This process of summarising should eventually leave you with a much less daunting set of memory-jogging revision notes. If the exam is still some way off, you may even have time to reinforce any particularly thin sections of notes or, if the problem is largely down to a lack of understanding, seek individual help from your teacher. Above all, remember that this book is only a revision *guide*. It is not a *substitute* for revision.

You must avoid at all costs:

1. **Staying at home when you should be at school attending the revision lessons that your teachers have organised.** *You may feel that you can 'do a better job yourself' but, in my experience, the vast majority of students who adopt this approach do not achieve their potential. However pointless the school revision lessons may seem to you, they are probably helping you more than you realise.*
2. **Revising for hours without a break or working for whole days on a single subject.** *A series of 45-minute sessions followed by 15-minute breaks can lead to more productive work and it is good to build some daily variety into your revision programme.*
3. **Question spotting.** *Although it is good to look at the kinds of questions that have turned up in the past, question spotting (trying to guess what the examiners will put on the exam paper) is a dangerous game.*
4. **Leaving out major topics.** *Leaving topics out when you revise can be disastrous. In my work as an examiner I have marked examination scripts where extremely intelligent candidates have scored 35/40 on one question, only to get 12/40 in the other question because they had clearly not revised the topic.*

'How should I set out my revision notes?'

Try presenting your notes in different formats. This book, for example, presents the information in the form of diagrams. You could try turning these diagrams into prose or into bullet-pointed lists. Equally, try turning some of your own hand-written notes into diagrams, to supplement the ones here. You will find that the very process of reformatting your notes in this way reinforces learning and develops a greater understanding of the material.

Getting started

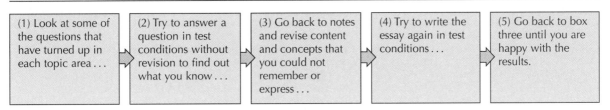

(1) Look at some of the questions that have turned up in each topic area...	(2) Try to answer a question in test conditions without revision to find out what you know...	(3) Go back to notes and revise content and concepts that you could not remember or express...	(4) Try to write the essay again in test conditions...	(5) Go back to box three until you are happy with the results.

On the examination day

The basics

1. **Make sure that you know which examination is on which day.** This might sound obvious but I have known candidates turn up for a British Politics examination thinking that they were about to sit a US paper – and having revised accordingly. It is your responsibility to make sure that you know which exam is on which day. These kinds of mistakes can cost grades.

2. **Make sure that you arrive on time for the examination.** If you arrive hours before the start you will probably get yourself into a state before anyone else arrives. If you arrive at the last minute, or even late, you will probably not be in the best frame of mind to tackle the examination paper.

3. **Bring the correct materials with you.** You should know what you need for the examination. Do not turn up without a pencil if you have spent your whole revision programme planning essays in pencil before you start. On a more serious note, think carefully about what pen you are going to use. I read a recent examiner's report that complained about the difficulty that the examiner had reading 'scratchy blue biro'. I would advise you to use **a black roller ball pen, a black gel pen or a black ink pen**. It would be a shame to lose valuable marks because your words of wisdom could not be read!

Timing

You must be fully aware of the total time available for the examination and the amount of time you have available to complete each question. It can be helpful to make a note of the times at which you should be starting each question at the start of the examination. This will help you to make sure that you do not fall behind schedule.

Question choice

It is tempting to start writing as soon as you open the paper but it is far better to have a good look at all of the questions first to make sure that you haven't missed anything. It might be that the question on the Prime Minister is there after all but that it is just worded unusually. It would be a shame to miss a 'favourite topic' in your rush to get started.

Writing good answers

In the examination you will need to demonstrate a sound understanding of political **theory** and show that you can **apply** this theory to current issues and events. For example, in answering a question on pressure groups you will be expected to know about ways of classifying pressure groups ('sectional/cause', 'insider/outsider' etc.). This is the theory. You will also need to show that you can apply this theory, perhaps by using it to assess the fuel protests, or the work of environmental pressure groups. Where stimulus material (cartoons, tables, extracts from books etc.) appears as part of the question you must make reference to it, where appropriate, putting it into context using your own knowledge of political theory and current affairs.

You must avoid at all costs

1. **Writing answers that ignore the question**
   You must do what is asked of you rather than simply writing what you want to write. If it says 'explain' do not simply 'describe'. If the question asks you to consider a particular period (e.g. the 1990s) then focus on that period rather than reeling-off all of your learnt examples from the 1960s. If you are asked to comment on a piece of stimulus material, do not simply copy out big chunks of it in your answer without comment.

2. **Writing answers that are totally theoretical . . .**
   and making no attempt to apply the theory by using appropriate examples.

3. **Writing answers that simply describe recent events . . .**
   without any attempt to bring in theory. Anyone can do this if they watch the news. You have been studying Politics for at least a year and you should, therefore, be able to bring political theory into your evaluation of events as well as putting these events into their historical context.

4. **Failing to answer the required number of questions or leaving too little time to answer the last question effectively**
   This can be a disaster. You must time yourself properly in the examination. The number of extra marks that you will gain by spending an extra ten minutes on a question that you have already answered well, will not make up for the marks that you lose as a result of your only having 15 minutes left to do the last question. Be strict with yourself!

6

How to answer comparative questions

Ordinary questions requiring comparative material

A lot of the questions that you will be asked to answer in the examination will be focused on a single country. Though you will be given credit for **illustrating your answers with relevant examples from other countries**, the focus will clearly be on one named country. For example:

- In an essay on 'electoral reform in the UK' you might be expected to mention the use of electoral systems in other countries; for example, AMS in Germany or STV in the Republic of Ireland, perhaps even commenting on whether such systems have worked for the countries concerned.

- In an essay on the 'use of referendums in the UK' you might be expected to mention countries that make greater use of referendums such as Switzerland.

This book provides you with the level of information that you need to answer these questions. On topics such as these, where there is an obvious need for comparative material, such material is provided on the relevant page alongside the UK content. Some questions, however, are more explicitly comparative and will require you to use both UK and US pages.

Genuine comparative questions

Whichever specification you are following, it is likely that you will have to face questions that are more explicitly comparative in nature. In the AQA Specification, for example, the whole of Module 4 is Comparative UK/USA Government, and questions will be set accordingly. Genuinely comparative questions are questions where the comparative material is not just there to provide illustrations with which to highlight the UK experience, but where the whole point of the question is to compare the experience in two different countries. For example:

1. Compare and contrast the roles and powers of the British Prime Minister and the US President.
2. Compare the importance of committees within the US Congress to those within the UK Parliament.
3. Would you agree that the elections in the US are decided largely by the same factors that decide elections in the UK?
4. How do UK political parties compare with their US counterparts?

Clearly, answering such questions requires a different approach – but what should it be?

Structuring answers to comparative questions

Structure is the key to answering comparative questions effectively. If we take as an example a comparative question on constitutions, we can illustrate two different approaches, one far better than the other.

Question:
What similarities and differences exist between the constitutions of the US and the UK?

Approach 1			
Candidate introduces topic by defining term 'constitution'. Makes some comments about codified and uncodified constitutions.	Candidate moves on to look at US Constitution and writes two short paragraphs: one on origins and sources and one on principles and main elements.	Candidate moves on to look at UK Constitution and writes two short paragraphs: one on origins and sources and one on principles and main elements.	The candidate concludes, comparing and contrasting the origins, sources and principles of the two constitutions.

Though this approach has some merits (it is, for example, fairly easy to do and allows you to reel off large chunks of pre-learnt material) it is **not really answering the question until the conclusion**. However accurate the answer is in terms of factual content, the candidate **should really be identifying similarities and differences from the start** for two main reasons:
Firstly, it is a higher-level skill than simply telling the examiner everything you know. It will score higher marks; and
Secondly, it is what the question asks candidates to do.

Approach 2		
Candidate provides an outline of the main areas of debate concerning constitutions. Perhaps addresses validity of terms such as codified/ uncodified, flexible/rigid etc.	The candidate writes four paragraphs. The **first** identifies similarities and differences between the origins of the two constitutions; the **second** looks at similarities and differences between the sources of the two constitutions; the **third** considers similarities and differences between the underlying principles of the two constitutions; and the **fourth** deals with main elements.	The candidate highlights the key similarities and differences already identified and offers a final assessment.

This is a far better response because the candidate is identifying similarities and differences from early in the essay. This type of structure also makes it far more difficult for the candidate to drift into lengthy passages of description without addressing the question. It is likely to lead to a more focused, analytical response.

AS/A2 specifications (as of April, 2002)

Introduction

It is very important that you familiarise yourself with the main elements of the specification that **you** are studying – the **content** for each module and the **format of the examination** (the number and type of questions that you will face and how much choice you will have). Your teacher will almost certainly have given you this kind of information at some point. If you do **not** have this information, most of it is available via the internet (see web addresses below).

On these sites you will find full specifications, sample papers and advice for teachers teaching the courses. These Teachers' Guides are worth having a look at because they will give you extra information about what you will be expected to know in the examination. **Remember, this page only provides an outline summary and could be out of date. Make sure that you have up-to-date information.**

The Specifications in outline

AQA www.aqa.org.uk/

AS	Module content	Assessment
Mod 1	Electoral systems and voting behaviour	33.33% of AS (16.67% of A) 1 hour
Mod 2	Parties and pressure groups	33.33% of AS (16.67% of A) 1 hour
Mod 3	Features of a representative democracy	33.33% of AS (16.67% of A) 1 hour

AS	Module content	Assessment
Mod 4	Comparative UK/USA government	15% of A-Level 1½ hours
Mod 5	Either: 1. Politics of the USA; or 2. Politics of Northern Ireland, Scotland and Wales; or 3. Ideas in contemporary British Politics	15% of A-Level 1½ hours
Mod 6	Synoptic module: 1. Power; 2. Participation and representation; 3. Political culture; 4. Continuity and change	20% of A-Level 2 hours Four sections (see left). Answer from one section.

EdExcel www.edexcel.org.uk/

AS	Module content	Assessment
Mod 1	People and Politics	33.33% of AS (16.67% of A) 1 hour
Mod 2	Governing the UK	33.33% of AS (16.67% of A) 1 hour
Mod 3	The changing UK system	33.33% of AS (16.67% of A) 1 hour

NB: for the A2, candidates must follow route a, b, c or d

AS	Module content	Assessment
Mod 4	4a UK political issues 4b Introducing ideologies 4c Representation in the US 4d International Politics	15% A-Level 1¼ hours
Mod 5	5a The EU and European issues 5b Other ideological traditions 5c Governing the USA 5d Issues in international Politics	15% of A-Level 1¼ hours
Mod 6	6a Policy-making in the UK 6b Ideological development in the UK 6c Comparative UK and US Politics 6d International Politics and the UK.	20% of A-Level 1½ hours

OCR www.ocr.org.uk/

AS	Module content	Assessment
Mod 1	Elections, electoral systems and voting behaviour in the UK	30% of AS (15% of A) 1 hour
Mod 2	Politics of the UK	30% of AS (15% of A) 1 hour
Mod 3	Government of the UK	40% of AS (20% of A) 1 hour

NB: for the A2, candidates must follow route a or b

AS	Module content	Assessment
Mod 4	Either: 4a US government and Politics; or 4b Political ideas and concepts	15% A-Level 1½ hours
Mod 5	Either: Government and Politics Research (coursework); or Government and Politics Research (written exam – see right)	15% of A-Level 1½ hours
Mod 6	Either: 4a Government and Politics (US option); or 4b Government and Politics (Political ideas and concepts option)	20% of A-Level 1½ hours

1.1 What is Politics?

Introduction

Within any society there will be conflicts of interests: situations in which individuals within the group might want to 'pull in different directions'. These conflicts might result from:

Scarcity
When there is a shortage of certain goods, conflict will result over the distribution of available resources.

Ideological differences
Individuals might take a radically different view of the way in which society should be organised.

Differences in approach
Individuals might share an ideology but have a different approach in achieving their common goals.

Divisions of labour and power
Individuals might be unhappy about their own position within society. Conflict might result from their desire to challenge the status quo.

The political process is the process by which these conflicts are resolved. Politics is, therefore, a study of conflict resolution. Part of this study must involve the way in which power is divided up between individuals, between individuals and the state, and between the different institutions that make up the state (Parliament, Cabinet, Prime Minister, police etc.) This is Politics on a 'macro' level, but even on a 'micro' level (family, school, friendship groups etc.) political activity is going on because power relationships exist at all of those levels.

In essence, therefore, Politics is about conflict resolution and the distribution of power.

Key terms

Power...
is the ability to do something: the ability to make something happen. Power can exist with or without authority. A bandit with a gun might have power without authority. An armed police officer might have power and authority.

Authority...
is the right to make something happen: the right to take a particular course of action. Authority can exist without much or any power. A teacher, for example, has a certain authority but little real power.

Laws...
are there to regulate society. They should serve to discourage behaviour that is detrimental to the common good and encourage that which is beneficial.

Justice...
is the exercise of authority in a manner that is morally right or fair (just). Many laws are just, but there can be a difference between what is legal and what is just. Consider the actions of Robin Hood!

What kind of activity is political?
Many different kinds of activity can be considered political. For example:

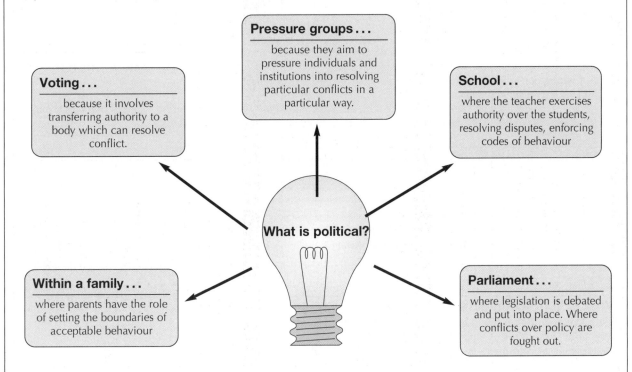

Voting...
because it involves transferring authority to a body which can resolve conflict.

Pressure groups...
because they aim to pressure individuals and institutions into resolving particular conflicts in a particular way.

School...
where the teacher exercises authority over the students, resolving disputes, enforcing codes of behaviour

What is political?

Within a family...
where parents have the role of setting the boundaries of acceptable behaviour

Parliament...
where legislation is debated and put into place. Where conflicts over policy are fought out.

1.2 What is democracy?

Introduction

The term democracy comes from the Greek – *demos* (meaning 'the people') and *kratia* (meaning 'power'). Literally, therefore, democracy is 'rule by the people' or 'people power'. Some argue, however, that the word demos could just as easily be defined as 'the mob'. This would leave democracy as 'mob rule'. John Kingdom sees a natural progression from the 'pure form' of democracy to the corrupt form of mob rule, in the same way that monarchy can descend into tyranny and aristocracy into oligarchy.

As a term, democracy – like 'justice' and 'freedom' – has become so widely misused as to become almost meaningless in itself. More commonly, it is qualified.

Different strands

Many writers draw a distinction between what they call 'representative democracy' and what is known as 'direct democracy'.

What is representative democracy?

Edmund Burke, in a speech to his Bristol constituents in 1774, summed up what many see as the essence of representative democracy in Britain.

'Your representative owes you not his industry only,' Burke noted, 'but his judgement; and he betrays you if he sacrifices it to your opinion.'

The Burkeian view is, therefore, that we elect individuals to represent us in Parliament and other assemblies. They then represent our interests to the best of their ability but they are not delegates sent with specific instructions or orders to follow. As a result, our elected representatives might make decisions which are contrary to our wishes.

V

What is direct democracy?

Direct democracy is said to have its origins in Athens around 500BC, where the 40 000 free men of the city had the right to attend forum meetings at which certain policies could be approved or rejected. The classic modern tool of direct democracy is the referendum. In a referendum voters are asked to voice their view on a particular issue. The result of this vote may be binding or advisory, depending on the nature of the referendum, but the question is normally framed by the government of the day. In some countries initiatives operate alongside referendums. Through an initiative a predetermined number of registered voters can initiate legislation.

Does direct democracy get in the way of representative democracy?

Some argue that referendums and other forms of direct democracy undermine our system of representative democracy. If we elect representatives to act in our best interests, it is argued, they should not have to come back to us on a regular basis to ask us what we want. Indeed, it is bad for them to do so because . . .

- *in doing so it could be argued that they are abdicating their responsibility to govern.*
- *we have elected them as individuals who we believe are capable of judging the issues on our behalf, and they need the space in which they can do this.*
- *our representatives will often have access to a far better body of information on which to make their judgements and a lot more time in which to do it.*
- *people are likely to make decisions which they see as being in their immediate interest, whereas politicians may be able to make decisions which are unpopular but which are in our long-term interests.*

Others argue that such tools of direct democracy actually help strengthen our representative democracy by . . .
- *helping to focus the mandate on particular issues.*
- *refreshing the mandate several years into a Parliament when circumstances might have changed.*
- *legitimising major constitutional changes that might appear to bind future Parliaments and governments and should not, therefore, be made without explicit public approval.*

NB. Referendums are dealt with more comprehensively in Ch 10.3 and Ch 24.4.

What is liberal democracy?

The essence of liberal democracy is limited government. In a liberal democracy the state stands back from the free market and imposes only minimal regulation. It does, however, preserve basic civil rights (expression, assembly, association, movement etc. – see Ch 14) and allow people to vote in regular free and fair elections. The term liberal democracy is applied to many western democracies.

2.1 Conservatism

Introduction
If an ideology is 'a system of ideas at the basis of an economic or political theory' (*Concise Oxford Dictionary*), it could be argued that conservatism is barely an ideology at all, based as it is in a reaction to the changes put forward by other ideologies. Conservatism is based firmly upon pragmatism and the belief in gradual improvements founded on experience and existing institutions, rather than a priori reasoning and radical change.

Approach
As a result of this, conservatives often take a different approach to solving problems than those coming from a more traditionally ideological perspective.

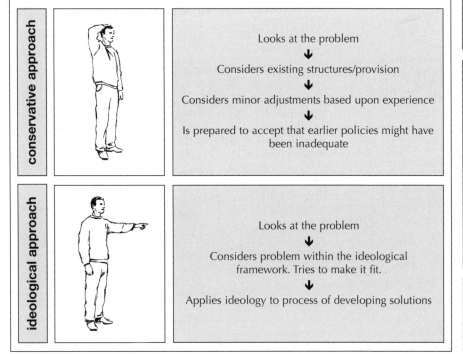

conservative approach

Looks at the problem
↓
Considers existing structures/provision
↓
Considers minor adjustments based upon experience
↓
Is prepared to accept that earlier policies might have been inadequate

ideological approach

Looks at the problem
↓
Considers problem within the ideological framework. Tries to make it fit.
↓
Applies ideology to process of developing solutions

Confusing terms

'conservative'
We often use this term to describe people who are unwilling to change or out of date.

'conservative ideology'
See left: this is a supposedly more coherent approach to directing government policy.

'Conservative'
The capital letter usually denotes a reference to the Conservative Party or its policies/position.

Human nature
This is a phrase used when referring to the natural human state; that is to say, what people are like in their pure state when one removes the influence of the societies in which they live. Some people have a positive view of human nature and believe that society can corrupt individuals. Those with a more pessimistic view would see people as flawed and society as a necessary regulating force.

Paternalism
Where authority is centralised but the state is benevolent; caring for the most needy.

Origins
Modern conservatism dates from the opposition to the popular radicalism prevalent around the time of the French Revolution in the 1790s. It was a reaction first to this radical change and later to liberalism (Ch 2.2) and socialism (Ch 2.3). Writers such as Edmund Burke in his *Reflections on the Revolution in France* (1790) highlighted the dangers of radical change and the need for societies to evolve in order to avoid the emergence of such destructive radicalism.

Conservatism today
Modern conservatism can be divided into two clear strands:

Liberal/libertarian conservatism
For example, the 'New Right' in the UK and US in the 1980s/1990s. In Britain, the advent of Thatcherism and 'neo-liberal' economic policy.

Collectivist/paternalist conservatism
Describing much of the post-war Conservative history in Britain. 'One-nation Tories'. Often marginalised under Thatcher as 'the wets'.

Free market economics ... deregulation ... privatisation ... restrictions on the power of the unions	Mixed economy (Keynesianism)
Limited state intervention ... 'rolling back the frontiers of the state'	More significant state intervention
Quick and radical change	Slow gradual change ... evolution not revolution
Maintaining national sovereignty	Increasing integration in Europe
Quite individualistic	Collectivistic ... pluralistic
Limited welfare provision ... low 'safety net' only	Support for universal welfare state ... paternalism (see above)

2.2 Liberalism

Introduction
Whereas conservatives traditionally emphasise the role of society in shaping individuals, liberals place a greater emphasis on the importance of the individual. Liberal society is to be formed of free individuals, autonomous and equally valuable. Government intervention in relations between individuals should be considered only when existing practices threaten individual autonomy or freedom. Therefore, legitimate government action centres on protecting the individual. Over time, this liberal view of deregulated 'small government', where people interact freely, has been tempered by a realisation that, without some regulation, abuses could occur. In practice, therefore, traditional ('classical') liberalism has become moderated by the need to protect people from a form of capitalism that appears to restrict freedom.

Main facets of liberalism

Rationality
John Locke believed in rational thought over dogmatism. He believed that differences of opinion were inevitable and that free and rational individuals should – as far as possible – be allowed to resolve problems without the need for oppressive state intervention. There would in effect be . . .

Government by consent
Jean Jacques Rousseau in *The Social Contract* (1762) put forward the idea that men gave up natural freedom in return for social freedom. They could not, therefore, do all that they could in their natural state, but they would gain from the greater protection afforded in a society in which all men gave up their freedom to certain things. This would lead to a . . .

Limited government
. . . where there might be a separation of powers – along the lines advocated by writers such as Montesquieu – between executive, legislative and judicial branches. There might then be a system of checks and balances between branches, which would protect the people from any one branch becoming dominant and infringing those . . .

Toleration
. . . would become the norm and different traditions could be valued and respected. There could be an equality of opportunity, regardless of background.

Inalienable rights
. . . considered vital for individual fulfilment: equality before the law, freedom of expression etc. (Ch 14). In so doing, liberals would create a society in which . . .

A liberal view of human nature
Liberals have a generally positive view of human nature. Some early liberals saw men as self-seeking and egotistical, but later writers believed that humans are rational and compassionate, if corruptible. Liberals place the emphasis on guidance (encouragement for individuals to develop in the right direction); they believe that individuals, given choices, can be helped to make the decisions that benefit them and society at large.

Different forms of liberalism

Classical liberalism
Particularly common in the nineteenth century, classical liberalism saw minimal state intervention as being the ideal. There was an emphasis on freedom, toleration and equality. Individuals were rational and had choices to make. Classical liberalism emphasised the desirability of self-help and self-improvement.

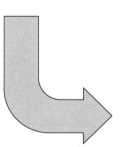

New/progressive liberalism
The social impact of industrialisation – particularly its more exploitative face – made many liberals realise that greater regulation might be needed. The market could not be allowed to go unchecked. Self-help would not be enough. There was a need for state provision of schools and hospitals. Pensions and unemployment benefit could be provided. Such ideas were put forward by writers such as T H Green and, later, L T Hobhouse. John Maynard Keynes and William Beveridge provided the basis for the mixed economy and welfare statism of the years following the Second World War.

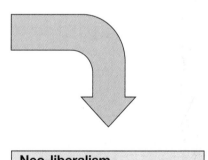

Neo-liberalism
Often associated with the 'New Right', neo-liberalism involved 'rolling back the frontiers of the state'; ending or at least minimising state provision/intervention. It was a return to classical liberal ideas of self-help and equality of opportunity rather than outcome. Neo-liberals once again emphasised the centrality of the market in providing for the needs of individuals.

2.3 Socialism

Introduction

Socialists traditionally place a greater emphasis on the importance of society as a whole rather that the specific needs of individuals. For socialists, individuals are social creatures who thrive in close proximity to others. As long as the society in which they live is supportive, they can live successfully and harmoniously, acting selflessly in the interests of all.

Socialists see capitalism and classical liberalism as damaging because they encourage individualism, selfishness and egoism. They create 'wants' and greed, while institutionalising inequality and the (sometimes even artificially perpetuated) scarcity of desired or necessary goods.

The impact of capitalism from a socialist perspective

Human cost
Capitalism is exploitative. Workers are not rewarded for the full value of their labour and are often exposed to unacceptable levels of harm.

Human spirit
Capitalism encourages greed, jealousy and an unhealthy form of competition. It acts against co-operation and altruism.

Democracy
Democracy is illusionary. It appears to offer real hope of change but merely acts to preserve the capitalist order through minor concessions and incentives.

Inequality
Capitalism entrenches inequality. Its main motivation is the accumulation of wealth and – given limited wealth – this ensures that there will always be losers as well as winners.

Resources
Capitalism is wasteful of resources. Products are designed to fail or be superseded at a certain points (fail-rates and inbuilt redundancy). The desire for ever-cheaper raw materials and ever-cheaper energy sources encourages the destruction of natural environments. Capitalism acts against long-term environmental planning in favour of short-term profits.

A socialist agenda

Socialists, therefore, have the desire to remould society rather than allowing it to evolve through interaction. Socialists favour: the redistribution of resources resulting in greater equality of outcome, an emphasis on co-operation and common goals rather than competition and individualism, state provision of education and welfare, and collective control of the means of production.

Different strands of socialism

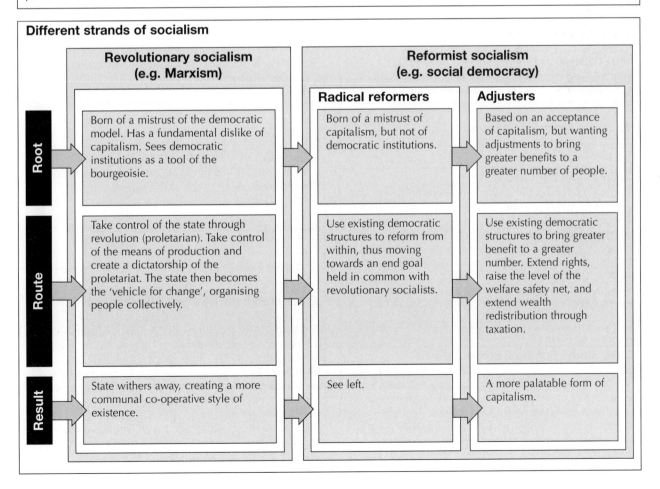

	Revolutionary socialism (e.g. Marxism)	Reformist socialism (e.g. social democracy)	
		Radical reformers	**Adjusters**
Root	Born of a mistrust of the democratic model. Has a fundamental dislike of capitalism. Sees democratic institutions as a tool of the bourgeoisie.	Born of a mistrust of capitalism, but not of democratic institutions.	Based on an acceptance of capitalism, but wanting adjustments to bring greater benefits to a greater number of people.
Route	Take control of the state through revolution (proletarian). Take control of the means of production and create a dictatorship of the proletariat. The state then becomes the 'vehicle for change', organising people collectively.	Use existing democratic structures to reform from within, thus moving towards an end goal held in common with revolutionary socialists.	Use existing democratic structures to bring greater benefit to a greater number. Extend rights, raise the level of the welfare safety net, and extend wealth redistribution through taxation.
Result	State withers away, creating a more communal co-operative style of existence.	See left.	A more palatable form of capitalism.

2.4 Environmentalism

Introduction

Environmentalism shares with socialism many of its criticisms of capitalism. However, whereas socialism and other ideologies tend to focus on the distribution of power and of resources between individuals within a society, and the relationship between individuals and the state, environmentalism takes as its starting point the central importance of the relationship between mankind as a whole and the environment. This provides a wholly different perspective on the state.

Environmentalist criticisms of capitalism

1. Capitalism is based upon the exploitation of people and other natural resources. Capitalism sees nature as something to be exploited.

2. Capitalism creates and nurtures false desires and demands through advertising. This leads to the production of unnecessary goods that waste finite resources. This waste, coupled to unnecessary advertising and packaging, is unjustifiable.

3. Manufacturers ensure that their products have deliberately high fail-rates in order to make sure that they have a constant demand for their products. They also ensure that their products have inbuilt redundancy. That is to say, even if they still work (i.e. have not failed), goods will in time become redundant because the manufacturers have a limited interest in maintaining old products compared to their interest in selling new products.

4. Within a market it is very difficult to make companies accountable for the environmental damage that they do because the environmental impact of their actions often only becomes apparent years later.

What does environmentalism involve?

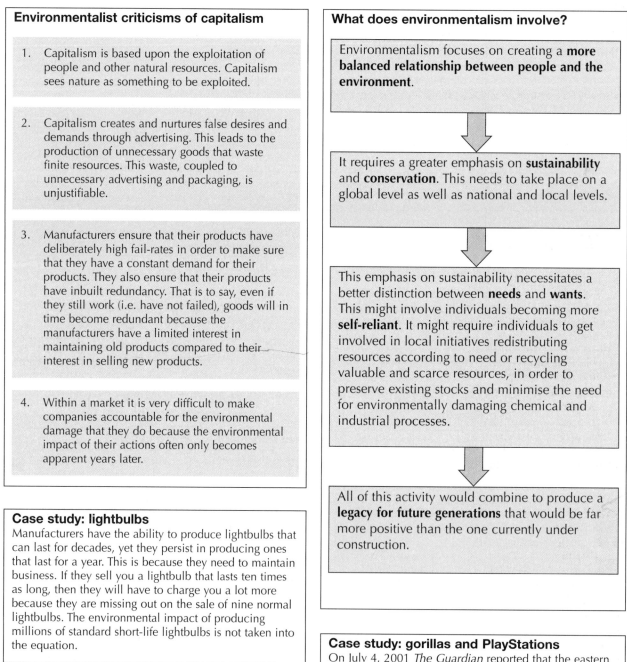

Environmentalism focuses on creating a **more balanced relationship between people and the environment**.

It requires a greater emphasis on **sustainability** and **conservation**. This needs to take place on a global level as well as national and local levels.

This emphasis on sustainability necessitates a better distinction between **needs** and **wants**. This might involve individuals becoming more **self-reliant**. It might require individuals to get involved in local initiatives redistributing resources according to need or recycling valuable and scarce resources, in order to preserve existing stocks and minimise the need for environmentally damaging chemical and industrial processes.

All of this activity would combine to produce a **legacy for future generations** that would be far more positive than the one currently under construction.

Case study: lightbulbs

Manufacturers have the ability to produce lightbulbs that can last for decades, yet they persist in producing ones that last for a year. This is because they need to maintain business. If they sell you a lightbulb that lasts ten times as long, then they will have to charge you a lot more because they are missing out on the sale of nine normal lightbulbs. The environmental impact of producing millions of standard short-life lightbulbs is not taken into the equation.

Case study: personal computers

Personal computers have an inbuilt redundancy and this is made more apparent when manufacturers produce software that will only run on computers with the latest specifications. Many computers over five years old simply end up in landfill sites even though they are still serviceable. Advertising is also used to create false demand for higher specification machines.

Case study: gorillas and PlayStations

On July 4, 2001 *The Guardian* reported that the eastern lowland gorilla population in the national park on the borders of Congo, Rwanda and Uganda has been made almost extinct by the destruction of their habitat caused by mining for Coltan (colombo tantalite), a mineral used as a hardening agent for metals in hi-tech industries. A shortage of this material in 2000 apparently led to the world-wide shortage of Sony PlayStation 2s at that time. Biologist Jane Goodall predicts that, at the present rate, great apes will be extinct in 10–15 years as a result of logging, the trade in 'bush-meat' and mining.

3.1 A post-war survey, 1945–1979

Introduction
A lot of what was done in 1945 was based on the 'new liberalism' of men such as William Beveridge and John Maynard Keynes (Ch 2.2). By 1945 it was clear that classical liberalism (Ch 2.2) and its emphasis on the individual through laissez faire policies (the free market) had failed because it had not offered sufficient protection to the individual. There was, therefore, a need for greater government intervention than might have been considered necessary by liberals in the nineteenth century.

John Maynard Keynes
Keynes believed that limited state intervention in the economy was necessary in order to avoid a spiral of recession. Keynes favoured intervention: a cash boost that might kick-start the economy. He did not believe, however, that the aim should be state-engineered equality. The inequalities of capitalism were a necessary incentive to hard work. This mixed economy would retain the benefits of the free market, while removing its worst tendencies.

William Beveridge and the Beveridge Report (1942)
Beveridge, a liberal civil servant, was commissioned by Churchill to produce a report on welfare provision and make suggestions for change. The Beveridge Report that followed in 1942 identified 'Five Giants' that needed to be defeated: want, disease, ignorance, squalor and idleness.

Beveridge recognised that these 'Giants' were linked, and that a concerted and co-ordinated effort would be required if they were to be conquered. Attlee's Labour Government, elected in 1945 with 393 seats – against the Conservatives' 213 – had the electoral mandate necessary to push ahead with such radical change.

The post-war consensus
Following the Second World War there was a broad agreement on the basis of future policy. In the social sphere, for example, there was an acceptance that:
- *full employment should be the goal;*
- *unions should be consulted over economic/ industrial policy;*
- *there should be public ownership of key industries;*
- *there should be public provision of welfare – covering health care, education, unemployment etc.*

This 'post-war consensus' clearly had its origins – in part – in the national coalition government in office during the war years.

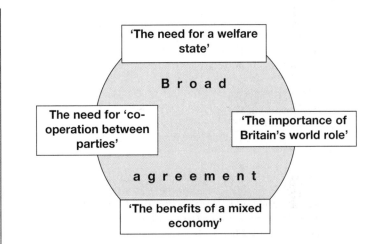

Broad agreement

- 'The need for a welfare state'
- The need for 'co-operation between parties'
- 'The importance of Britain's world role'
- 'The benefits of a mixed economy'

Attacking the 'Five Giants'
The post-war years saw a mass of legislation aimed at defeating the 'Five Giants' identified by Beveridge. The National Insurance Act of 1946 provided for the unemployed, the sick, dependants of the dead and those in maternity. The Butler Education Act of 1944 provided free secondary education, compulsory up to the age of 15. The 1946 National Health Act provided for the creation of the National Health Service.

Post-war Prime Ministers

1945–1951	Attlee
1951–1955	Churchill
1955–1957	Eden
1957–1963	MacMillan
1963–1964	Home
1964–1970	Wilson
1970–1974	Heath
1974–1976	Wilson
1976–1979	Callaghan
1979–1990	Thatcher
1990–1997	Major
1997–present	Blair

The breakdown of the post-war consensus.
By the 1970s it was clear that not all was well. Wilson had been forced to devalue the pound, and although unemployment had not risen above 1 000 000 between 1945 and 1974, it hit 1 500 000 in 1979. The co-operation between business, politicians and unions – the tripartism or corporatism of the earlier decades – was under real pressure as wage demands spiralled out of control and inflation became a real problem. Though the Winter of Discontent of 1978–79 brought the Labour Government crashing down, the problems had been there for some time.

3.2 Thatcherism and Majorism, 1979–1997

Introduction

By 1979 the post-war consensus was already dead (see Ch 3.1). The 1978–79 Winter of Discontent had signalled the end of Callaghan's Labour Administration, and the new government under Margaret Thatcher from 1979 followed a clear neo-liberal, 'New Right' agenda, offering more dogmatism and confrontation than pragmatism and co-operation. Thatcher had emerged from the Conservative Party leadership contest in 1975 following the failure of the former leader Edward Heath in the elections of 1974. A 'dark horse' in the first ballot, she had swept to victory upon the votes of those waiting for the entry of other candidates in the second ballot. Her election as leader in 1975 put an end to any lingering ideas of co-operation between parties.

Key elements of Thatcherism

Domestic policy

Economic
* Monetarism rather than Keynesianism
* Full employment not seen as possible or – necessarily – desirable
* An end to 'tripartism'. The reduction of union power
* Aims of controlling public expenditure and improving productivity; low inflation (2.5% by 1986) and low direct taxation

Social
* NHS spending was increased by one-third between 1979 and 1990 but did not keep pace with demand caused by changing demographics.
* A lower benefits safety net
* The sale of council houses to established tenants ('right to buy legislation')
* A focus on law and order
* The Community Charge ('Poll Tax')

Political
* Talk of 'rolling back the frontiers of the state' (small government) but increasing centralisation
* Civil service reform – increasing 'agencification' (see Ch 7)
* Major local government reform (see Ch 9). Abolition of Greater London Council – seen as a blatant attack on the left

Foreign policy

The 'special relationship'
Thatcher emphasised the importance of the 'special relationship' between the UK and the US. More than any Prime Minister and President since the Second World War, Thatcher and Reagan appeared to be 'singing from the same hymn-sheet'. The UK was a base for US air attacks on Libya.

Europe
Thatcher suspected the motives of other EEC states and forced rebates to compensate the UK for its net contribution to the Community. However, she still signed the 1986 Single European Act and, reluctantly, approved entry into the ERM in October 1990 (see Ch 5).

Defence policy
An important plank in the Thatcherite programme. Thatcher allowed the siting of US Cruise and Pershing missiles in the UK and upgraded our own missiles from Polaris to Trident. In 1986 defence spending was 5% of GDP, and had increased by 27% since 1978. 'Fortress Falklands' was established following the war in 1982.

Style

Image conscious
Thatcher received voice coaching, became famous for her power-dressing, and relied heavily upon speech writers and her Press Secretary, Bernard Ingham.

Confrontational
Thatcher's style was based on confronting opposition inside her party, in the country as a whole, and abroad. She described the miners as the 'enemy within' at the time of the Miners' Strike (1984–85).

Dogmatic
Thatcher was not often prepared to back down. Though she eventually accepted entry to the ERM in October 1990, her support for and defence of the 'Poll Tax' was more typical of her belief in her chosen course.

Domineering
Thatcher became famous for the way in which she controlled and sometime belittled Cabinet colleagues, culminating in high-profile resignations such as those by Heseltine, Lawson and Geoffrey Howe (see Ch 6).

Majorism

Context
Major's rise was meteoric. Although only elected to Parliament in 1979, he became Minister for Social Security in 1983, Chief Secretary to the Treasury in 1987, Foreign Secretary in June 1989, Chancellor in October 1989, and Conservative leader and Prime Minister in November 1990. Michael Heseltine, the man who had initially challenged Thatcher for the leadership, was passed over in favour of a man who could unify the Party after the divisions and infighting of the later Thatcher years. Thatcher's legacy demanded a different style – a more consensual approach – as well as some policy changes.

Continuity
Privatisation was continued, as were civil service reforms (the Next Steps Programme, see Ch 7). There remained a focus on low inflation and cuts in direct taxation, though the Party's reputation for economic competence was damaged by Black Wednesday and the UK's subsequent withdrawal from the European Exchange Rate Mechanism. As the Major premiership came to its close, it became apparent that many of the key elements of the Thatcherite agenda had – in fact – been realised and that there was a need for new direction. The Party, it was said, needed a spell on the back benches to refocus itself.

Change
There was a marked change in style and tone; a more consensual style as opposed to a confrontational one. This was partly due to the context of the administration and partly due to the fact that the Major Government was having to operate with an ever-shrinking Parliamentary majority. There were key policy changes. The 'Poll Tax' was shelved in favour of the property-based Council Tax. A slightly more sympathetic stance was taken on Europe, approving Maastricht while securing opt-outs on the Social Chapter and the Single Currency. Major was accused of a lack of vision but did have his 'big idea': the Citizen's Charter.

3.3 Blairism, 1997 to present

Introduction
In the same way that Majorism must be seen in the context of Thatcherism, and Thatcherism was itself a result of the failures of Heath and the apparent redundancy of the post-war consensus, Blairism must be seen as a reaction to the failure of the Labour Party in the 1980s – especially in the 1983 general election, where its hard-left manifesto was described as the 'longest suicide note in History'.

Ideology or pragmatism?
It has become fashionable in recent years to refer to the 'end of ideology'. Political parties have moved to the centre. Pragmatic populist policies, rather than ideological dogma, have become the norm. Some writers have hailed the emergence of a 'new consensus' around the centre–right. They cite Labour's jettisoning of Clause 4 (indeed the Party's reluctance to talk about socialism at all) and Tony Blair's pitch for 'middle England'. This, coupled to Iain Duncan Smith's appeal for the Conservatives to become a more inclusive party in the wake of a second humiliating general election defeat, has, for many, signalled the end of adversarial party politics as we know it.

Is there now more of a focus on style and presentation than on doctrine and dogma? Is it all about 'spin'? (See Ch 6.)

Catch phrases
Part of the new emphasis on presentation has been an increased awareness on the importance of catch phrases. This is by no means totally new, but some argue that it has become particularly apparent in recent years..The Blair administration has employed a large number of these phrases, for example:

'a stake-holder society'; 'welfare to work'; 'joined-up government'; 'economic prudence'; 'a third way'.

Such phrases are, by their very nature, difficult to pin down and define even when leading figures attempt to do so. Tony Blair, for example, tried to outline the 'third way' in a speech to the French National Assembly in March 1998. 'When I talk of a third way, I mean neither laissez faire nor state control and rigidity' he asserted. Yet explaining what the third way *is* has proved more difficult than asserting *what it is not*.

Tangible changes (?)

Policy
Social – Increased spending on public services: health, education and welfare. Extensive programmes unveiled before the 2001 general election, including greater support for single working mothers and partial nursery funding for pre-school children. A complete ban on fox hunting has not been forced through as anticipated.

Political/constitutional – The Human Rights Act, the Freedom of Information Act, partial reform of the Lords and devolution, including the use of new electoral systems in the Scottish Parliament and Welsh Assembly. Lots of unfinished projects and half-way houses. A coherent programme?

Economic – In 1997 Gordon Brown accepted Conservative spending plans for the first two years and has placed an emphasis on 'economic prudence' since. Low direct taxation and low inflation have been maintained (control over interest rates was given to the Bank of England with a 2.5% inflation target upon taking power). Controlled public expenditure, with a realisation that full employment is hard to achieve.

The Blair project

Power (see also Ch 6)
The last five years have seen a centralisation of power around Downing Street. Blair has reduced the number of full Cabinet meetings held each week, preferring instead to use 'bilaterals', meetings between himself and another minister. He has attended the Commons less frequently than most other post-war Prime Ministers and has reduced Prime Minister's Questions from two to one (albeit longer) session on Wednesdays. Blair has taken personal control of certain key issues (for example, 'foot and mouth') and has become reliant on an ever-increasing band of policy advisors. The overall effect has been a much more central role for the Prime Minister above and beyond Cabinet.

Style/presentation (see also Ch 6)
A lot has been made of the importance of presentation and spin. At the centre of much of the criticism has been Alastair Campbell, now Director of Communications, through whom so much political information was filtered during Blair's first term. The activities of the Press Office – for example, the use of pagers to brief Labour MPs in the Commons during debates – gave the impression of an extremely controlling administration. Some spoke of Blair's 'control freak' tendencies, and fears of these were reinforced by briefings against Ken Livingstone as the Party first tried to force its preferred candidate for London Mayor onto the ballot paper as the official Labour candidate, and then tried to discredit Ken Livingstone's independent candidacy.

4.1   Sources

What is a constitution?

A constitution is a body of rules that defines the manner in which a state or society is organised. It sets out the way in which sovereign power is distributed between the government and the people, and between the government's constituent parts. In so doing, a constitution provides a framework upon which more complex rules, structures and processes can be built.

Codified and uncodified constitutions

Within the broad definition given above, it is possible to discern two styles of constitutions: those which consist of a full and authoritative set of rules written down in a single place (*codified* – for example, the US Constitution) and those which are less tangible, often having evolved over time and having become as much reliant on traditions and customs as any written documents (*uncodified* – for example, the UK Constitution). The fact that the UK Constitution is uncodified does not mean, however, that it is 'un-written'; some of its sources are indeed in written form. What then are the main sources of the UK Constitution?

Statute law

Acts of Parliament are referred to as statutes. Some of these statutes play a significant role in outlining the extent and distribution of government powers; the Parliament Acts of 1911 and 1949, for example, limit the power of the House of Lords. Other statutes outline our rights within a democracy; in the various Representation of the People Acts, for example, rules governing elections and the franchise are set out.

Statute law is generally regarded as taking precedence over all other constitutional sources and this is linked to the idea of parliamentary sovereignty (see Ch 4.2).

Some argue that our membership of the EU limits the importance of statute law (and parliamentary sovereignty) but others maintain that this is untrue, as long as Parliament retains the power to withdraw from the EU by repealing the 1972 European Communities Act.

Common law

Common law consists of established customs and precedent developed through the actions of judges. This 'precedent' is often referred to as 'case law' or 'judge-made law'. When a case is heard, the court will generally look for previous examples of similar cases and look to follow precedent when arriving at a decision. Where no precedent exists, the decision made will itself set precedent; though in areas such as this, it is common for the case to be passed around through the appeals process before a final judgement is made. A lot of the original law concerning civil liberties and a good deal of consumer protection rests upon common law.

The royal prerogative (including the power to declare war and agree treaties) is also based in common law. When John Major signed the Maastricht Treaty, he was doing so under the prerogative powers exercised by the Prime Minister in the name of the monarch. He could, therefore, have argued that there was no need for Parliament to approve this Treaty.

Treaties and EU law

The increasing globalisation of politics and UK involvement in supra-national organisations have led some to question the extent to which statute law is still the overriding source of our constitution.

Our membership of the EU is particularly significant. In passing the 1972 European Communities Act, European law and regulations were given precedence over our own national laws. Thus, it is argued, statute law no longer conquers all and Parliament is no longer sovereign.

Some argue that power has only been delegated to the EU and that Parliament still has the power to repeal the 1972 Act, thereby removing us from the Union. In this sense, Parliament is still theoretically sovereign and statute law is still theoretically pre-eminent. Such a withdrawal would, however, be extremely difficult to execute.

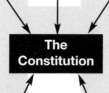

The Constitution

Conventions

Conventions are traditions or customs that have evolved over time and have, through deference to precedent, become accepted rules of behaviour. Unlike common law, however, conventions will not stand up in a court of law.

Important conventions include the doctrines of individual and collective ministerial responsibility, as well as the rule requiring the royal assent before a bill passed by both Houses of Parliament can pass into law.

Works of authority

As Philip Norton has noted, whereas statute law takes precedence over all other sources, works of authority have only a persuasive authority; a role in settling disputes. When politicians want to ascertain correct procedure, they may call into play certain specialist works dealing with the constitution. Over time, therefore, some of these books have themselves become part of the constitutional framework because they codify practices not outlined on paper elsewhere. Such works include:

Fitzherbert's *Abridgement* (1516); Coke's *Institutes of the Law of England* (1624–44); Erskine May's *Parliamentary Practice* (first published in 1844); A V Dicey's *An Introduction to the Study of the Law of the Constitution* (1885).

4.2 Doctrines and principles

Key principles

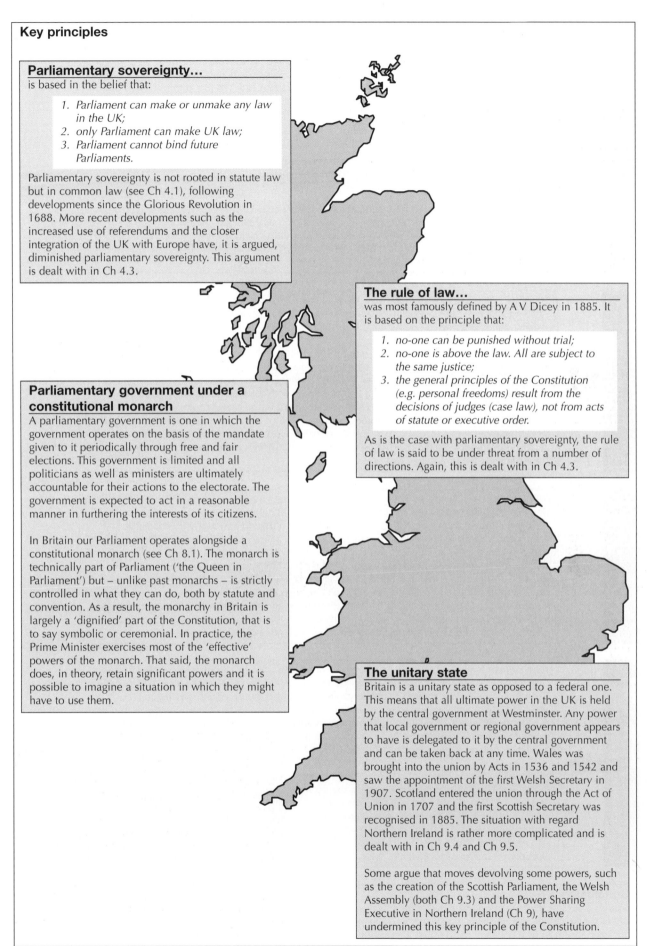

Parliamentary sovereignty...

is based in the belief that:

1. *Parliament can make or unmake any law in the UK;*
2. *only Parliament can make UK law;*
3. *Parliament cannot bind future Parliaments.*

Parliamentary sovereignty is not rooted in statute law but in common law (see Ch 4.1), following developments since the Glorious Revolution in 1688. More recent developments such as the increased use of referendums and the closer integration of the UK with Europe have, it is argued, diminished parliamentary sovereignty. This argument is dealt with in Ch 4.3.

The rule of law...

was most famously defined by A V Dicey in 1885. It is based on the principle that:

1. *no-one can be punished without trial;*
2. *no-one is above the law. All are subject to the same justice;*
3. *the general principles of the Constitution (e.g. personal freedoms) result from the decisions of judges (case law), not from acts of statute or executive order.*

As is the case with parliamentary sovereignty, the rule of law is said to be under threat from a number of directions. Again, this is dealt with in Ch 4.3.

Parliamentary government under a constitutional monarch

A parliamentary government is one in which the government operates on the basis of the mandate given to it periodically through free and fair elections. This government is limited and all politicians as well as ministers are ultimately accountable for their actions to the electorate. The government is expected to act in a reasonable manner in furthering the interests of its citizens.

In Britain our Parliament operates alongside a constitutional monarch (see Ch 8.1). The monarch is technically part of Parliament ('the Queen in Parliament') but – unlike past monarchs – is strictly controlled in what they can do, both by statute and convention. As a result, the monarchy in Britain is largely a 'dignified' part of the Constitution, that is to say symbolic or ceremonial. In practice, the Prime Minister exercises most of the 'effective' powers of the monarch. That said, the monarch does, in theory, retain significant powers and it is possible to imagine a situation in which they might have to use them.

The unitary state

Britain is a unitary state as opposed to a federal one. This means that all ultimate power in the UK is held by the central government at Westminster. Any power that local government or regional government appears to have is delegated to it by the central government and can be taken back at any time. Wales was brought into the union by Acts in 1536 and 1542 and saw the appointment of the first Welsh Secretary in 1907. Scotland entered the union through the Act of Union in 1707 and the first Scottish Secretary was recognised in 1885. The situation with regard Northern Ireland is rather more complicated and is dealt with in Ch 9.4 and Ch 9.5.

Some argue that moves devolving some powers, such as the creation of the Scottish Parliament, the Welsh Assembly (both Ch 9.3) and the Power Sharing Executive in Northern Ireland (Ch 9), have undermined this key principle of the Constitution.

4.3 The Constitution in transition?

Parliamentary sovereignty

The doctrine of parliamentary sovereignty has, it is argued, been undermined by a number of factors.

1. Increasing European integration has seen significant power delegated to the EU. The European Communities Act of 1972 gave European law precedence over UK law, and the Maastricht Treaty of 1991 broadened and deepened the Community significantly, creating the European Union. While a simple Act of Parliament (probably backed up with a referendum) could remove us from the EU – thus, in theory, meaning that Parliament is still technically sovereign – such a move would be difficult to achieve in practice and extremely expensive.

2. Others argue that Parliament as a whole has become dominated by the Commons, the Commons by the majority party, the majority party by the government, the government by the Cabinet and the Cabinet by the Prime Minister. In reality, therefore, the idea of a sovereign parliament is questionable and some maintain that our government is effectively an 'elected dictatorship'. Against this argument one could bring in examples of the fate of Prime Ministers and governments who consistently and systematically appeared to repress the power of Parliament, party and government – Margaret Thatcher's downfall is a good case in point.

The rule of law

There are numerous long-standing exceptions to the rule of law and these are documented in all standard textbooks: the favourable treatment of accused foreign diplomats, for example, or the specific limitations placed upon the rights of those accused of acts of terrorism (under the various pieces of anti-terrorism legislation). More recent developments have also brought some key aspects of the rule of law into question: the suggestion that trial by jury could be further limited, for example, or the removal of the 'presumption of innocence' or the 'right to remain silent' without having inferences drawn from one's silence. At the same time, we are seeing the creation of what some have hailed as a 'rights culture' with the Human Rights Act and the Freedom of Information Act being passed. These apparent rights, however, are still not entrenched in a codified constitution and, as such, they can be repealed as easily as any other act. In the case of the HRA in particular, the courts only have the power to highlight inconsistencies between the rights offered in the Act and other legislation. They cannot invalidate laws infringing the protected rights. See Ch 14.4.

The unitary state

Although the UK remains, in theory, a unitary state, some power has been delegated in such a way that it would be very difficult to get it back. This is particularly true of the Scottish Parliament and the Welsh Assembly, though the Northern Ireland Power Sharing Executive has been suspended from time to time as a tactic during the peace process. Opinions differ as to the extent to which these institutions remain an end in themselves or steps on a path to a federal system. The principle of subsidiarity – enshrined in the Maastricht Treaty – states that decisions should be taken at the most appropriate level and this, together with the EU's use of 'regions' for other purposes (such as economic development) and the use of the regional list system in elections to the EU Parliament, has fuelled demands for greater regional government in the UK. Such demands have been further heightened by a sense that England and its regions are now under-represented in relation to Scotland, Northern Ireland and Wales.

Parliamentary government under a constitutional monarch

The nature of Parliament is changing. Reform to the Lords, though incomplete, is likely to lead to a second elected chamber. This would lead to issues such as the division of power between the Commons and the new second elected chamber. Eurosceptics and some others argue that, in any case, parliamentary government is undermined by the increasing delegation of power to the EU. Those who speak of 'elective dictatorship' also question the worth of the term 'parliamentary government'. The increased use of referendums in recent years is also said to undermine the principle of representative government. See Ch 10.3.

The monarch has been said to be under threat in recent years, though approval ratings for the Queen herself remain high. In the wake of the death of Diana, Princess of Wales, the monarchy took a good deal of criticism, but there has been an attempt to rehabilitate leading figures in recent years and there has been no significant move towards republicanism despite the efforts of some newspapers. The abolition of the monarchy or the removal of its residual powers/responsibilities would also create significant knock-on constitutional effects. Who, for example, would give the assent to bills (a president perhaps) or act as a national figurehead?

Conclusion

Although the Constitution has evolved over time, it is now clearly entering a phase of major change. Many of the key elements of the state are being reassessed, as is the relationship between the state and the individual. There does not appear to be a coherent master-plan. Progress is unpredictable and crab-like.

5.1 The origins and organisation of the European Union

Historical context

At the end of the Second World War there was a widely-held desire to bind states together in some kind of economic organisation in order to prevent Europe from descending into war once again. The European Coal and Steel Community was formed in 1952 and included France, Germany, Italy, Belgium, the Netherlands and Luxembourg. In 1957 these six member states signed the Treaty of Rome, creating the European Economic Community (EEC) and the European Atomic Energy Community. This treaty broadened the Coal and Steel Community to include foreign trade and agriculture. At that time the UK favoured retaining close trading links with the US ('the special relationship') and the newly- formed Commonwealth.

Economic union into European Union

By the 1980s it was widely accepted that the EEC had achieved many of its initial objectives. Peace between the major European powers had been preserved for over 35 years and the Common Agricultural Policy (Ch 5.2) had, for the most part, succeeded in regulating production of key 'products' through the use of subsidies and quotas. Many felt that the EEC needed to set itself new targets; ones that reflected how far Europe had come since the war.

In 1986 the Single European Act created a single European market where the 'four freedoms' of goods, persons, services and capital could be preserved; all four would be able to move freely across the borders of European Community states. The Maastricht Treaty of 1992 took things a stage further. It created the European Union (EU), extending the Community beyond the economic into areas such as justice and home affairs, foreign and security policy. The EU was, therefore, to be based on three pillars:

The European Community	Foreign and security policy	Justice and home affairs

The Treaty of Amsterdam built upon Maastricht, extending cooperation. This left the Treaty of Nice (see Ch. 5.2) to address EU enlargement and the reform of EU institutions.

Key Steps

1952	Coal and Steel Community
1958	Treaty of Rome – EEC formed
1973	UK (plus Denmark and Ireland) joined
1981	Greece joined
1986	Single European Act
1986	Spain and Portugal joined
1992	Maastricht Treaty
1995	Austria, Finland and Sweden joined
1997	Amsterdam Treaty
2001	The Nice Treaty

The main institutions of the European Union

The Council of the European Union

Often referred to as the Council of Ministers, this body consists of ministers from the 15 member states. The actual minister involved will depend on the nature of the issues being discussed. If, for example, defence policy were being discussed then the 15 national defence ministers might meet. The presidency of the Council operates on a rota (2002 first half-year Spain; 2002 second half-year Denmark; 2003 first half-year Greece) The Council is the main decision-making institution. Its work is supported by COREPER (the Committee of Permanent Representatives). COREPER is made up of officials from each country and it undertakes the necessary preparation in between the various Council meetings. COREPER oversees the work of around 100 more specialised working groups. Some decisions must be taken unanimously but others operate under qualified majority voting (see right).

The European Commission

The Commission consists of 20 commissioners: two from each of the larger countries (France, Germany, Spain, Italy and the UK) and one from each of the remaining ten member states. Each commissioner is responsible for a certain area. Britain's commissioners are Neil Kinnock (Vice-President of the Commission and Commissioner for Administrative Reform) and Chris Patten (Commissioner for External Relations). The commissioners are appointed for a fixed term of five years; the current Commission will sit until 2005. Under the commissioners work a staff of around 15 000 people divided up into over 30 Directorates-General. Around one-fifth of the staff are employed in the translation and interpreting services. These people ensure that the texts of treaties and directives are available in the native languages of all member states. The Commission has the role of initiating legislation and making proposals to the Council and the Parliament. It also acts as the guardian (enforcer) of EU treaties and holds power to execute agreed policies.

Qualified majority voting

In areas such as foreign and security matters and enlargement of the EU, a unanimous vote is required in the Council of Ministers. This means that states effectively have a veto over such issues. In most areas, however, a system of QMV operates. Under this system, countries' votes are weighted roughly in relation to their population. The UK, France, Germany and Italy, for example, hold ten votes, whereas The Netherlands only holds five and Luxembourg only two. In any vote under QMV a successful proposal must secure at least 62 of the 87 votes available. No one country, therefore, can reject proposals under QMV. Under Nice, QMV will be extended into far more areas.

Other EU institutions

Court of Justice; Court of Auditors; European Central Bank; Economic and Social Committee; Committee of the Regions; European Investment Bank; European Ombudsman.

The European Parliament

The European Parliament is the only EU institution that is democratically elected by citizens in each of its member states. In the UK elections now operate under the regional party list system. The Parliament has a total of 626 MEPs, with the larger states electing more than the smaller. The UK has 87 members, for example, whereas Luxembourg only has six. Initially, Parliament only had the power to advise, but in recent years it has been given some powers to amend legislation. This increased power – the co-decision procedure – sees the Parliament on an equal footing in some areas of policy; for example, health and the environment, where Parliament has been able to secure improvements in fuel quality with a view to reducing pollution (from 2000). The Parliament also has control of the purse strings: each year, the President of the Parliament has to approve the budget before it can come into effect. As a result the EU can, in theory, reject the EU budget. MEPs also have a role in approving the Commission President and the Commission, and can censure the entire Commission – forcing it to resign. This might well have happened in 1999, following allegations of corruption, had not the 20 commissioners resigned en masse on March 15 – removing the need for Parliamentary censure.

5.2 The Treaty of Nice and the future of the European Union

Enlargement

One of the key issues facing the EU over the next few years will be the extent to which it can enlarge, while retaining cohesion and meaning. Enlargement will have a significant impact on the nature, composition and operation of the three key institutions (see below).

Current members	Proposed members
Belgium, Germany, France, Italy, Luxembourg, Netherlands, Denmark, Greece, Spain, Ireland, Austria, Portugal, Sweden, Finland and the UK.	12 nations are already in negotiations: Bulgaria, Cyprus, the Czech Republic, Estonia, Hungary, Latvia, Lithuania, Malta, Poland, Romania, Slovakia and Slovenia. Turkey has also been accepted as a candidate.

The Treaty of Nice and EU institutions

The Council of the European Union (Council of Ministers)

The enlargement of the EU as outlined above will have an impact on the workings of the Council because it will become almost impossible to reach unanimous decisions with over 30 member states. As a result, QMV is to be extended into over 30 areas which are currently decided on the basis of unanimity. The weighting of each state's votes will also have to change as each of the proposed states meets the criteria and joins the Union. Tthe Treaty of Nice therefore outlines the numbers of votes that will be allocated as these changes are made. The UK will get 29, for example, as will Germany, France and Italy. Of the proposed new members, Poland will get the most votes (27) and Malta the least (three). The number of votes required to pass a measure will change as the Union expands, but member states will be able to insist that ministers representing 62% of the EU population approve of a measure for it to pass.

The Commission

If the current system for allocating commissioners were retained along with the expansion of the Union envisaged under Nice, the Commission would end up with over 30 members. As a result, from 2005, the Commission will only include one representative from each member state up to a maximum of 27. When this figure is reached, the Council of Ministers will have to take a unanimous decision to set the size of the Commission thereafter – but it will have to be below 27. The expansion of the Commission will also see greater executive powers for the President of the Commission, currently Romano Prodi of Italy. In the future the President will be able to hand out portfolios at will, as well as changing commissioners' portfolios on their own initiative. The President will also have the power to demand the resignation of a commissioner, subject to the Commission's approval.

The European Parliament

The Treaty of Nice enhances the Parliament's role as a co-legislator (the co-decision procedure). It limits the number of MEPs to 732 (currently 626) and allocates seats from the next election (2005) to current member states as well as the new member states proposed under the Treaty. The UK, for example, will have 72 seats (currently 87), Germany 99 (99). Poland will have 50 and Malta will have five. The Council gains the power to regulate the organisation (particularly the funding) of political parties at a European level.

The single currency

The timetable for moving towards a single currency was set out in the Maastricht Treaty along with the so-called convergence criteria that countries would have to meet before being admitted. From January 1, 1999 11 EU member states were participating in the euro: Belgium, Germany, Spain, France, Ireland, Italy, Luxembourg, Netherlands, Austria, Portugal and Finland. Greece participated from January 1, 2001. These countries make up the so-called eurozone. From January 1, 2002 the euro became the legal currency in these countries and on February 28, 2002 their old national currencies became obsolete.

The UK, Sweden and Denmark remain outside the eurozone at the time of writing.

The Common Agricultural Policy (CAP)

The CAP was introduced in the 1960s. It worked on the principle that when market prices were low, the EEC would buy up surplus produce, stabilising prices. Some of this material was stored: the so-called grain mountains, butter mountains and wine lakes. When goods were in short supply the EEC could release some of their stores or offer subsidies to farmers to increase production. For many products a farmer would need to hold a 'quota' in order to produce, and in some cases the EEC would pay farmers to farm nothing (set-aside). The CAP has always been incredibly expensive; according to the Consumer Association, the policy costs the UK £5 billion each year. It estimates that each household pays nearly £16 per week in taxes and higher food prices. Some reform took place in the 1990s but, as the EU expands, it is likely that the programme will have to undergo a major rethink.

Deepening the Union(?)

The Maastricht Treaty (1992) extended the possibility EU co-operation into new areas (see below). The Treaty of Nice (2001) called for greater co-operation, and made this easier by requiring that a minimum of only eight EU states agree before 'enhanced co-operation' can take place. Other states can then join as and when they see fit. This might lead to different groupings of states moving at different speeds on different issues: a 'multi-track Europe'.

Common Foreign and Security Policy (CFSP)

The Maastricht Treaty offered the prospect of some kind of European Defence Force, and Germany and France – in particular – seemed keen to put together a joint force. The collapse of Yugoslavia in the 1990s and the ongoing problems (Kosova/Serbia etc.) led many to believe that a European-wide peace-keeping or quick-reaction force might be the best way to deal with problems on the Continent. Some progress is likely in the future, though concerns over the chain of command for such a force and its relationship to NATO remain. More likely is foreign policy co-operation in the form of Europe-wide economic sanctions against suspect regimes, as has happened in the case of Zimbabwe.

Home affairs and justice

Some progress has already been made (for example, the Social Chapter and increased cross-border co-operation on crime). The Union is likely to develop further in this area.

6.1 The Prime Minister

Origins of the office

The office of Prime Minister is based largely on convention. Once the monarch stopped attending Cabinet meetings (under George I, who reigned 1714–27), the First Lord of the Treasury began chairing Cabinet meetings. This is the formal title still held by Prime Ministers today. Robert Walpole is generally regarded as the first Prime Minister (1721–42), though in reality Robert Peel (1841–46) has a better claim as the first modern Prime Minister. The powers of the Prime Minister have evolved gradually, largely as a result of the assimilation of royal prerogative powers (see right). While the monarch still retains these power in theory, in practice the Prime Minister acts in place of the monarch.

The royal prerogative

These powers, formally held by the monarch but – in practice – exercised by the Prime Minister include the power to:

declare war; make treaties; annex and cede territory; control the armed forces; control patronage; control the workings of the civil service; make use of emergency powers.

The powers of the Prime Minister

Patronage and the control of Cabinet

The Prime Minister has massive powers of patronage over the Church of England (archbishops, bishops etc.), senior judges (e.g. the Lord Chief Justice), Privy Councillors and civil servants. It is in Cabinet and government, however, that the power of patronage becomes crucial. The Prime Minister ultimately decides who gets what at all levels of the government. He or she also controls the timing and agenda of Cabinet meetings as well as 'taking the feeling of the meeting'.

Limitations: the seniority of colleagues might demand their inclusion (e.g. Jack Straw), as might a need for balance (e.g. John Prescott) or a need to reward those who have supported your rise (e.g. Gordon Brown). If the Prime Minister excludes or forces out key figures they can often become dangerous enemies on the back benches (e.g. Heseltine under Thatcher). There are also the questions of availability for office, ability and experience. Margaret Thatcher was often criticised – particularly in the latter years of her administration – for passing over or forcing out more experienced ministers in favour of 'yes-men'. Some items also demand inclusion on the Cabinet agenda.

Party and Parliament

As the leader of the majority party in the Commons (most often), the Prime Minister has considerable power. They can control the parliamentary timetable and pursue the government's programme. They are the public face of party and government. They control key appointments within their own party as well as within government, and can rely on a certain amount of loyalty from the party simply by virtue of the fact that they are in government. When backs are against the wall, they can even threaten to ask the Queen to dissolve Parliament and call an election (a threat made by John Major in 1992).

Limitations: the party will not always remain loyal (back bench support for Thatcher failed in 1990). Parliament can also – in theory – call errant governments to account (e.g. through Prime Minister's Questions on Wednesdays, or debates and motions).

What is the core executive?

The term 'core executive' is a collective term usually taken to refer to the key institutions and processes involved in co-ordinating the work of central government: the Prime Minister, Cabinet, Cabinet Committees and Cabinet Office, Treasury and Foreign Office bodies, law, security and intelligence officers, and certain other top civil servants.

Models of executive control

Cabinet government

This places the Cabinet at the centre of decision-making, while accepting that some decisions might need to be made elsewhere. Cabinet is seen as a unified body, operating under the doctrine of collective responsibility. The Cabinet acts as a check against any attempts by the Prime Minister to dominate the process. The Prime Minister is merely 'primus inter pares' – first among equals. John Major's administrations (1990–97) are often offered as examples.

Prime Ministerial cliques/kitchen cabinet

In this model, the Prime Minister works within a reduced (kitchen) cabinet or clique of key advisors. The composition of this clique is fairly fixed, but key additional individuals might be brought into the circle on certain issues. Cabinet is reduced to a rubber stamp, being informed of and then approving those decisions made in the smaller meetings. Some feel that the Blair administrations (1997–present) have worked in this way, though he prefers 'bilaterals' to cliques.

Prime Ministerial government

Writers such as Richard Crossman in the 1960s and Tony Benn in the 1980s (both former Labour ministers) spoke of the rise of Prime Ministerial power. They saw the increasing dominance of the Prime Minister within Cabinet. This, they argued had been achieved largely as a result of the increasing centralisation of the party machines and the civil service in the hands of the Prime Minister. Since then, the media has further focused attention on the Prime Minister (see Ch 3.2, Ch 3.3).

Departmentalised/ministerial government

Under this analysis, government departments have control over their respective areas and the ministers in charge can act with a fair degree of autonomy upon the advice of those more junior politicians and civil servants within their departments. The Prime Minister bows to departmental expertise but holds ministers to account for their decisions (an aspect of ministerial responsibility). Cabinet becomes an arena for resolving conflicts between departments.

Differentiated/segmented decisions

This model accepts that the distribution of power within the executive might vary in different policy areas. The Prime Minister might dominate the heights of government – foreign policy, defence, key economic policy decisions – whereas the Cabinet might be given a considerable degree of autonomy in all other areas. The Prime Minister only interferes in these low-priority areas when ministers make mistakes, or when events move the issue further up the agenda (e.g. Blair and the 'foot and mouth' crisis).

A general model of executive power

In reality, any attempt to provide a simple model explaining the distribution of power within the core executive is likely to be flawed. The interrelationships between the various offices and institutions depend largely upon the characters and approaches of the incumbent politicians/officials as well as circumstances (e.g. the size of the government's majority in the Commons). Administrations do not always fit into a box, much less studies of particular episodes within the term of an administration.

The Sheffield College
Hillsborough LRC
Telephone: 0114 260 2254

6.2 The Cabinet

Introduction

As is the case with the office of Prime Minister, the Cabinet has evolved over time; from a group of individuals linking the King and Parliament into what Walter Bagehot (1867) saw as an institution central to the decision-making process. The Prime Minister, it was argued, was merely 'primus inter pares' (first among equals). Even at that time, however, this argument would have been open to question, and over the last 20 years the apparent expansion of Prime Ministerial power has led some to question how significant a role the Cabinet still retains in the process of government. The modern Cabinet consists of around 23 paid members and fulfils a number of important functions (see below). Traditionally, Cabinet Ministers have been expected to work within the principles of collective responsibility and ministerial responsibility (see Glossary).

The various roles of the Cabinet

Decision-making

Traditionally, Cabinet has been seen as central to the decision-making process. The Cabinet's role in this area, however, has been undermined by the development of Prime Ministerial power that has come with the increased centralisation of bureaucratic controls and the increased importance of the media.

Co-ordinating departments

Cabinet always had a role in co-ordinating the activities of government departments. While the decision-making role of Cabinet has been diminished somewhat, its position as an arena in which individuals can report on their activities and bring colleagues up-to-date remains significant.

Forward planning

Cabinet retains a role in addressing problems arising from policy and/or events. Cabinet provides a 'talking shop' where the direction of policy can, if necessary, be discussed and where the broad direction of policy can be re-focused. It is also a place where ministers can raise genuine concerns.

Recent Cabinets

The Cabinet under Thatcher

Thatcher's first Cabinet contained a good number of ministers who had served under Heath – the old guard of 'one-nation Tories'. Using the hire-and-fire power ruthlessly, she gradually brought in her own people to a point where many felt there was greater talent on the back benches than on the front. Her confrontational style led to high-profile resignations, such as Heseltine (right), Lawson and Howe in particular. The style of Heseltine's resignation in 1986 (walking out of a Cabinet meeting) and the savage attack on Thatcher made by Geoffrey Howe in his resignation speech contributed to her eventual downfall in 1990.

The Cabinet under Major

Following Thatcher's fall in November 1990, John Major emerged as the compromise candidate. Including his rivals for the leadership (Heseltine and Hurd) in the Cabinet, he sought to develop a more consensual style. After the general election of 1992, Major was working with a small majority and, as it shrank further, infighting became more apparent – particularly over Europe. Describing his opponents in Cabinet as the 'bastards' for briefing the press against him, he invited them to 'put up or shut up' in a leadership election in which he defeated John Redwood (above). This victory did not, however, stop the infighting, and accusations of sleaze further contributed to an appearance of an administration in crisis.

The Cabinet under Blair

Blair's first Cabinet included many heavyweight politicians who had their own power bases within the Party (Cook, Prescott and Brown for example). While all were retained post-2001, only Gordon Brown (right) kept a high-profile office, as Blair moved in more of his own people and promoted other Blairites within Cabinet – as a block, some suggest, against Brown's ambitions. Mo Mowlam has spoken of the 'crippling' battle at the top between Blair and Brown. *The Guardian* claimed that the administration had 'a bad case of the TB-GBs' (November 20, 2001). Blair continues to favour bilateral meetings over larger cliques. He dominates key decisions, but in many less important policy areas ministers are allowed to act fairly independently – although he has often taken personal control during major crises.

What is the Cabinet Office?

The Cabinet Office consists around 2000 staff and is the key player in co-ordinating the activities of government. The Office was strengthened by Labour in 1998. This strengthening involved creating new elements and also bringing together a number of previously independent bodies under the Cabinet Office umbrella. The result was what amounted to a Prime Minister's Department, in all but name; a power base to challenge Gordon Brown's in the Treasury, perhaps. The new Cabinet Office comprised:

a Cabinet Office Minister (the so-called 'Cabinet Enforcer') as well as the Cabinet Secretary (Sir Richard Wilson), four separate Secretariats (Economic and Domestic, Defence and Overseas, European (EU), Constitution), the Performance and Innovation Unit, the Women's Unit, the Centre for Management and Policy Studies, the Head of the Government and Communication Service, and the Chief Scientific Advisor.

There was also a physical centralisation of the Cabinet Office, with the staff from around 17 former Cabinet Office buildings being relocated to new accommodation in Downing Street. *The Guardian* saw these bureaucratic developments as a major threat to Cabinet government.

Cabinet committees

As the pressures on the work of Cabinet increased after the Second World War – both in volume of work and in its complexity – the Cabinet was forced to delegate significant aspects of its work to Cabinet committees and sub-committees. These committees are given authority over specific areas and, as far as possible, decisions are then taken at that level, so as to lighten the burden on full Cabinet meetings. Committees are generally chaired by senior Cabinet members; sometimes the Prime Minister of the day. The rest of the members are drawn from the Cabinet as appropriate. The many committees generally fall into one of three categories: foreign and defence, domestic/home affairs, and economic. Some ministers will attend committees in all three categories (the Leader of the Commons or the Home Secretary, for example), whereas other ministers will only be involved in committees that are more directly linked to their portfolios (the Health Secretary, for example). As a result of the expansion of committee work, the full Cabinet has increasingly become a body for reporting and reviewing decisions taken at committee level rather than making decisions itself. It has also been noted that the full Cabinet only rarely fully debates matters that have already been dealt with at committee level.

6.3 Special advisors, spin and control

Introduction

One of the key features of the Blair Administrations has been their emphasis on presentation and control; the importance of keeping everyone 'on-message' (i.e. maintaining the appearance of unity in Cabinet, government, parliamentary party and beyond). One aspect of this has been the high profile attained by the Prime Minister's Press Secretary (now Director of Communications), Alastair Campbell. Another has been the attempt to control the selection of Party candidates for high office (Alun Michael, Donald Dewar and Frank Dobson) – often with disastrous results. At the same time, there has been a physical concentration of resources in Downing Street with the strengthening of the Cabinet Office. All of this, and much more, has led to claims that Blair has 'control freak tendencies' and that the Government is 'spinning out of control'. What are the foundations for such fears?

What are special advisors?

There were five so-called special advisors in 1990, a figure that increased to around 36 in the last year of John Major's Government, 69 by the end of the first year of the new Labour Government in 1997, and 81 by March 2002. Special advisors have two key roles:

- *to make the government less reliant on the work of the Civil Service;*
- *to help the Prime Minister keep up-to-date with government departments that are often far better staffed and resourced.*

Blair has made extensive use of special advisors. Jonathon Powell was appointed as a 'US-style' Chief of Staff, Alastair Campbell holds the role of Director of Communications, and Sally Morgan is the Director of Government Relations. She replaced Anji Hunter following the 2001 general election. Other ministers have also made extensive use of such advisors. Stephen Buyers, for example, relied heavily on Jo Moore prior to her resignation.

Task forces

Such groups generally consist of 'outsiders' (in particular, business people), who examine a particular area or policy. The Labour Government has been accused of becoming over-reliant on task forces since returning to office.

Some have suggested that the Government has set up task forces and working groups as a way of avoiding actual 'action'. Others suggest that the Government only chooses to act on the recommendations of the task forces when they fit in with the Government's own preconceived agenda. Some task forces, such as the Advisory Group looking into Citizenship Education under Bernard Crick, have seen their recommendations taken up almost word for word. Others, such as Lord Rogers' report on urban renewal, have been rejected or put on the back burner.

The Government had instituted 50 separate task forces by the end of 1997, and 75 by the end of 1998. As early as 1997, Labour had over 500 people working in government-appointed task forces.

The role of government whips

The role of the government whips is to ensure that the government maintains a majority in votes taken in Parliament. The Chief Whip attends Cabinet meetings and has the status of a senior minister. The whips' ultimate sanction, removing the whip from an MP and thus effectively expelling him or her from the party, is used only rarely. In 1994 under John Major, however, eight Conservative MPs (the so-called 'whipless wonders') had the whip removed for disloyalty in matters connected to the Party's policy on Europe.

More recently, the Labour Chief Whip Hillary Armstrong found herself under fire over her disastrous attempts to force Shrewsbury MP Paul Marsdon into line. Marsdon had questioned the manner in which the Government was pursuing the 'war on terrorism'. Armstrong's approach was widely criticised; according to *The Times* (October 23, 2001), former Tory Whip Andrew MacKay believed that she was simply not up to the job. Marsdon defected to the LibDems in December 2001.

The Prime Minister's Office

Over the last few years the Prime Minister's Office has taken on a clearer and more substantial structure. The Office comprises a total of around 150 staff divided between a number of different Office groupings. Until 2001 these were:

the Private Office, the Political Unit, the Strategic Communications Unit, the Press Office, and the Policy Unit.

It is the latter two that have probably provoked most discussion.

Alastair Campbell and the Press Office

The Press Office traditionally operates under the control of the Chief Press Officer (a role filled by Alastair Campbell from 1997). The role of the Office, and the Chief Press Secretary in particular, is to govern the Prime Minister's relations with the media. Prior to Alastair Campbell's appointment, the role of Chief Press Secretary was often associated with Bernard Ingham, who held the post under Margaret Thatcher and who was noted for his combative, no-nonsense style. Under Blair, Campbell has become a central figure, as a greater emphasis has been placed upon presentation and spin. Campbell, officially the Prime Minister's Director of Communications following the 2001 election, continues to control access to the Prime Minister, as well as regulating media access to Government ministers. He has a central role in efforts to manage the public perception of the Government's efforts and now has two civil service deputies for lobby briefings (Godric Smith and Tom Kelly).

The Policy Unit

In 1997, Tony Blair appointed David Miliband as the Head of the Policy Unit. The Policy Unit originated under Prime Minister Harold Wilson in 1974 and was supposed to be a planning and research body, consisting mainly of outside specialists. The staff of the Policy Unit were politically appointed. Each new Prime Minister had the opportunity to replace the entire Policy Unit Staff. After the election victory in 2001, the Policy Unit was merged with the Prime Minister's Private Office, forming the Number 10 Policy Directorate under civil servant Jeremy Heywood.

The Times's slant on Hillary Armstrong

7.1 Role of the Civil Service

Introduction

The Civil Service is often described as the administrative side of the UK Government (the bureaucracy). In reality, however, top civil servants are increasingly politicised and active in the policy-making process. This has undermined the idea of **neutrality**; one of the three principles which was traditionally said to characterise civil servants. The other two principles – **anonymity** and **permanence** – have also been undermined by recent changes: the former as some civil servants become publicly known and are, in some cases, identified as being responsible for the execution of policy (for example in government agencies such as the Child Support Agency); the latter as incoming governments find it impossible to work with the civil servants appointed by the previous administration (or vice versa) or civil servants are forced to resign over policy failures (most obviously in Government agencies). Sir Richard Mottram, the senior civil servant at the heart of the Jo Moore row, for example, complained that Stephen Byers had compromised his position by forcing him to release a public statement clearing Byers of any wrongdoing (*Guardian*, March 8, 2002).

The Structure of the Civil Service

The Administrative Group, which is probably the most significant part of the Civil Service is dealt with more thoroughly in Ch 7.2. This box provides a basic outline of the structure of the Civil Service as a whole.

Service-wide Generalists
These generalists work in various or all departments. The majority work in the Administrative Group which is dealt with on the next page.

Service-aide Specialists
Specialists such as economists and those working in the statisticians group work across the service providing specialist information.

Departmental Groups + Agencies
Some civil servants are tied to particular government departments. Many (380 000 or 75% of the Civil Service 1998) are hived off into agencies such as the Prisons Service.

The Impact of Civil Service Reform

Growing discontent in the 1950s and early 1960s led to the Fulton Report. The Report criticised the Civil Service for its amateurish approach and tendency to promote on seniority rather than merit. The Report recommended the creation of a Civil Service Department, the abolition of Civil Service Classes, the creation of a unified grade structure with a clear career path, and the establishment of a Civil Service College. The implementation of the Reports recommendations in 1968 was incomplete and short-lived. The grade structure was never full adopted, the College was downgraded and the Civil Service Department was abolished by Thatcher in 1981. Thatcher reduced the size of the Civil Service from 750 000 staff in 1979 to 600 000 in 1990 and 534 000 by the end of 1991. Derek (later Lord) Rayner was given the responsibility of improving financial management. His Efficiency Unit led to the Financial Management Initiative (FMI). Accompanying these developments was a closer scrutiny of top level Civil Service appointments. Some accused Thatcher of politicising the Civil Service. The pace and scale of policy changes during the Thatcher years was also said to have kept the Service on its toes.

'Agencification'

The Ibbs' Report grew out of the failure of earlier reforms to address the root of the problem. Sir Robert Ibbs began work under Thatcher producing the so-called 'Next Steps' programme published in 1988. This report criticised the Civil Service for its size, poor efficiency and conservative outlook. Its recommendations were accepted in February 1988 and have remained influential since. The main impact of the programme has been the hiving-off of Government services into semi-autonomous agencies. This agencification has progressed at great pace. In April 1990 there were 12 agencies. By April 1998 there were 124 a number that had increased to 138 by the autumn (employing 380 000 staff – 75% of the Civil Service). Though the changes have been far-reaching and dramatic not all have been convinced by the results. The Child Support Agency and the Prison Service Agency have been a particular focus of attention and criticism.

How Can Civil Servants Control?

As Tony Benn remarked in 1981

'They [Civil Servants] are always trying to steer incoming Governments back to the policy of the outgoing Government, minus the mistakes that the Civil Servants thought the outgoing Government made. And remember, when a Government is elected it has maximum energy and minimum knowledge. Just before it is defeated it has maximum knowledge and minimum energy.'

There are six distinct advantages that civil servants have over ministers:

1. **Civil Servants control information** (and can either deny ministers essential information or drown the minister in paperwork);
2. **Ministers have other Commitments**;
3. **Top Civil Servants outnumber Ministers** (10:1);
4. **Networking** (civil servants can have informal meetings – often cross-departmental – and outmanoeuvre an awkward minister);
5. **Ministers can go 'native'** (becoming surrounded by the civil service and cut off from the reality outside their departments);
6. **'Outliving' ministers** (top civil servants tend to stay in the department a lot longer than the ministers do).

The Future of the Civil Service

John Major, previously criticised for lacking both vision and a flagship policy, launched his 'big idea' – the Citizen's Charter in 1991. Though it was often criticised at the time, many facets of the scheme were retained under Labour, not least the central emphasis on the quality of provision in public services. Labour has also emphasised the need for greater forward planning and the development of a less risk-averse culture in the Civil Service. Their championing of 'joined-up government' has seen encouragement for a more co-operative and collaborative approach across traditional (often departmental) boundaries. This is likely to continue, as is the trend towards increasing reliance on political advisors and politicisation at the top of the Civil Service. Further changes in the Civil Service may be prompted by the fallout from the programme of devolution started in 1997.

7.2 Departments, ministers and 'their' civil servants

Introduction
Cabinet consists largely of the leading ministers from each Governmental Department. These Secretaries of State head Departments consisting of other Ministers of various ranks and Civil Servants. It is the relationship between top Ministers and their top Civil Servants that has often provoked the most debate.

Departmental Hierarchy
Departments are headed by a Secretary State under which there are two ranks of Junior Ministers and the position of Parliamentary Private Secretary. All three ranks serve as apprenticeships or testing grounds for MPs with ambition or potential for higher office.
As of March 2002:

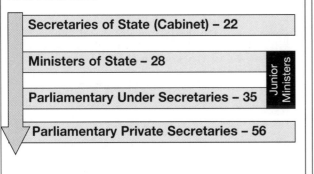

Secretaries of State (Cabinet) – 22

Ministers of State – 28

Parliamentary Under Secretaries – 35

Parliamentary Private Secretaries – 56

Junior Ministers

The Civil Service
As we have seen on the previous page a lot of Civil Servants have no real role in the policy making process. In the top 5 grades of the Administration Group however and particularly amongst those 1000 individuals who make up the top 4 grades there is significant policy input.

Administration Group Civil Servants
The top 5 Grades in the Administration Group have been known as the Senior Civil Service (SCS) since 1996. In 1998 this SCS consisted of 4000 staff with the top 4 Grades (those with key policy input) numbering about 1000.

Grade	Title
1	First Permanent Secretary
1a	Second Permanent Secretary
2	Deputy Secretary
3	Under Secretary
4	Executive Directing Bands
5	Assistant Secretary

Models of Ministerial – Civil Service Relations
Theakston, in his article 'Ministers and Mandarins' (Talking Politics Vol.4 no. 2 1991/2) outlined four models of ministerial-civil servant relationship:

The Formal Constitutional Model
This model views the Civil Service as what it was always expected to be – a service, providing the information that Ministers need, making them aware of the various permutations and problems, yet essentially remaining non-political. This model would allow for the three principles traditionally attached to the Civil Service – neutrality, anonymity and permanence. Whilst this model fits in nicely with the traditional view, it is at best only theoretical.

The Adversarial Model
This model characterises the relationship as something of a struggle for power and control. In the 1960s and 1970s Labour Ministers such as Richard Crossman and Tony Benn felt that the Civil Service was obstructing the Government's policy programme (see the quotation from Benn on the previous page). In the 1980s Margaret Thatcher felt that the Service was similarly unwilling to move ahead quickly on her radical policy programme. She, like Benn before her, accused them of having their own agenda.

The Village Life in the Whitehall Community Model
This model affords the Civil Service a greater input than that offered in the Formal Constitutional Model outlined above, yet essentially retains the idea of a close and co-operative relationship. The Ministers within the Department would provide the vision and drive, the Civil Servants would put the whole thing together based upon their long knowledge and experience of what would work. Thus, when questioned over the Maastricht Treaty, Kenneth Clarke defended the fact that he had not read the Treaty by highlighting the role of the Civil Service in addressing the detail of such legislation.

The Bureaucratic Expansionism Model
This model shares some of its suspicion of the Civil Service with the Adversarial Model, yet moves further. In the Bureaucratic Expansionism Model the Civil Servants are trying to serve their own interests by creating bureaucratic empires which are financially inefficient and get in the way of clear and effective government. It was partly a belief in this view that led to the appointment of Derek Rayner in the 1980s and the launch of the Financial Management Initiative (see Ch 7.1).

Ministerial and Collective Responsibility
In theory Ministers are bound by a number of doctrines and codes of behaviour. Under the doctrine of Collective Responsibility all Cabinet Ministers are bound to publicly stand by decisions taken collectively in Cabinet – regardless of their own personal views. Thus Michael Heseltine resigned from Cabinet over his unwillingness to remain publicly silent over the Westland Affair and Nigel Lawson and Geoffrey Howe also made high profile exits under Thatcher. In reality, however ministers now rarely resign on matters of principle, favouring instead the tactic of briefing the press against their opponents within Cabinet. The doctrine of Ministerial Responsibility can be divided into two distinct strands: role responsibility and personal responsibility. The former dictates that Ministers are responsible for what goes on in their Departments and should resign if they fail in their job. The latter concerns their personal conduct and might, for example, demand resignation over sexual of financial scandals. In reality, both aspects of Ministerial Responsibility have been undermined in recent years – not least by the unwillingness of ministers to go. Norman Lamont's failure to resign over Black Wednesday in 1992 (or by what followed) could be taken as a case in point.

What are Quangos?

The term quango is normally taken to mean …

quasi autonomous non-governmental organisation

quasi (or semi) autonomous (independent) because they tend to work with a degree of independence, non-governmental because their members are not normally drawn from the ranks of elected politicians or the Civil Service. While this may appear straightforward, there is a good deal of debate concerning precisely which groups fall inside this definition. Some take a more **exclusive** view, preferring to use the term NDPB (non-departmental public body) whereas others adopt a more **inclusive** definition and include many more groups under the broader term EGO (extra-governmental organisation). Which interpretation one favours has a dramatic affect on the numbers of quangos that one sees as existing and on attempts to discover whether overall numbers are going up or down. The narrower (exclusive) view would support the idea that there had been a fall in the number of quangos (NDPBs) from around 2000 in 1979 to around 1200 today. The broader (inclusive) definition would place the number at nearer 7000, perhaps more.

Quangos and Party Politics

Though parties in opposition are often critical of the use of quangos, they invariably become more sympathetic towards them once they are in government. In 1979, for example, Margaret Thatcher criticised the number of quangos in existence, seeing them as yet another unnecessary layer of bureaucracy. By 1994, however, quangos accounted for nearly a fifth of all government expenditure and by 1997 the Labour Party was actually accusing the Conservatives of creating a 'quango-state' (or 'quangocracy'). In 1998, the new Labour Government produced two documents, *Opening up the Doors* and *Opening up Public Appointments*, following their 1997 consultation paper, *Opening Up Quangos*. Both initiatives were, however, limited in their scope and in terms of the number of quangos affected. In addition, Labour created almost as many quangos as they removed between 1997 and 1999.

Classification of Quangos

1. Advisory Quangos

Bodies that are formed from specialists with a view to providing advice and guidance to government. Examples include the CRE (the Commission for Racial Equality) or SEAC (The Spongiform Encephalopathy Advisory Committee that advised the government on BSE, 'mad-cow disease').

2. Regulatory Quangos

Bodies that apply and in some cases formulate regulations governing particular areas of activity. Examples include OFSTED (the Office for Standards in Education that organises the inspection of state schools) and the Monopolies and Mergers Commission.

3. Administrative Quangos

Bodies that manage or administer certain activities or services on behalf of the government. A good example is QCA (the Qualifications and Curriculum Authority that manages various aspects of assessment in education).

4. Spending Quangos

Bodies that are set up to spend or distribute funds on the behalf of government. Examples include the Sports Council and the various National Lottery Boards that allocate the money raised by the Lottery for good causes.

Quangos – A Balance Sheet

Positive Uses

1. Their virtual independence from government and the secrecy in which they often work allows quangos to make the right decisions rather than politically motivated or expedient ones.
2. In certain areas, regulation for example, a certain degree of independence is particularly helpful.
3. The appointment process **can** allow the creation of bodies that are more socially representative than would be achieved through election.
4. Specialists are more suited to dealing with many areas of policy than ministers or most top civil servants.
5. By focusing on one area, quangos often avoid problems caused by conflicting priorities in government.
6. Quangos reduce the workload of ministers and departments.
7. Many quangos operate at a local level where decisions can be made more relevant to those that they affect.

Limitations

1. Quangos are not accountable to voters for their decisions. There is, therefore, a democratic deficit – especially when jobs are transferred from elected bodies to quangos.
2. Membership can be problematic. Quangos are often appointed in an atmosphere of secrecy and there have been accusations of nepotism. Sometimes key individuals are left out and there is a sense that this may be for political reasons. For example, the omission of Professor Richard Lacey from SEAC (see above) raised some concerns.
3. Quangos' meetings are often secretive and their recommendations are often not fully made public. There is a lack of transparency.
4. The proliferation of quangos has created a further unnecessary level of bureaucracy.
5. Some quangos have been accused of waste, inefficiency or corruption.

8.1 The monarchy

The role of the monarchy

The monarchy has existed in its hereditary form since the tenth century AD, if not before. According to Philip Norton, Elizabeth II can trace her own claim back to King Egbert who was said to have united England under his rule in AD829. Although the only break in the reign of monarchs came as a result of the English Civil War and the subsequent execution of Charles I (1649), the last 400 years have seen the gradual transformation from the medieval and early modern monarch, claiming the 'divine right' to rule, to the modern 'constitutional monarch'. The same period has, of course, seen a parallel growth in the power of Parliament as well as the emergence and growth of the power of the Prime Minister. The royal prerogative powers (see Ch 6.1) still offer a monarch considerable, if largely theoretical, powers. The monarch is the head of the executive, a key figure in the legislative process, the head of the judiciary, the Commander in Chief of the armed forces and the Supreme Governor of the Church of England. In reality, however, most of these powers are now exercised by the Prime Minister on behalf of the monarch. Despite this, the monarch still retains key powers:

The power to dissolve Parliament

Though the Queen generally dissolves Parliament (resulting in a general election) on the Prime Minister's request, she could refuse if, for example, a minority government was trying to gain an unfair advantage by timing an election favourably against the wishes of a clear majority of MPs. In such an instance the Queen might instead choose to offer the leader of another party the chance to form an administration.

The power to appoint the Prime Minister

This is normally straightforward. However, in the event of a 'hung parliament' (where no single party had an overall majority of seats in the Commons), the Queen would have to choose whom she should invite to try and form a government. If two or more parties were equal in strength, this decision could prove pivotal.

Turning points

1215	Magna Carta – King John accepted certain limits on the manner in which he could govern.
1280s	Edward I needed money regularly for wars. This led to Parliament being called more frequently.
1327	Edward II was deposed, partly as a result of his attempts to govern without taking advice from leading nobles.
1530s	Increasing legislative role for Parliament (Reformation Parliament, 1529–36).
1649	Charles I was executed, after maintaining the 'divine right' and quarreling with Parliament.
1689	William and Mary accepted the so-called 'Bill of Rights'. A monarch could not suspend laws or levy taxation without Parliament.
1707	Queen Anne became the last monarch to reject a bill.
1714	George I did not speak English. The role of the King's 'Prime Minister' emerged (Walpole) and, by the nineteenth century, became central.
1854	Queen Victoria became the last monarch to give the royal assent in person.

Arguments for and against the monarchy

For

Tradition
The monarchy provides a link with our past, a way of understanding where the country has come from.

The need for a non-political figurehead
The monarch is above party politics. They can unite the nation in times of crisis without appearing to look to gain politically.

Lack of a suitable alternative
The abolition of the monarchy would create a vacuum. The Prime Minister's powers might expand and/or we would have to create an elected head of state. The result would not be any better than the monarchy and could be worse.

The monarchy is cost-effective
The monarchy is good value, both in terms of the amount of money it costs and in terms of the revenues it brings into the country through tourism and overseas trade. The Princess Royal alone had 505 official engagements in 2001 (*The Observer*, December 3, 2001).

The monarchy is popular
Despite everything, the Queen is more popular than most politicians: 71% of the population think that she is hardworking (*The Observer*).

Against

The monarchy is a relic of the past
Tradition is not an argument for keeping an out-of-date institution. It is time to move on.

The hereditary principle is abhorrent
It is wrong that people should hold positions of power and authority simply as a result of an accident of birth. We should create a society that is based more on ability.

The figurehead role is outdated
The current royal family have shown themselves to be unsuitable figureheads through their dysfunctional relationships, public scandals (sexual and financial) and inappropriate interventions into the political arena. Some royals (Edward, for example) have even been accused of trying to profit from their name. They are not 'figurehead material'. Such behaviour has also affected their popularity.

The monarchy is a waste of money
The Civil List costs £8.9 million per year and other costs may be as high as £80 million. This is unacceptable when the Queen's wealth is estimated at £1.1 billion.

Introduction

Parliament comprises the monarch, the House of Commons and the House of Lords. Though the Commons has changed in size periodically – most recently as a result of the activities of the Boundaries Commission in creating new constituencies – it is the House of Lords which has seen the most dramatic changes in its composition in recent years.

The House of Commons

The Commons currently consists of 659 MPs. Each MP represents a single-member constituency, being elected using the first past the post electoral system – either in the general election or, where a vacancy has arisen, in a by-election. At the time of writing, the composition of Parliament is as follows. It includes the 2001 by-election result in Ipswich as well as the defection of Labour MP Paul Marsdon to the Liberal Democrats on December 11, 2001.

Labour	411	Plaid Cymru	4
Conservative	166	Sinn Fein	4
Liberal Democrat	53	SDLP	3
Ulster Unionists	6	Independent	1
UDUP	5	The Speaker	1
SNP	5	Total	659

The House of Lords

Until 1999 the House of Lords consisted of around 750 hereditary peers and 500 life peers. In 1999 the House of Lords Act removed the right of most hereditary peers to sit and vote in the Lords. At the same time, it allowed them to vote and stand as candidates in parliamentary elections (privileges that had previously been denied them due to their status). The intention had been to remove the voting rights of all hereditary peers, but the Weatherill Amendment allowed 92 hereditary peers to stay on a transitional House until the the completion of Lords reform; 75 who had been elected by fellow hereditary peers, the Earl Marshal, the Lord Great Chamberlain , and 15 Deputy Speakers who were retained by right. Of the 75 elected peers, 42 were Conservatives, 28 Crossbenchers, three LibDems and two Labour. Ten other hereditary peers were granted life peerages. As of May 2000 the Lords consists of:

558 life peers	92 hereditary peers	26 bishops

At the time Labour came to power in 1997, the Conservatives had 476 peers to Labour's 120. Following appointments since that time and the removal of the majority of hereditary peers the chamber currently comprises:

Conservative 222	Labour 197	LibDem 62	Crossbenchers/others 216

Socio-economic background of MPs

Ethnicity

In the general election of 7 June 2001 there were 57 ethnic minority candidates. This was up by one-third on the 1997 figure and represented a continuation of the upward trend in ethnic minority candidature since 1979, when there were only five such candidates. In 2001, 12 ethnic minority MPs were elected – all representing the Labour Party.

Education

The proportion of Conservative MPs who attended public school is 66%, compared to 16% of Labour MPs and 41% of LibDem MPs. Of the MPs in Parliament in December 2000, 153 (23%) went to Oxford or Cambridge (97 Oxford, 56 Cambridge). Sixty Labour MPs went to Oxford or Cambridge, as did 76 Conservatives and 15 Liberal Democrats.

Occupation

Following the 1997 election, 43.2% of MPs were from the professions, 18% from business, 29% miscellaneous, and 8.9 manual. Within the professions, 10.3% of MPs are trained teachers, 5.7% are barristers, and 7.5% are involved in publishing or journalism by trade.

Age

The average age of an MP is currently 50.3 years. This compares to 49.3 following the 1997 election and 50 in 1992. There are only four MPs between the ages of 18 and 29, whereas there are ten over-70s. Only 80 MPs are under 40, and 340 are over 50.

Gender

In 1987 only 6% of MPs (41) were women. This figure increased to 10% (60) in 1992 and 18.2% (120) in 1997, before falling back to 17.9% (118) in 2001.

Sexual orientation

Then Agriculture Minister Nick Brown's 'outing' in the face of allegations from a former lover brought the total of openly 'gay' MPs to nine; six by their own admission and a further three as a result of media attention and the activities of other groups. 'Outrage' claims that there are up to 30 other 'closeted' MPs vulnerable to tabloid exposure.

For comparison: Socio-economic background of local councillors

Average age:	57
Gender:	70% male, 30% female
Ethnicity:	Only 2.5% from ethnic minorities
In full time work:	52%
Retired:	38%

Source: The Improvement and Development Agency (IDeA). Quoted in *The Guardian* (February 22, 2002)

8.3 The passage of legislation

Different Types of Bill

Private Bills
Generally affect a particular area of policy or an organisation as opposed to the population as a whole. Some Private Bills only affect one or two people and these are sometimes referred to as Personal Bills.

Personal Bills
Personal Bills normally deal with regulations affecting one or two people. Sometimes they grant individuals a dispensation from existing law.

Public Bills
Public Bills affect the entire population. The vast majority of Public Bills are Government sponsored bills but there is also limited time available for Private Members Bills sponsored by Backbenchers.

Government Bills
Government Bills often seek to fulfil manifesto commitments and are much more likely of success because the Government controls the parliamentary timetable. Ministers pilot these Bills through the legislative stages.

Private Member's Bills
A Private Members Ballot allocates slots for such bills and MPs who have entered the ballot and been successful can then advance their legislation. Private Members Bills offer a way of legislating on controversial issues (eg the Abortion Act) without dividing parties.

Passage of a Government Bill

Preparation
Before a bill is introduced it will normally go through a consultation stage. This Can start with a Consultation (Green) Paper. This may then be turned into a firm proposal (White Paper) before the bill is eventually drafted.

Commons Stages

First Reading
Bill introduced. Date set for Second Reading. Bill printed up ready for Second Reading.

Second Reading
Minister outlines proposals and deals with general questions. Principles of Bill discussed.

Committee Stage
Bill sent to Standing Committee. Separate committees formed for each bill

Report Stage
Amended bill reported out of committee and voted through to....

Third Reading
No major amendments at this stage. Look at bill as a whole. Pass or reject.

Lords Stages

First Reading

Second Reading

Committee Stage
As in the Commons, the Bill passes into its committee stage following the Second Reading. In the House of Lords, however, this is normally done in the Chamber as a committee of the whole House.

Report Stage

Third Reading
If the Bills is passed it moves towards the Royal Assent. If it is rejected or significantly amended then it will return to the Commons for consideration

Under the Parliament Act (see Glossary) the Lords can only delay bills

Royal Assent
Before a Bill becomes law it must receive the Royal Assent. By convention the monarch does not refuse. The last monarch to refuse was Queen Anne (1707) over the Scottish Militias Bill.

The Work of Committees
There are two broad types committee in the House of Commons

Standing Committees
Standing committees usually have the role of considering legislation (see left) or documents. They are made up of 15–60 members, the numbers from each party reflecting the composition of the House itself. Where formed to consider a piece of legislation, standing committees can last for several months, suggesting minor changes and more serious amendments before reporting out to the House.

Select Committees
Select committees are not often as involved in the passage of legislation. Since 1979 departmental select committees have had the role of scrutinising the work of the various government departments. Of the non-departmental select committees, the Public Accounts Committee is one of the most high profile and has the role of ensuring value for money in government. This Committee has developed a fearsome reputation for making departments accountable for their spending.

8.4 The role of an MP

The representative

MPs are representatives rather than delegates (see Ch 1.2). Most MPs hold regular surgeries in order to deal with constituency issues and gauge opinion. Some MPs (such as the Prime Minister and members of the government) may have difficulty in representing their constituents as effectively, due to the demands on their time. Others (such as the Speaker and Deputy Speakers) might be restricted in what they can say due to the nature of their jobs. Voters can remove MPs through the ballot box, but in reality most MPs owe their positions more to those who selected them as their party's candidate. Few MPs have sufficient personal support to be elected without the party label (Martin Bell in 1997 and Dr Richard Taylor in 2001 being recent exceptions) and many can be said to have been elected purely due to their party label.

The loyal party drone

Most MPs are elected by virtue of the party label that they carry during the election. It is logical, therefore, the parties would argue, that MPs should toe the party line once in Parliament. To this end the party whips (see Ch 6.3) cajole and punish troublesome MPs. Such MPs might find their chances of promotion limited. Those that persistently ignore the whips might have the whip withdrawn. This effectively throws the MP out of the parliamentary party and leaves them vulnerable to de-selection in their constituency. Some MPs choose to resign the whip or even cross the floor of the House and join another party by taking that party's whip. They can do this without seeking re-election because – in theory – **they** are elected, not the party.

The watchdog

Traditionally, MPs within Parliament have had the role of holding government accountable through the various debates, committees, Prime Minister's and Ministers' Questions and – ultimately – by voting on government bills. This is crucial, but a government usually has a big enough majority to over-ride rebellions and MPs, controlled by whips, are often too fearful to act as a watchdog, particularly in the age of the 'career politician' (see below). Though there have always been MPs who prioritise this role (Tony Benn and Dennis Skinner, for example), individuals such as the Parliamentary Commissioner and bodies such as the Public Accounts Committee probably carry more weight than individual MPs.

Conscience?

The local trouble-shooter

Regardless of whether or not MPs ever follow the views of their constituents rather than the party whips, all MPs play an important role in trouble-shooting within their constituency and representing the interests of constituents facing problems either within the constituency or abroad. In recent months, for example, MPs have been at work making representations on behalf of the British plane spotters arrested and charged in Greece. MPs can also intervene in disputes between constituents and local government bodies. Many MPs also find that domestic problems are brought to their surgeries. This troubleshooting role has seen some MPs described as glorified social workers.

The legislator

For a bill to become an act, it must be passed through the House of Commons. As a result, MPs have total power over legislation. In reality, however, the situation is far different. MPs, as we have already noted, are under pressure to conform. Parliamentary debates can be cut short, committees and committee chairmen leaned on. Ironically, as the passage of the recent anti-terrorism legislation has shown, it is often the Lords who offer the more spirited opposition to government policy; a fact particularly true during the Thatcher years.

The future for MPs

Many writers have observed the increasing number of what are called 'career politicians' in the House. Whereas MPs in the 1940s served an average of only five years in Parliament, today's MPs often linger for 15 or 20 years. The job has changed: MPs now often have more comfortable office accommodation in Portcullis House, they receive a reasonable salary and over £50 000 in allowable expenses on top of that salary, and the hours of debate have been moderated. The accompanying desire to secure and then retain such a position is likely to lead to greater party loyalty within the Chamber. At the same time, however, many voters are becoming unhappy with the extent to which their representatives represent them and by the continual allegations of sleaze and scandal. The resulting disillusionment has – it is argued – contributed to lower turnout in 2001 as well as to the election of non-party parliamentary candidates (for example, Martin Bell and Dr Richard Taylor). This disaffection with MPs will need to be addressed.

8.5 Parliamentary reform

Roles and criticisms of Parliament

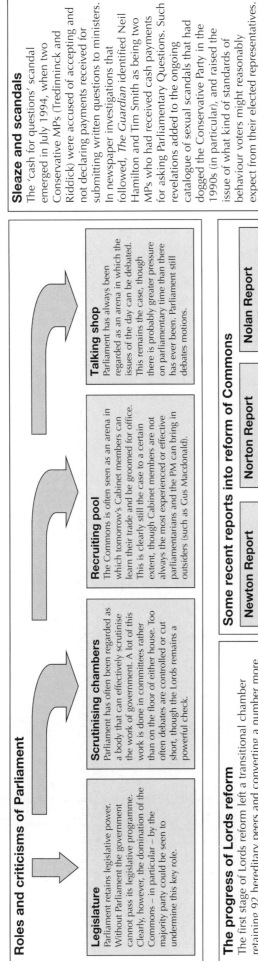

Legislature

Parliament retains legislative power. Without Parliament the government cannot pass its legislative programme. Clearly, however, the domination of the Commons – in particular – by the majority party could be seen to undermine this key role.

Scrutinising chambers

Parliament has often been regarded as a body that can effectively scrutinise the work of government. A lot of this work is done in committees rather than on the floor of either house. Too often debates are controlled or cut short, though the Lords remains a powerful check.

Recruiting pool

The Commons is often seen as an arena in which tomorrow's Cabinet members can learn their trade and be groomed for office. This is clearly still the case, though there are Cabinet members who are not always the most experienced or effective parliamentarians and the PM can bring in outsiders (such as Gus Macdonald).

Talking shop

Parliament has always been regarded as an arena in which the issues of the day can be debated. This remains the case, though there is probably greater pressure on parliamentary time than there has ever been. Parliament still debates motions.

Sleaze and scandals

The 'cash for questions' scandal emerged in July 1994, when two Conservative MPs (Tredinninck and Riddick) were accused of accepting and not declaring payments received for submitting written questions to ministers. In newspaper investigations that followed, *The Guardian* identified Neil Hamilton and Tim Smith as being two MPs who had received cash payments for asking Parliamentary Questions. Such revelations added to the ongoing catalogue of sexual scandals that had dogged the Conservative Party in the 1990s (in particular), and raised the issue of what kind of standards of behaviour voters might reasonably expect from their elected representatives. The accusations made by Mohamed Al Fayed against Neil Hamilton in *The Guardian* were particularly damning, and contributed greatly to Hamilton's exit from Parliament at the hands of Martin Bell (the anti-sleaze independent candidate) in 1997. The Nolan Committee on Standards in Public Life was set up to investigate the whole area and produced the Nolan Report.

Elizabeth Filkin …

replaced Gordon Downey as PCS and gained a reputation for the thoroughness of her investigations into complaints against – amongst others – Peter Mandelson and Keith Vaz. When she was not re-appointed in 2001, she accused some of those who had criticised her style of organising a 'whispering campaign' against her. Filkin was eventually succeeded by Phillip Mawer.

The progress of Lords reform

The first stage of Lords reform left a transitional chamber retaining 92 hereditary peers and converting a number more into life peers. In its autumn 2001 White Paper on converting Lords reform, the Government envisages a second chamber consisting of 600 members, 120 (20%) of whom would be directly elected. The remainder would be appointed members. An independent appointment commission will be created as the Wakeham Report (see below) envisaged, but it will not have sufficient power to stop all political appointments to the chamber. In January 2002 Conservative Leader Iain Duncan Smith, supported by the LibDems, called for an upper chamber of 300 (called the 'Senate') with 240 (80%) being directly elected and the remainder being appointed by the independent commission.

The Wakeham Report

On January 20, 2000 the Wakeham Commission published its recommendations on Lords reform. It proposed:
- a house of around 550 members;
- a powerful and independent appointments commission;
- fixed terms of office for members;
- an elected element (under PR) numbering 65, 87 or 195, depending on the model adopted.

Some recent reports into reform of Commons

Newton Report (2001)

A commission set up by the Hansard Society, chaired by Tony Newton (Lord Newton of Braintree), produced the Newton Report.

The Newton Report's focus was on improving government accountability. Like the Norton Report (see right) it concluded that what was needed was the strengthening of the select committee system, as well as a greater willingness to communicate to the broader public in a sincere and comprehensible manner.

Norton Report (2000)

The Norton Report was commissioned by the Leader of the Opposition in 1999 and chaired by Philip Norton (Lord Norton of Louth).

The Report recommended, amongst other things, the strengthening and broadening of the system of select committees. This would allow for greater scrutiny of legislation and might also help to improve financial efficiency. It would make the work of government and Parliament more transparent, allowing for greater public appreciation of Parliament's work.

Nolan Report (1995)

The Nolan Committee (see right) was set up by the Government and chaired by Lord Justice Nolan.

In its first report (1995) it recommended, amongst other things, that there should be a 'code of conduct' for MPs and an Independent Parliamentary Commissioner for Standards. In November 1995 the House introduced a number of key changes. Crucially, it created a Select Committee on Standards and Privileges and appointed a Parliamentary Commissioner for Standards (PCS), Sir Gordon Downey.

9.1 The history and organisation of local government

Introduction

The basic units of local government – parish, county and borough – date back to the end of the Middle Ages. Even in the 1960s, however, there was little uniformity. In some areas authorities were too small to provide services effectively or efficiently, while in others they were too big to allow a good degree of democratic accountability. This problem of accountability was also emphasised by the unclear division of roles between different tiers of local government – the voters simply did not know who was responsible for what. All of these problems were further aggravated by the fact that the authority boundaries often dated back many years and no longer bore any relation to what was on the ground. Such inefficiency, inconsistency, unaccountability and inappropriateness led to calls for reform.

Recent local election results

Turnout and voting patterns

In 2002, experiments in postal voting raised turnout by 28% in those wards included in the trial. Similar trials in text voting and online voting also increased turnout (by 5% and 1% respectively). Overall, however, turnout for local elections in non-general-election years is poor.

% Local election turnout in non-general-election years (rounded)

1996	1998	1999	2000	2002
34%	28%	31%	29%	35%

In addition, voters often use local elections to register protest votes against the party in office nationally. This normally benefits the LibDems.

% voting by party (general elections shaded for comparison)

Party	1997	1998	2000	2001	2002
Lab	43%	37%	29%	42%	33%
Con	31%	33%	38%	33%	34%
LibDem	17%	25%	28%	19%	27%

The 2002 local elections also saw the Kidderminster Health Concern Party gain overall control of Wyre Forest district council and the Hartlepool FC mascot, the monkey *H'Angus* (Stuart Drummond), elected as the new mayor of Hartlepool, commanding a budget of £106 million.

Local government reform

1960s and 1970s

The Maud Report of 1967 sought to address many of the criticisms outlined above. Although it recommended unitary (one tier) authorities in most areas, the Labour Government fell before its implementation and the Conservative Government provided for a two-tier system in the 1972 Local Government Act that came into force in 1974. In London, the GLC operated above the London Boroughs. In the six other metropolitan counties, Metropolitan County Councils operated above Metropolitan Districts. In the other (non-metropolitan) areas, County Councils operated above District Councils. In all areas, the 10 000 or so lower councils (generally parish councils in England) remained relatively untouched.

1980s

Margaret Thatcher abolished the GLC and the Metropolitan Counties in 1986, encouraging the formation of joint boards to deal with big services, and devolving all other powers down to the London Boroughs and Metropolitan Districts. Many saw this as an attempt to attack predominantly Labour-dominated councils who were pursuing radical policy agendas out of step with central government. These changes and the changes in local taxation are dealt with in Ch 9.2.

Local government in the 1990s

The local government review announced by Michael Heseltine in 1990 sought to address some of the problems that were seen as central to Thatcher's fall (for example, the 'Poll Tax' debacle), as well as considering broader questions of local government structure. The Banham Commission from 1992 investigated the possibility of introducing a greater number of unitary authorities (as Maud had recommended in the 1960s). Though the Secretary of State for the Environment was keen on the extension of unitary authorities for some areas and a retention of the old two-tier structure in other areas, the Commission gradually moved towards a position where it favoured unitary authorities, the result of the Commission's work has been the creation of a greater number of unitary authorities where it has been shown that such authorities can make sense economically, in terms of what is on the ground, and in terms of local accountability. The return to office of the Labour Party in 1997 and the appointment of Hillary Armstrong as Local Government Minister promised a more co-operative and collaborative relationship between local and central government. This and the current state of play is addressed in Ch 9.2.

Do we need local government?

YES

Political participation
The existence of local government encourages people to get involved in making the decisions that will affect them the most.

Representation
Local government can represent local people more effectively than Westminster.

Relevance
Local councils know what the local area needs. It makes sense to delegate power

NO

Participation rates in local government are extremely low and voter turnout is poor.

Councillors rarely have the resources or the time to **represent** local people properly. Local government is amateurish.

Local governments often get lost in the detail and fail to see the bigger picture. Central government can often be more objective and, therefore, more **appropriate.**

9.2 Central–local government relations

Outline

The reality for local government is that it is largely at the mercy of central government. Despite the devolution of certain powers to Scotland, Wales and the Northern Ireland Assembly, the UK remains a unitary state. Any or all of these powers could in fact be returned to Parliament at any time. Local government can only do what it is given the authority to do by central government. A significant chunk of local government funding still comes in the form of central government grants (though less of a proportion of total local authority spending than was the case in the 1970s, when it stood at around 60%). Moreover, the role and status of local government has been eroded as a result of a series of changes largely brought about under the Thatcher Administrations (see below) but continued under Major and Blair. The key to the relationship between central and local government lies in the powers that the former holds over the latter. These allow central government to determine whether central and local government are partners or whether local government is merely an agent of central government.

Legislation

Central government has total power to legislate over the range and extent of local government power. If it wanted to, it could abolish local government altogether.

The doctrine of ultra vires

Local authorities are only allowed to do what is authorised by law. Anything else is 'ultra vires' (beyond their authority). Councillors can be prosecuted and fined.

Inspections

Central government can inspect the delivery of local government services directly, or through organisations such as OFSTED.

Acting in default

Ultimately, central government can act in default, taking control of a particular local service under the direct control of central government.

Central–local government relations under Thatcher

Local government taxation

The government decided to replace the rates (a property-based tax) with the Community Charge (a tax on all local adults). Thatcher believed that making local authorities directly accountable for their spending to all adults (and therefore voters) in their area would encourage high-spending councils to make efficiencies and cuts, for fear of not being returned to office. The public reaction to this policy contributed to Thatcher's fall and it was abandoned in 1991 in favour of the property-based Council Tax.

Changes in education and housing

The introduction of the National Curriculum reduced the power of local advisors, and the introduction of local management for schools and then grant maintained status diminished the role of local authorities in education massively. The sale of council houses through the right to buy legislation of the early 1980s removed local authorities from another major aspect of people's lives. Taken together, such changes diminished local government responsibilities (and therefore its status) significantly.

Municipal socialism and the abolition of the Greater London Council (GLC)

Faced by the reality of a lengthy Conservative period in office, many urban Labour-controlled councils tried to do as much as they could on a local level to create the kind of society that they wanted. The right ridiculed this so-called 'municipal socialism', and these 'loony left' councillors were criticised for their poor controls over spending. The central government used the tactic of 'capping' to limit local tax revenues and, therefore, spending. The GLC, headed by 'red Ken' Livingstone, was also abolished and members of Liverpool Council were prosecuted.

New Labour and the future of local government

In 1998 and 1999 the Government produced a key White Paper, 'Modern Local Government: In Touch with the People' (1998) and a number of bills and future proposals. Collectively, these moves amounted to a commitment to develop local government in two distinct areas in the years ahead:

To improve the quality of local services

This aim was embodied in the Government's so-called 'Best Value' programme. During the last years of the Conservative administration there had been an extension of Compulsory Competitive Tendering. That meant that local services had to be put out to tender and that local authorities were then bound to accept the lowest acceptable tender regardless of other considerations. Under 'Best Value' authorities would not be forced to put services out to tender, but they would still be expected to plan for excellence and use the private sector where it provided the best way of delivering services. Another part of the programme was the opportunity for councils to apply to become Beacon Councils based solely upon the excellence of their service. This reflected similar changes made in education, where Beacon Schools were supposed to show others the way forward.

To undertake a programme of democratic renewal

There has long been a feeling that local government has been overtaken by apathy. This second part of the Labour agenda is aimed at re-invigorating local government institutions and practices, with a view to encouraging greater public involvement, understanding and interest. One plank of this programme is the move towards allowing local authorities to change the structure of their executives. Under the policy, authorities have the option of adopting a structure incorporating an elected mayor supported by a local cabinet that could provide clear vision and direction at a local level. In line with this policy, a new Greater London Assembly was set up under the newly-elected Mayor; ironically, one Ken Livingstone. Other elements of the programme involve increasing voter turnout in local elections by bringing greater flexibility and innovation to the process – including internet voting, more postal voting and having polling stations situated in supermarkets and other public places. There is also a desire to improve standards of ethics amongst local councillors and to deliver greater accountability, making decision-making more open, inclusive and transparent.

9.3 Devolution: the Scottish Parliament and the Welsh Assembly

Introduction

For many, devolution was one of the 'hot' issues of the 1970s. The successes of the nationalists in Scotland in the 1974 elections put the issue firmly on the agenda, and the referendums of March 1979 offered both the Scots and the Welsh the opportunity to achieve a degree of devolved government. In the event, the referendum showed little support for such a move in Wales. In Scotland the 'yes-campaign' won the majority of votes but the regulations governing the referendum stated that there needed to be support from 40% of the electorate for the plans to go ahead. Though the 'yes' camp had the majority of votes cast, the turnout was not sufficient to take them over the 40% of electorate threshold. The failure in the referendums took some steam out of the campaign for devolution but support grew again in the late 1980s, and by the time of the 1997 general election the Labour Party was committed to new referendums in Scotland and in Wales. In September 1997 these referendums ran on the basis of a simple majority of those voting; that is, without the 40% of electorate requirement that had caused so many problems in the 1979 Scottish Referendum.

The Scottish Parliament

The Referendum

In its 1997 election manifesto the Labour Party had committed itself to a referendum on the question of devolution for Scotland. The Referendum that took place in September 1997 presented the Scottish electorate with two questions: whether there should be a Scottish Parliament and whether the Parliament should have tax-varying powers. The questions offered voters the chance to vote 'no, no', 'yes, no' or 'yes, yes':

Parliament	Yes 74.3%	No 25.7%	Tax-varying	Yes 63.5%	No 36.5%

Election and composition

The 1999 election was completed under an AMS (FPTP-TU) system (see Ch 10)

Party	FPTP seats	List top-up	Total MSPs
Conservative	0	18	18
Labour	53	3	56
LibDem	12	5	17
SNP	7	28	35
Others	1	2	3
Totals	73	56	129

Function and effectiveness

The Scottish Parliament had significant power devolved to it at the time of its creation. Though areas such as foreign policy, employment legislation and control of the monetary system were reserved for the Westminster Parliament, Scotland took total control of areas such as education, agriculture, and law and home affairs. The second 'yes' in the 'yes, yes' referendum result also gave the Parliament income tax-varying powers.

No party won an overall majority in the Parliament elections so the LibDem and Labour groups went into coalition to form an administration headed by First Minister Donald Dewar (later Henry McLeish and – at the time of writing – Jack McConnell). Though the administration has been criticised in some areas (for example, the debacle over Scottish public examination results) it has been made significant moves in other areas (for example, addressing the issue of student loans).

NB the number of Scottish MPs in the **Westminster Parliament** is likely to be reduced from 72 to 58. This is a partial remedy for what was once called the 'West Lothian Question' – the problem of what to do about the 'double representation' of Scottish voters once devolution had occurred.

The Welsh Assembly

The Referendum

As was the case with Scottish devolution, the Labour Party had a 1997 manifesto commitment to bring forward proposals for and a referendum on devolving power to a Welsh Assembly. The election of the Labour government led, therefore, to the 1997 Referendum. Unlike in Scotland, where voters were faced with two questions, Welsh voters simply had to decide whether or not they supported the government's proposals:

Yes	50.3% (559 419 votes)	No	49.7% (552 698 votes)

Election and composition

The 1999 election was completed under an AMS (FPTP-TU) system (see Ch 10)

Party	FPTP seats	List top-up	Total MWAs
Conservative	1	8	9
Labour	27	1	28
LibDem	3	3	6
Plaid Cymru	9	8	17
Others	0	0	0
Totals	40	20	60

Function and effectiveness

The Assembly was not given the same powers as the Scottish Parliament. The Assembly has no primary legislative powers but can recommend legislation to the UK Parliament and has a role in overseeing Welsh quangos. It can also implement Westminster legislation in Wales. The Assembly does not have the income tax-varying powers afforded the Scottish Parliament.

As was the case in Scotland, the Assembly Elections did not provide any one party with an overall majority. Unusually, however, the Labour group under Alun Michael decided to go it alone in a minority administration. Michael was widely regarded as someone who had been imposed on the Welsh Labour Party from Westminster and he struggled to achieve any real degree of control. In 2000 he resigned and was replaced as First Secretary by Rhodri Morgan, the man who many felt should have been given the job at the outset. Morgan took the Labour group into coalition with the LibDems.

9.4 Northern Ireland (part 1): historical context and main political parties

Historical context

Ireland came under the effective control of England during the Tudor period, following a policy of extending colonisation beyond the Pale, the area around Dublin which had been under English influence for some time. By the end of the Tudor period, Ireland had been all but conquered, but opposition to the nature and style of English rule continued beyond 1603. Between 1800 and 1921 the whole of Ireland was part of the UK under the terms of the Act of Union, but in 1921 the Westminster Government gave in to pressure from nationalists and agreed the Irish Treaty which split the country into two. The south initially became a self-governing dominion (much in the same way as countries such as Canada and Australia had been) but in 1949 it became the Irish Republic. The six North-Eastern counties remained part of the UK, though governed by a devolved assembly at Stormont. The partition of Ireland led to a civil war in the newly-created free state, between those who accepted the partition (the 'Free-Staters') and those who saw the non-inclusion of the remaining six counties as a betrayal. The Assembly, initially intended to be little more than 'a glorified county council' according to the British Prime Minister Lloyd George, became a Protestant-dominated parliament for a Protestant-dominated 'state' under its own Northern Ireland Prime Minister.

Between 1922 and 1972 the British Government was reasonable happy to allow the Stormont Parliament to rule the Six Counties as it saw fit. The Stormont Parliament remained a Protestant-dominated body, the police force (the Royal Ulster Constabulary) was a Protestant-dominated organisation and the vast majority of Northern Irish MPs returned to the Westminster Parliament represented unionist parties. During this period, however, tensions grew between the Protestant community and the Catholic minority – increasingly resentful of the inequalities in the treatment they received, not only at the hands of the RUC but also in terms of employment opportunities. Increased tension led to an increase in protest and, ultimately, violence. This violence was made worse by the emergence and growth of armed paramilitary groups. On the nationalist side the Official Irish Republican Army (IRA) had favoured legitimate protest, using armed force largely for self-defence. In 1969, disillusioned with the failure of the Official IRA to act more decisively, some of the more militant members of the organisation split to form the Provisional IRA. On the unionist side, the Ulster Defence Association (UDA) and the Ulster Volunteer Force (UVF) were active. As a result of the increasing tension between the various groups and the British Government's loss of confidence in the Stormont administration's ability to address the associated problems, the Assembly was dissolved in 1972 and replaced by direct rule.

Political parties in Northern Ireland

Unionist

Ulster Unionist Party (UUP)

The UUP was the party that effectively governed the North from 1922–72. The Party's members at Westminster tend to vote with the Conservative Party, with whom they were closely aligned before the decision to bring in direct rule in 1972. They signed up to the Good Friday Agreement (see Ch 9.5) and are generally regarded as the moderate of the two unionist parties.

Democratic Unionist Party (DUP)

Ian Paisley formed the DUP in 1971 as an offshoot of the UUP. The Party opposed the Good Friday Agreement and generally takes a more extreme unionist stance, being unwilling to make concessions to the Catholic community in the North.

General election performance (seats)

Party	1992	1997	2001
UUP	9	10	6
DUP	3	2	5

Nationalist

Social Democratic and Labour Party (SDLP)

The Party was founded in 1970 as a nationalist rather than a Catholic party, but it is fair to say that the vast body of its support comes from the Catholic community. The SDLP played a leading role in brokering the Good Friday Agreement and it is widely regarded as the more moderate of the two main nationalist groups.

Sinn Fein

Sinn Fein's military wing is the IRA and prior to the 1980s it refused to legitimise Westminster elections by putting up candidates. Since then, however, it has stood in elections and in recent years – particularly as it has taken a more active role in the peace process – its support has increased significantly.

General election performance (seats)

Party	1992	1997	2001
SDLP	4	3	3
Sinn Fein	0	2	4

The Good Friday Agreement

The Good Friday Agreement came at the end of more than a decade of substantial negotiations, reviews and proposals. The Anglo–Irish Agreement of 1985 established the right of the Republic of Ireland to have a say in policy-making in Northern Ireland, and this paved the way for the Downing Street Declaration in 1993. This joint declaration from the British and Irish Governments and the framework document that followed in 1995 provided the basis for further negotiations and for the setting up of an international commission under Senator George Mitchell, which was given the task of addressing the question of arms decommissioning (see right). Following Labour's general election victory in 1997, it became obvious that the Northern Irish peace process was high on the agenda. The IRA restored its cease-fire on July 19, 1997 and this opened the way for the all-party talks that resulted in the Good Friday Agreement of April 1998. The Agreement was confirmed by referendum. In Northern Ireland, 71.1% voted in favour of the Agreement and in the Republic support was at 94.4% for an agreement that involved giving up their constitutional claims to Northern Ireland.

The terms of the Good Friday Agreement

The final Agreement included seven key elements

An elected Northern Ireland Assembly Made up of 108 elected members (see below) and holding legislative powers	**A Governing Executive Committee** Made up of 12 ministers and headed by a First Minister
A prisoner release programme In light of the peace process, terrorist prisoners from both sides of the divide were to be released on licence.	**A Council of the Isles** Drawing together representatives from Dublin, Belfast, Westminster, the Scottish Parliament and the Welsh Assembly
Arms decommissioning See right.	**A North–South Ministerial Council** Allowing ministers from Dublin and Belfast to co-ordinate and promote joint policies
	RUC reform Eventually the subject of the Independent Commission on Policing under Chris Patten. Included, symbolically, changing the name of the force

The Northern Ireland Assembly and Executive

The Good Friday Agreement called for an elected Assembly of 108 members. The elections for the Assembly took place in June 1998 under STV. The turnout was 69% and the results are shown below left.

Party	Seats
UUP	28
SDLP	24
DUP	20
Sinn Fein	18
Alliance	6
UK Unionists	5
Independent Unionists	3
Progressive Unionists	2
Women's Coalition	2
Total	**108**

The Executive

The Executive consists of 12 ministers including a First Minister (initially David Trimble UUP) and a Deputy (initially Seamus Mallon SDLP) plus the heads of the various departments including Health, Education, Environment, Economic Development, Agriculture and Finance. The decision of Sinn Fein to nominate Martin McGuinness as Education Minister caused some disquiet due to his admission that he had been active in the IRA earlier in his career.

Arms decommissioning

The issue of decommissioning paramilitary arms was and remains central to the long-term chances of success in the peace process.

The Mitchell Report

An international commission into the decommissioning of weapons was set up under Senator George Mitchell in 1995. Its report (the Mitchell Report) was published in 1996 and recommended that some decommissioning should take place during but not necessarily before all-party talks. John Major insisted that decommissioning should take place first, an assertion that might have prompted the IRA to break its cease-fire the following month by bombing Canary Wharf.

The Mitchell Review

In July 1999 Senator Mitchell was persuaded to return to conduct a review of the Good Friday Agreement. This review (the Mitchell Review) was completed by November and was generally favourable, encouraging unionists – in particular – to moderate their position. The International Commission on Decommissioning was to be headed by John de Chastelain (a Canadian general). It would be his task to assess the progress towards decommissioning and play a role in the verification of such decommissioning. With this in prospect and Sinn Fein making the right noises, David Trimble was able to carry his party with him – just.

What has followed has been a game of brinkmanship on both sides. Indeed, on several occasions the Northern Ireland Secretary has been forced temporarily to suspend the Executive. By the time of writing, however, the Commission has been satisfied that the IRA has put some weapons permanently beyond use.

Sinn Fein MPs

Sinn Fein MPs elected to the Westminster Parliament have, traditionally, not taken up their seats. In December 2001, however, following a heated debate in the chamber, Sinn Fein MPs were given access to Commons facilities even though they are not formally sworn in as MPs. They took up this right in January 2002.

10.1 The electoral system

General Elections (The First Past the Post System)

The UK is divided into 659 Parliamentary Constituencies. Each Constituency elects a single MP to represent them in the House of Commons. In a General Election, voters cast a single vote for the Candidate that they would like to represent their Constituency. At the end of the voting process, the votes are totalled and the candidate with the largest number of votes wins. The winning candidate needs only one vote more than their nearest rival to secure victory; hence 'first past the post' (FPTP). Where a vacancy arises (through death or resignation for example), a by-election takes place in the affected constituency using the same rules. Local elections also operate under FPTP.

Quirky Results

1935 was the last year in which the winning party in a General Election secured more than 50% of the votes cast.

In the General Elections of 1950, 1951 and February 1974 the winning party gained less votes nationally than the party that ended up forming the official opposition.

In 1983 the Labour Party gained 27.6% of the votes nationally and won 209 seats. The Liberal/SDP Alliance, in contrast, gained 25.4% of the votes but only won 23 seats.

The Majority of 2 votes achieved by the LibDems in Winchester in 1997 was the lowest constituency majority in any seat for 50 years.

The voter turnout in the 2001 General Election – 59% – was the lowest since 1918.

In Focus – 2001 Election

(a) Largest Majority: Easington (Lab. Hold)
53.7% turnout
Conservative 3 411 (10.3%)
Labour 25 360 (76.8%)
LibDem 3 408 (10.3%)
Socialist Labour Party 831 (2.5%)

A Labour majority of 21 949 votes (66.5%)

In Focus – 2001 Election

(b) Smallest Majority: Cheadle (LibDem gain)
65.5% turnout
Conservative 18 444 (42.3%)
Labour 6 086 (14%)
LibDem 18 477 (42.4%)
UK Independence Party 599 (1.4%)

A LibDem majority of 33 votes (0.1%)

European Elections (*A Regional List System*)

European Parliament Elections in Northern Ireland have operated under Proportional Representation (PR) since 1979. 1999 saw the first European Parliament (EP) Elections in Britain to be conducted under a system of PR. Under the d'Hondt or Closed Party List system (see p41) voters in each British region voted for their preferred party. The 84 British EP seats were then divided up within regions according to votes cast. This led to a result which was more proportional than FPTP, for the main parties at least:

Party	% Votes	No. Seats	% Seats
Labour	28	29	34.5
Conservative	35.8	36	42.9
LibDem	12.7	10	11.9
UKIP	7	3	3.6
Green	6.3	2	2.4

Scottish Parliament and Welsh Assembly Elections (*First Past the Post Top Up*)

1999 saw the first elections to the new Scottish Parliament and Welsh Assembly, conducted under the First Past the Post Top Up system (FPTP-TU). This system gives a top up number of seats to parties that lose out through the First Past the Post system. It does this by awarding top-up seats in proportion to the votes cast for each party. Each voter casts two votes, one for their chosen candidate in their constituency and one for their chosen party. The second 'party' votes are then totalled within each region and the regional top-up seats are awarded proportionally; whilst taking into consideration the constituency seats that the party has already won before FPTP. Top-up seats are then filled from lists of candidates drawn up before the election by each party. For example, If a party wins two top-up seats then the first two candidates on their list are duly elected. In Scotland there are 129 MSPs in total (73 FPTP and 56 TU). In Wales there are 60 MWAs (40 FPTP and 20 TU).

Party	Scottish Parliament			Welsh Assembly		
	FPTP	TU	Total	FPTP	TU	Total
Labour	53	3	56	27	1	28
Conservative	0	18	18	1	8	9
LibDem	12	5	17	3	3	6
SNP	7	28	35			
Plaid Cymru				9	8	17
Others	1	2	3	0	0	0

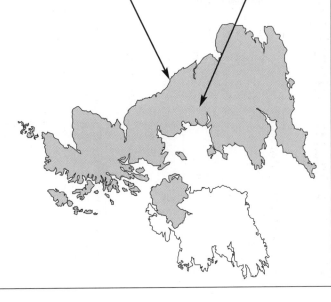

10.2 The case for and against electoral reform

What is an electoral system?

In the British context, an electoral system is a set of rules by which popular votes are translated into seats in a legislature. Electoral systems can be broadly divided into those which are *majoritarian* (i.e. require the winner to secure a majority), those which are *proportional* (i.e. attempting to distribute seats in proportion to votes cast), and those which are a combination of the two – *hybrid* systems.

What should an electoral system seek to offer?

According to Lord Jenkins' Independent Commission on Electoral Reform, an effective electoral system should seek to address four main objectives. These scores (out of five) are only for purposes of discussion and are adapted from the report:

Objective	FPTP	AV	STV	List	AMS
Proportionality	1	2	4	5	5
Stable government	4	3	2	2	2
Voter choice	1	3	5	2	3
The MP–constituency link	5	5	3	1	3
Total	**11**	**13**	**14**	**10**	**13**

First past the post: arguments for/arguments against

Arguments for:

- The system is part of our traditions.
- The system is cheap and easy to operate.
- The system is easily understood, which helps voters and contributes to greater confidence in the result.
- The single-member constituency allows for a close MP–constituency link.
- The system normally produces strong, majority governments, making coalitions less likely.

Arguments against:

- The system distorts the popular vote to an unacceptable degree.
- It leads to large numbers of wasted votes.
- It disadvantages small parties.
- It provides too little voter choice.
- It leads to artificially polarised adversarial politics. Coalition government would be more constructive in the long term.
- It perpetuates the current geographical strongholds of some parties.

Electoral reform in favour of what?

Alternative vote and AV+

AV is a *majoritarian* system whereas AV+ is a *hybrid* system.

AV retains the single-member constituencies present in FPTP but requires the winning candidate in each constituency to gain 50%+ of the votes cast. Instead of putting a cross in a single box, voters have the opportunity to rank candidates in order of preference (1,2,3 etc.). Any candidate achieving 50%+ of the votes when the first preferences are counted is elected. If no candidate wins on first preferences, the bottom candidate is eliminated and their votes are transferred to the second preferences indicated on each ballot paper. This continues until a candidate crosses the 50%+ winning line. AV+ operates in the same way as FPTP-TU (with the voter voting once for candidates and once – the '+' bit – for their preferred party) but the FPTP element is replaced with the AV system above.

AV used in Australia.
AV+ recommended by the Jenkins Commission.

Single transferable vote

STV is a *proportional* system.

STV is probably the most complicated system. Its aim of achieving clear proportionality and eliminating wasted votes requires a fairly complex system of counting and vote transference. STV replaces single-member constituencies with larger multi-member constituencies. Voters indicate their preferences for a number of candidates in order (1,2,3 etc.). In order to be elected, a candidate must achieve a quota. Once this quota is achieved, any surplus votes for that candidate are transferred in accordance with second preferences. If no candidate is elected on first preferences, then the lowest-polling candidate is eliminated and their votes are redistributed in the same way. This process continues until enough candidates have achieved the quota for all of the seats in the multi-member constituency to be filled.

STV used in: Northern Ireland Assembly elections, Irish Republic.

Party list (regional or national)

PL is a *proportional* system.

Under PL voters cast their vote for a party, either on a regional (RL) or a national basis (NL). Each party draws up a list of candidates in the order (top down) that the party would want to see them elected. Each party will often include as many candidates on their lists as there are seats available. An 'open list system' allows voters to express preferences between candidates standing for the same party, whereas a 'closed list system' only gives the voter the chance to vote for their party of choice, the candidate order already having been decided by the party. After the voting process, the votes are totalled and the seats are then distributed in proportion to votes cast. In a closed list system, a party achieving a 20% share of the vote would achieve 40 seats in a 200-seat parliament. The top 40 names from that party's list would, therefore, be elected.

Used in: Israel (NL), European elections in UK (RL).

Additional members system

AMS is a *hybrid* system.

Under AMS a proportion of seats are contested using the FPTP system and the remainder are used to reward parties in proportion to the number of votes that they achieve. This second, proportional, element can be organised on a national or a regional basis. In Germany, for example, 50% of seats are elected under FPTP with the remaining 50% being distributed proportionally. In the Scottish Parliament and Welsh Assembly elections another variant of AMS, FPTP top-up, was used (see Ch 10.1). In Germany there is a threshold of 5% which parties must cross before they are entitled to any of the additional/top-up seats.

Used in: Germany, Scottish Parliament and Welsh Assembly, Greater London Authority.

Conclusions: Prior to the 1997 general election, the Labour Party offered an independent report on electoral reform, to be followed by a referendum on any resulting proposals. Lord Jenkins duly led the investigation, which selected AV+ as the most appropriate system. Had this system been operating in 1997, it is estimated that the actual Labour majority of 179 would have been reduced to 60. The Labour Government has not implemented the Jenkins Report but it has brought in a variety of new systems for elections to, amongst others, the European Parliament, the Scottish Parliament, the Welsh Assembly and the London Assembly. Under many of these systems, Labour has fared worse than it did under FPTP in 1997. Some have argued that this has dampened the Party's enthusiasm towards the introduction of PR for parliamentary elections. Many more feel that the introduction of so many different systems in such a short space of time has been counterproductive.

What is a referendum?

A referendum is a popular vote in which the electorate decides an issue by answering 'yes' or 'no' to a question. In the UK context, the questions are set by the government. In some countries, however, there are mechanisms which allow citizens to initiate referendums on their own questions. Referendums can be either 'advisory' (i.e. only for the purpose of giving the government a clear view of the public mood) or 'binding' (committing the government to legislate in line with the referendum's outcome). Referendums are often held when a major constitutional change is on the cards but many countries use these mechanisms far more frequently (see bottom right).

Arguments for

- Referendums offer a greater degree of 'direct democracy'. Citizens can have a real input into key decisions.
- They encourage political participation. People are more likely to participate when they care about the issues involved and the choices are black and white.
- They provide a way for governments to 'test the water' before making certain changes.
- They allow government to focus on other issues, rather than getting bogged down in long-running squabbles.
- They can be used to provide a clear and final answer.
- They can prevent dangerous divisions within political parties over controversial issues. This prevents governments from collapsing and, therefore, provides greater continuity in government.
- They provide a way of focusing or renewing the mandate on a particular issue.
- They provide a method for resolving tricky moral questions.
- They provide a way of legitimising major constitutional changes.

Arguments against

- Referendums are inconsistent with our system of parliamentary government and they undermine the principles of a representative democracy.
- Far from encouraging participation, regular use of referendums could lead to apathy and low turnouts that might distort the results.
- They undermine collective responsibility in Cabinet.
- Governments can use referendums to duck their responsibility to make decisions – to 'govern'.
- Most issues are too complicated to be condensed into a simple yes/no question.
- Funding differences between the 'yes' and 'no' camps might mean that the referendum is not played out on a level playing field.
- The questions might be biased; phrased in such a way as to encourage a certain response.
- Governments can time referendums to make a favourable result more likely.
- Decisions are not always considered final. Governments sometimes go back again and again until they get the result that they want.
- Referendums create a tyranny of the majority.

UK referendums to date

All of the referendums in the UK thus far have been concerned with the distribution of power between the various tiers of government: supra-national, national and sub-national.

Summary

	Date	Who voted	Questions	Turnout (%)	Yes (%)	No (%)
1.	1973, March	N Ireland	Should NI stay in the UK?	58.1	98.9	1.1
2.	1975, June	UK	Should UK stay in the EEC?	63.2	67.2	32.8
3.	1979, March	Scotland	Should there be a Scottish Parliament?	63.8	51.6	48.4
4.	1979, March	Wales	Should there be a Welsh Parliament?	58.3	20.3	79.7
5.	1997, Sept.	Scotland	Should there be a Scottish Parliament?	60.4	74.3	25.7
			With tax-varying powers?		63.5	36.5
6.	1997, Sept.	Wales	Should there be a Welsh Assembly?	50.1	50.3	49.7
7.	1998, May	London	A London Mayor and London Assembly?	34	72	28
8.	1998, May	N Ireland	Approval for the Good Friday Agreement.	81	71.1	28.9

Future UK referendums?

The government is committed to a referendum before entry into the European Currency (euro). In the past there has been a commitment to a referendum before any change to the electoral system used in general elections. Referendums could also be employed to decide other key constitutional changes concerning institutions such as the monarchy. In 1998 Lord Neill's Committee on Standards in Public Life recommended that future referendums in the UK should be state-funded and that the 'yes' and 'no' campaigns should share a £1.2 million pot. It is also likely that the precise wording of any future referendum would have to be approved by the Electoral Commission, in order to avoid any dangers associated with biased wording.

The experience in other countries

Referendums are widely used in other countries. For example:

- In the **United States** many states operate a system of initiatives (propositions). Citizens often have the opportunity to raise questions for public vote if they can gain the support of a specified proportion of the state's population. Though not all of these propositions are passed, many have been significant. For example, Proposition 184 in California created a mandatory 25-year sentence for those convicted of a serious felony for the third time (the so-called 'three strikes and you're out' rule).
- In **Ireland** a 1995 referendum legalised divorce (by a margin of only 9124 votes). The 1998 referendum authorised constitutional changes in line with the Good Friday Agreement. The Irish referendum of 2001 rejected the Treaty of Nice. In March 2002 the Irish rejected a further tightening of their strict anti-abortion laws by 629 041 votes to 618 485.
- In **Switzerland** a referendum on a law can take place if 50 000 voters sign a petition and 100 000 voters can initiate a referendum on a constitutional amendment. Since referendums started in Switzerland 135 years ago there have been over 450. The current rate is four per year. In December 2001, for example, the Swiss rejected a proposal to abolish their armed forces. A similar proposal had been rejected three years earlier. In March 2002 the Swiss voted to join the UN by 55% to 45%. In 1986 they had rejected a similar proposal 3:1.
- In **Italy** 500 000 of the country's electors can initiate a referendum.
- In **New Zealand** the 1993 Citizen's Initiated Referenda Act requires support of 10% of the electorate to initiate a non-binding referendum.

11.1 The origins and development of the British party system

Introduction
Political parties have a long history in Britain, but modern mass political parties have their origins in the waves of electoral reform, starting in 1832, that extended the franchise (right to vote). Before the 1830s the two parties – the Whigs and the Tories – existed not as mass political parties with formal institutions outside Parliament and a mass membership, but merely as groups of like-minded individuals within Parliament, bound together by ideas, friendship or family ties. With electoral reform, however, came a need to organise – to mobilise the (however slowly) expanding electorate in support of one's party. Certainly, by the time the Labour Party was formed at the start of the twentieth century, political parties were organisations that would be more familiar to anyone studying their modern counterparts.

Different types of party systems
It is often said that Britain operates as a two-party system. The truth or otherwise of this statement will be discussed below, but the statement itself does beg the question 'what other kinds of party systems exist?'

The two-party system
Where a two-party system operates, two fairly equally matched parties compete for power. Smaller parties might also be involved in elections but they will have no realistic prospect of breaking the monopoly held by the big two.

Britain is often cited as a two-party system (see debate below). The US would be another good example.

The single-party system
In some countries a single party is able to monopolise government, ban other political parties and exercise total control over all candidates, where elections occur at all.

This type of system operated in the USSR and in many Eastern European states after the Second World War and in Nazi Germany.

The dominant-party system
This system exists where many parties may exist but only one ever gets elected, or at least forms the senior member in a coalition government.

In Japan the Liberal Democratic Party remained in power for 38 years following its formation in 1955.

The multi-party system
In a multi-party system many parties compete for power and the government will often pass between coalitions formed by different combinations of parties.

Prior to electoral reform in 1993, Italy was often seen as a classic multi-party system. Israel is another good example.

Is Britain a two-party system?

YES
The Labour and Conservative Parties are the only parties that have a realistic chance of forming a government in the near future or being the senior partner in a coalition.

Even in the 2001 general election the Labour and Conservative Parties secured 75% of the popular vote and around 90% of the seats in Parliament.

Despite making progress, the third party (the Liberal Democrats) is still a long way behind the second party (the Conservatives), even when the latter is probably at one of its lowest ebbs.

There is a good deal of stability in the 2001 result when compared to that of 1997. The swing from Labour to Conservative was only 1.8% and numbers of seats for each party hardly changed. Less than 30 seats changed hands.

NO
The Labour Party won 246 seats more than the Conservative Party in 2001, whereas the Conservative Party only won 114 seats more than the LibDems. Do we really have two parties capable of winning power?

Of voters, 25% backed a party other than the big two, and the 90% share of seats gained by Labour and the Conservatives remains artificially exaggerated by the electoral system.

The rise of the Liberal Democrats as a third party ignores the fact that they are often second to Labour in the North and West and the Conservatives in the South and East.

Although there appears to be a good deal of stability in the system, the raw figures mask a lot of localised swing (differential swing) as well as a massive fall in turnout. A party that could mobilise the 41% of the population who chose not to vote could clearly break the two-party system.

Could Britain become a multi-party system?
Many of the countries said to have multi-party systems have electoral systems more geared towards creating multi-party outcomes. It is no coincidence that countries that abandon PR systems (Italy, for example) often see a decline in minor party support. The introduction of PR in Britain could, therefore, bring about a multi-party system where coalition government would become the norm – though even in countries such as Ireland (using STV) they could not be said to have a true multi-party system. It could also be argued that we already have a three-party system or (more accurately) three two-party systems in different constituencies: Labour v. Conservative, Labour v. LibDem, and Conservative v. LibDem. In other areas we see genuine three-way races and in some Scottish constituencies four-way races, where the Conservatives are the outside bet.

11.2 The Conservative Party

The origins of the party

The Conservative Party emerged from the Tory Party in the 1830s. Many date its birth to Robert Peel's Tamworth Manifesto in 1834. In the twentieth century, the Party was in office (either alone or in coalition) for 67 years and enjoyed two extended periods in office: 1951–64 under Churchill, Eden, MacMillan and Home, and 1979–97 under Thatcher and then Major. During the latter period, in particular, the Conservative administrations brought massive changes to government, the economy and society as a whole (see Ch 3.2). This period also saw the Party move away from its consensual post-war 'one-nation Tory' position to a more neo-liberal 'New Right' approach.

The policy-making process

The party leader has the major role in policy-making within the Party, though the leader is expected to take some notice of the views of backbenchers (represented by the 1922 Committee), party elders, members of the front bench and the broader membership. The 'Fresh Future' initiative launched by William Hague following the 1997 general election defeat was supposed to make policy-making more inclusive. Two new bodies – the National Conservative Convention and the Conservative Political Forum – were formed, but both remain merely advisory. Hague did make use of ballots of the members to endorse his policies but – as is the case with referendums generally – these votes were all on issues and at times chosen by Hague, where he could feel confident of success.

Conservative landmarks

1830 Conservative Party emerges

1867 National Union established

1870 Central Office established

1923 The 1922 Committee formally established to co-ordinate and articulate views of backbench Conservative MPs

1951–64 Conservatives in office

1975 Margaret Thatcher defeats Edward Heath in leadership election

1979–97 Conservatives in office

1990 Thatcher fails to secure sufficient votes in first ballot of leadership election over Heseltine. Resigns. John Major becomes leader/PM

1992 Election victory

1995 Major survives John Redwood's leadership challenge

1997 Worst election defeat for 165 years. Major resigns and is replaced by William Hague

1999 Party wins European elections

2001 General election defeat. Hague resigns. Iain Duncan Smith elected as new leader.

Choosing the party leader and parliamentary candidates

Choosing the party leader

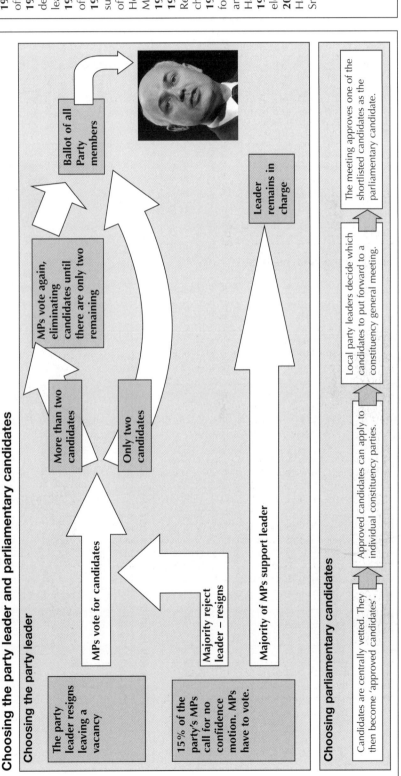

The party leader resigns leaving a vacancy

MPs vote for candidates

15% of the party's MPs call for no confidence motion. MPs have to vote.

Majority reject leader – resigns

Majority of MPs support leader

More than two candidates

Only two candidates

MPs vote again, eliminating candidates until there are only two remaining

Ballot of all Party members

Leader remains in charge

Choosing parliamentary candidates

Candidates are centrally vetted. They then become 'approved candidates'.

Approved candidates can apply to individual constituency parties.

Local party leaders decide which candidates to put forward to a constituency general meeting.

The meeting approves one of the shortlisted candidates as the parliamentary candidate.

11.3 The Labour Party

The origins of the party

It is important not to underestimate the role of the Trade Union Congress in establishing the Labour Party. In 1900 94% of the Labour Representation Committee's affiliated membership was from the unions, and well into the 1990s the unions still controlled around 80% of the votes at Party Conference and provided over 80% of Party funding. The Party was formed to represent working people at a time when the franchise was being extended to include many of its potential members. The decision to give all adult men the right to vote in 1918 was central in providing the Labour Party with the potential base of support from which to launch a serious electoral challenge. This also coincided with the adoption of the new Labour Party Constitution with its Clause Four, providing clear commitments to public ownership and the redistribution of wealth.

The policy-making process

Unlike the leader-dominated ('top-down') system of policy-making operating within the Conservative Party, the policy-making process in the Labour Party has traditionally been decidedly 'bottom-up'. This meant that Labour Party Conferences of the past were often genuinely policy-making events at which serious discussions and often heated arguments took place. Since 1997, however, the Party has adopted a policy-making cycle that runs over two years. The National Policy Forum appoints policy commissions to make proposals which are then formalised within the National Executive Committee (NEC) before being passed on to the Party Conference for final approval. Though this change was aimed at producing more considered policy and avoiding the kind of public rows that had become common at the Annual Party Conferences, some have seen it as a thinly-veiled attempt by the leadership to gain a greater control over the policy-making process and avoid nasty surprises.

Choosing the party leader and parliamentary candidates

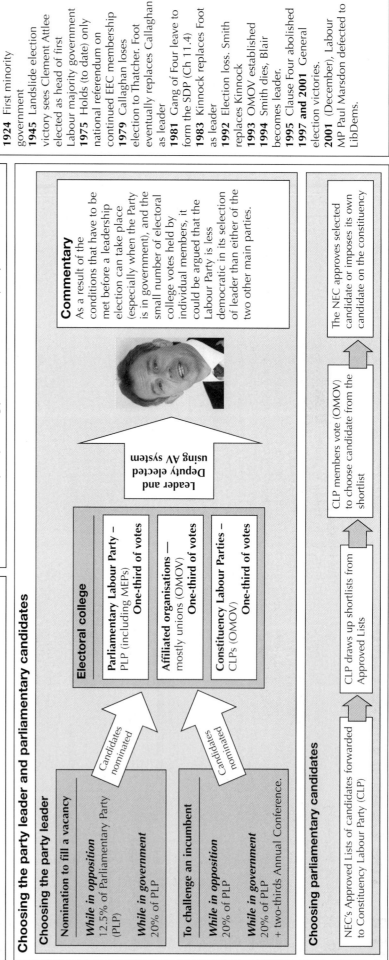

Choosing the party leader

Nomination to fill a vacancy

While in opposition
12.5% of Parliamentary Party (PLP)

While in government
20% of PLP

To challenge an incumbent

While in opposition
20% of PLP

While in government
20% of PLP
+ two-thirds Annual Conference.

Candidates nominated

Candidates nominated

Electoral college

Parliamentary Labour Party – PLP (including MEPs)
One-third of votes

Affiliated organisations — mostly unions (OMOV)
One-third of votes

Constituency Labour Parties – CLPs (OMOV)
One-third of votes

Leader and Deputy elected using AV system

Commentary

As a result of the conditions that have to be met before a leadership election can take place (especially when the Party is in government), and the small number of electoral college votes held by individual members, it could be argued that the Labour Party is less democratic in its selection of leader than either of the two other main parties.

Choosing parliamentary candidates

NEC's Approved Lists of candidates forwarded to Constituency Labour Party (CLP)

CLP draws up shortlists from Approved Lists

CLP members vote (OMOV) to choose candidate from the shortlist

The NEC approves selected candidate or imposes its own candidate on the constituency

11.4 The Liberal Democrats

The origins of the party

The Liberal Party had been the main party of government in the early twentieth century but was, by some distance, the third party by the middle of the century – rarely polling more than 10% of the vote. The SDP, in contrast, was formed as a result of the decision of leading Labour politicians to leave the Party in 1981. Roy Jenkins, David Owen, Bill Rogers and Shirley Williams (collectively known as the Gang of Four) launched the SDP with their Limehouse Declaration of that year. With the Labour Party in disarray, the SDP formed an electoral alliance with the Liberals (the SDP–Liberal Alliance) in 1983 and rode high in the polls. They secured 26% of the popular vote yet only gained 23 seats in Parliament. Following a similarly disappointing return for the Alliance in 1987, the parties merged in 1988 to form the Social and Liberal Democrats with Paddy Ashdown elected as leader. The following year the party renamed itself the Liberal Democrats. Charles Kennedy became leader in 1999.

The policy-making process

The Party is federal in structure comprising English, Scottish and Welsh State Parties. The State Parties are further subdivided into tiers (England has four, Scotland and Wales three each). Policies that only affect the area covered by one level of the Party would be dealt with at the appropriate level. Thus, a policy only affecting Scotland would be dealt with at a conference organised by the Scottish State Party. The English State Party has delegated its policy-making power to the Party's Federal Conference. The Federal Conference (meeting twice a year) is the supreme policy-making body in the Party but limits itself to dealing with policies that affect the UK as a whole (or England alone). The Conference deals with policy proposals from the Federal Policy Committee, State, regional and local parties. Once accepted, proposals become Party policy. The Party leadership has a good deal of control over the Federal Policy Committee and, therefore, policy.

LibDem landmarks

1906 Landslide Liberal victory (377 seats)

1915 Wartime coalition with Conservatives

1922 Coalition breaks up forcing Liberals out of government. Labour becomes main opposition party

1931–59 The wilderness years. Liberals never poll more than 10% in general elections

1977–78 LibLab pact

1981 The Social Democratic Party (SDP) formed by Labour dissidents (see left)

1983 Liberal/SDP Alliance wins 26% of votes in General election but only 23 secures seats

1987 Alliance secures 23% of votes but only 22 seats

1988 Alliance parties merge to form Social and Liberal Democrats

1989 Renamed Liberal Democrats

1992 18% votes, 20 seats

1994 LibDems return two MEPs

1997 17% votes, 46 seats

1999 Return ten MEPs. Kennedy succeeds Ashdown. LibLab coalition in Scotland

2000 LibLab coalition in Wales

2001 Party secures 52 seats in general election (18% votes)

2001 (December)LibDems have 53 MPs, after Paul Marsdon defects from Labour

Choosing the party leader and parliamentary candidates

Choosing the party leader

The party leader resigns or is incapacitated

A majority of MPs or 75 local parties demand an election

Two years have elapsed following a general election

Candidates are nominated

Candidates must be:
- MPs;
- *Proposed and seconded by other MPs;*
- *Nominated by no fewer than 200 members drawn from at least 20 different local parties.*

An election under an STV system. **One member one vote**

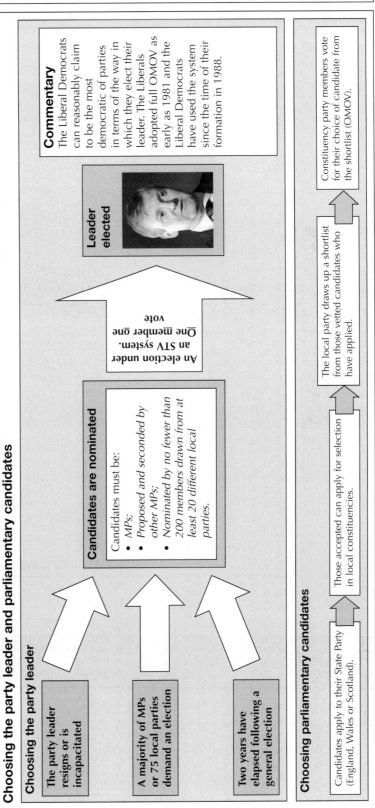

Leader elected

Commentary

The Liberal Democrats can reasonably claim to be the most democratic of parties in terms of the way in which they elect their leader. The Liberals adopted full OMOV as early as 1981 and the Liberal Democrats have used the system since the time of their formation in 1988.

Choosing parliamentary candidates

Candidates apply to their State Party (England, Wales or Scotland).

Those accepted can apply for selection in local constituencies.

The local party draws up a shortlist from those vetted candidates who have applied.

Constituency party members vote for their choice of candidate from the shortlist (OMOV).

11.5 Minor parties

Introduction

Mainstream political parties generally have the belief that they might eventually secure enough votes to win the seats necessary to carry them into government. Even the Liberal Democrats – who won only 52 seats in the 2001 general election and currently have 53 MPs – can imagine a time when they have built up enough of a parliamentary party to allow them to form an administration or, at least, become the minor party in a coalition government following an inconclusive election. There are, however, a great number of political parties who have no real hope of becoming part of a government or even returning a single MP. Such parties may use elections as a way of applying pressure to mainstream political parties or providing media exposure for what will inevitably be less mainstream ideas. There are also those nationalist parties who only stand in their respective areas and, therefore, have no ambition to secure control of Parliament.

Nationalist parties

Some of the largest minor parties are not, in fact, minor in the areas in which they operate. In Scotland, Wales and Northern Ireland parties unique to each area operate with considerable success. Northern Ireland parties are dealt with in Chapter 9.4.

The Scottish National Party (SNP)

Introduction

The Party was formed in 1934 and has the central aim of achieving an independent Scotland. It campaigned for a 'yes, yes' vote in the 1997 Referendum – supporting the creation of a devolved parliament with tax varying powers.

Though it performed well in the elections for the Scottish Parliament, it has been excluded from the administration by the LibLab coalition in place since 1999.

General election performance

Year	% votes (1)	MPs (659)
1992	21.5	3
1997	22.1	6
2001	20.1	5

Scottish Parliament election

Year	MSPs (129)
1999	35

(1) NB % of votes in Scotland

Plaid Cymru

Introduction

The Party was formed in 1925 and has the central aim of achieving an independent Wales as well as encouraging Welsh culture and, in particular, the use of the Welsh Language.

The Party supported the 'yes' campaign in the 1997 Referendum but has been excluded from the administration by the LibLab coalition in place since 2000.

General election performance

Year	% votes (2)	MPs (659)
1992	8.9	4
1997	9.9	4
2001	14.3	4

Welsh Assembly election

Year	MWA (60)
1999	17

(2) NB % of votes in Wales

The Green Party

The Green Party is often remembered for its impressive showing in the 1989 European elections – securing 15% of the votes, though winning no seats. In the 1999 European elections, under a more proportional electoral system, the Party secured 6.3% of the votes and returned two MEPs. Some argue that the group is more pressure group than party.

Fascist parties

The National Front (NF) was founded in 1967 and was claiming the support of about 20 000 members within 10 years. The British National Party (BNP) was born out of the NF split in the 1980s and has continued to campaign vigorously in elections – particularly in urban areas with significant ethnic minority populations. In the 2001 general election the BNP gained significant numbers of votes in a number of North-Western constituencies. In Oldham West, for example, BNP leader Nick Griffin gained 16.4% of the vote, claiming third place ahead of the Liberal Democrats. In Oldham East the BNP secured 11% of the vote. The Party has also achieved success in local elections. In 1993 their candidate Derek Beackon won a local council by-election in Tower Hamlets, and in the 2002 local elections the Party won three council seats in Burnley. The successful candidates were Carol Hughes, David Edwards, and Terence Grogan.

Other minor parties

There are numerous other minor party candidatures. The UK Independence Party (UKIP), for example, won 7% of the votes in the 1999 European elections, enough to win them three seats under the regional list system. They also gave credible performances in the 1997 and 2001 general elections. James Goldsmith's Referendum Party averaged 3.1% of the vote in each of the 547 seats where it stood in the 1997 general election. The anti-abortion ProLife Alliance (formed by Bruno Quintsvalle) put up 53 candidates in 1997 (securing 18 545 votes nationally) and 37 candidates in 2001 (9453 votes nationally). All 90 candidates lost their deposits. The Party has, however, raised its profile and become active in the courts over embryo experimentation, abortion and the separation of the conjoined twins 'Jodie' and 'Mary'.

12.1 The electorate

Introduction

Before studying voting behaviour, it is helpful to have some understanding of the composition of the electorate in socio-economic and demographic terms. This page considers areas such as gender, class, age and ethnicity as well as highlighting changes in occupational structure

The extension of the franchise (right to vote)

In 1831 only 5% of adults (over 18) or 450 000 individuals out of a population of around 25 million were able to vote. The 1832 Great Reform Act only increased the electorate to around 700 000, but many see it as important because it opened the door to later reforms. Around a million voters were added in 1867 as the property qualification for voting was lowered in boroughs. The Act of 1884 extended this to counties and added 2.5 million more voters. The 1918 Act enfranchised all adult men (over 21), and women over 30. The 1928 Act enfranchised all other women over 21. In 1969 the voting age was lowered from 21 to 18. By 1969, 99% of adults (over 18) or around 40 million individuals out of a population of 58 million had the vote.

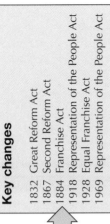

Key changes

1832	Great Reform Act
1867	Second Reform Act
1884	Franchise Act
1918	Representation of the People Act
1928	Equal Franchise Act
1969	Representation of the People Act

Socio-economic trends and issues

The North–South Divide?

During the 1980s political scientists focused on the growing divide between the prosperous South and the declining Northern parts of the country. During the 1980s many Northern-based primary (e.g. mining) and manufacturing (e.g. textiles) industries were in decline, whereas the 'service sector' and financial sectors (often based in the Home Counties) were booming. Sociologists also noted marked health and life expectancy differences between North and South.

In 1994 the average income per head in the North was only 89% of the average for the UK as a whole (the South-Eastern average income was 117% of the UK figure). Northern unemployment was 10.8 % compared to the UK figure of 8.6%. Though the phrase is still used, some argue that differences such as those identified are now less pronounced.

Gender

The traditional gender stereotypes have been broken down somewhat over the last few decades. Many more women now work (they made up 38% of the workforce in 1971, and 44% in 1996), though they are still more likely than men to be working in part-time employment, and 26% of women workers are still employed in clerical and secretarial occupations (compared to only 8% of men). Women also, therefore, have a lower average weekly income (in 1995, £374.60 for men, £269.60 for women).

Changing patterns of occupation

The 1980s and 1990s saw a decline in traditional heavy and manufacturing industries (36% of GDP in 1951; 27% in 1980; 22% in 1995) and a rise in the service sector (51% in 1951; 55.3% in 1980; 71% in 1995). The numbers of workers involved changed accordingly. Between 1955 and 1996 employment in the service sector increased from 36% to almost 76%, while manufacturing employment fell from 43% to 18%. By 1996 only 0.9% worked in heavy industry compared even to the 1991 figure of 1.7%.

At the same time, many nationalised industries (e.g. steel, gas, water, BT etc.) were transferred to the private sector. Individual share ownership jumped from 7% of adult population in 1979 to 22% in 1997. More women came into the workforce and there was an increase in part-time work (20% of jobs by 1996). The number of people who are self-employed increased by 75% between 1979 and 1990.

Home ownership

The Housing Act of 1980 gave long-term council house tenants the 'right to buy' their homes at discounts of between 50% and 70% of market value. After 1988 most of the remaining housing stock was transferred to Housing Associations or Housing Action Trusts. As a result, the rate of home ownership increased from 52% to 67% (1971–95) and the number of people living in rented accommodation decreased from 48% to 32% during the same period.

Ethnicity

In 1996 the ethnic minority population of Great Britain numbered 3.3 million (6% of the population). Of these 3.3 million:

Indian = 27%; Pakistani and Bangladeshi = 23%; Afro-Caribbean and other groups = 26%; Arab, Chinese, mixed and other origins = 24%

Members of ethnic minorities are still subject to considerable discrimination, and are more likely to be victimised, achieve less in school, be unemployed or in low-paid employment. A survey reported in *The Guardian* in 1997, for example, showed that 32% of white people still said that they would mind if one of their close relatives were to marry an Afro-Caribbean (as did 13% of Jews and 29% of Asians). There have also been numerous studies showing unequal treatment in the justice system.

Age

Britain has an ageing population. There has been a marked decrease in the birth-rate since the early part of the century but people are, on average, living longer. Women tend to live around three years longer than men do and for both sexes the average life expectancy is well over 70. This has already had and will increasingly have a massive impact on the health and welfare systems.

Social class

A social class is best defined as a group of people sharing a similar social position. Market researchers tend to divide people up into six socio-economic classes, though AB and DE are normally grouped together:

Class band:	% 1964	% 1992
A Professional/senior managerial	7.0	11.6
B Middle managers/executives	12.3	16.3
C1 Junior managers/non-manual	23.1	31.3
C2 Skilled manual	7.6	4.8
D Semi-skilled/unskilled manual	50.2	36.0
E Residual and casual workers. Those on benefits.		

12.2 Political participation and abstention

Different kinds of participation

Studies of political participation often – rightly – focus on levels of voter turnout. It is, though, important to remember that there are other forms of political participation; not least, involvement in political parties and pressure group activity (see Ch 13). This page, however, focuses largely on voter turnout, factors that affect it and the implications of low turnout in elections.

Levels of political activism

The fact that fewer people are voting and that the membership of most political parties is significantly lower than it was in the 1950s does not necessarily mean that people are not politically active. As Noreena Hertz remarked in *The Independent* (June 2001), 'it's not about apathy ... while voting is waning, other forms of political expression are on the rise'.

The membership of mainstream pressure groups such as Greenpeace has risen as the membership of the major political parties has fallen. Greenpeace's membership rose from 30 000 in 1981 to over 400 000 in 1992, whereas the Conservative Party's membership fell from 2.8 million in the 1950s to 780 000 in 1992 and 335 000 by the end of 2000. There has also been a marked increase in direct action. This is dealt with in Ch 13.

Voter turnout

One of the most obvious ways in which an individual can participate within a political system is to vote. Levels of turnout are, therefore, one important measure of political participation. There was widespread concern at the low voter turnout figure in the 2001 general election, but we should remember two things. Firstly, the overall figure masks massive regional variation. In Wyre Forrest, for example, the independent Dr Richard Taylor won on a 68% turnout. Secondly, turnout in other forms of elections is often far lower than in general elections.

European elections

Turnout at European elections is notoriously low. In some voting districts in Sunderland for example, turnout was as low as 1.5%. In 1999 the overall national turnout for UK elections to the European Parliament was only 24%. This was the lowest for any EU member state.

Local elections

In the 2000 local government elections turnout was 29% nationally and in 2002 it was 35%. This slight improvement was brought about by experiments with postal voting, text voting, and e-mail voting that improved turnout in some wards to over 50%.

Scottish Parliament, Welsh Assembly elections and Greater London Assembly elections

The turnout for elections for all these bodies was considered poor (though perhaps not now in light of the general election turnout). In Scotland 59% of voters turned out. In Wales only 40% voted. In London the turnout for the GLA elections was only 32%.

By-election turnout

It is hard to generalise on the subject of by-elections because of the variations caused by so many factors: the cause of the by-election, the nature of media coverage, and topical local issues – to name three. What we can say is that over the last 18 months, turnout in by-elections has been around the 30–40% mark.

In the 2001 by-election in Ipswich there was serious media coverage concerning the effect that the scheduling (on the same night) of the home leg of the UEFA Cup tie between Ipswich Town and Inter Milan might have on voter turnout, given the fact that the match had a sell-out crowd of over 20 000. In the event, turnout was not far off what it had been in the general election.

Why is turnout so low?

Intelligent voters

Voters are more likely to turn out to vote when they can see that the resulting institutions are important. They are also aware of other contextual factors. Voters didn't vote in 2001 because Labour was 'bound to win', whereas they had voted in 1997, 'when it mattered'.

Apathetic voters

Voters can't be bothered to vote. There is, some argue, a need for compulsory Citizenship lessons.

Disaffected voters

Increasing numbers of voters are coming to the conclusion that elections don't matter. All parties are the same and it is more profitable to spend one's time engaged in direct action on single issues.

Media-driven voters.

Only vote when the media brings the elections to their attention and makes them want to vote. Do not vote in low-profile elections.

Does it really matter?

Legitimacy – a government elected on the votes of a small proportion of the electorate might not have the same degree of legitimacy as one elected on a high turnout.

Mandate – it could be argued that a government elected on a low turnout does not, therefore, have as strong a mandate for its policies as a government elected on a high turnout.

Voter turnout in general elections 1945–2001

Year	%	Year	%
1945	73	1974 (Feb)	79
1950	84	1974 (Oct)	73
1951	83	1979	76
1955	77	1983	73
1959	79	1987	75
1964	77	1992	78
1966	76	1997	71
1970	72	2001	59

NB: Figures rounded.

12.3　An introduction to voting behaviour

Introduction

Psephologists have always tried to explain voting behaviour by constructing theoretical 'models'. Different writers favour different models but most of the models share some common elements – they simply have a different emphasis. The easiest was to explain voting behaviour is to think about **long-term** and **short-term** factors, where the long-term factors might include issues such as the social background of the individual voter (see Ch 12.1) and the short-term factors might include issues such as which party leader they may prefer at a particular time, or particular events which are linked to a particular time. Most political scientists however, take the analysis of voting behaviour a little further.

The primacy and recency approaches

The primacy model:

The primacy model suggests that factors such as age, gender, ethnicity and class (i.e. social divisions) can determine electoral outcomes. Such an analysis of voting behaviour would lead one to believe that stability is a major feature of voting behaviour, because such social factors only change very slowly. People who support this model would argue that although short-term factors are important, they do not really do enough to prevent the underlying social forces from shaping an individual's political outlook.

The recency model:

Other writers believe that voting patterns are in fact more volatile and that developments such as partisan dealignment and embourgeoisement have reduced many individuals' loyalty to a particular political party. As a result, they argue, short-term factors (issues, events, leaders, competence etc.) are much more important. They argue that the fact that the same numbers of voters tend to vote for the same parties does not mean that the same voters vote for the same party. There is a certain amount of 'churn' and many voters don't make up their minds until the last minute. In 1997 for example, 8.5 million voters changed their minds in the three-week period prior to the election, but the overall levels of support stayed the same.

Stability v. volatility

If you believe that long-term factors are more important in determining voting behaviour, then you will tend to feel that there is a certain amount of stability in voting behaviour because such factors do not change quickly. If, however, you believe that short-term factors are more significant in the present day, then it is inevitable that voting patterns will be more volatile because short-term events are less predictable. Some have argued that trends such as partisan dealignment (the weakening of the bonds between voter and party) have led to a greater number of floating voters and that this has increased volatility. Others have pointed to the similarity between the 1997 and 2001 general election results and emphasised the stability in the system. The latter judgement is, however, dangerous. Though the results in terms of seats won might be similar in each election, this does not mean that the voters voted in the same way or indeed voted at all in each election. Many voters might have voted differently with only the net result in terms of votes or seats remaining unchanged. This is known as **churn**.

Voting behaviour in by-elections

Voting behaviour in by-elections – as noted above – can be extremely volatile. This is a partly a result of the greater tendency towards protest voting and tactical voting in such elections, but also a result of the media focus often afforded such events. Though the 'swing' in by-elections is, therefore, often impressive, many seats are recaptured by their original holders at the next general election, when the context is different and the stakes are often considered higher.

Key terms

Tactical voting

Tactical voting is where an individual chooses to vote for a candidate that is not his or her preferred candidate in order to prevent his/her least favourite candidate being elected. It occurs most often where Labour voters vote LibDem in seats where the LibDems stand the best chance of defeating the Conservative candidate or where LibDems vote Labour in Labour/Conservative marginals.

Tactical voting was particularly prevalent in the 1997 and 2001 general elections, often encouraged by newspapers. *The Independent* (in its 'Rough Guide to the Election') produced two lists of 33 Conservative-held seats. The first 33 were seats in which LibDems should vote Labour if they wanted to unseat the Conservative MP. The second list of 33 seats were those in which Labour supporters should vote LibDem to achieve the same end.

A number of vote-swapping websites also appeared during the 2001 general election. On these sites people could agree to vote for a party other than their natural choice in their own constituency in return for someone voting in a similar fashion in their constituency. Thus, Labour voters in Labour no-go areas could see their vote – effectively – transferred into a constituency where it might matter.

Protest voting

In some cases voters choose to vote for a candidate or party other than their normal choice in order to send a message – often to their 'natural' party or to the government of the day. Protest voting often takes place in elections where the outcome is less crucial to the voter. Thus, the LibDems achieved spectacularly impressive results in supposedly safe Conservative seats towards the end of the Tories' 18-year spell in office. In the same way, the Conservatives secured impressive results in the 1999 European elections, despite having lost the general election so comprehensively only two years before. This was at least partly attributable to protest voting.

Swing

Swing is the movement of votes from one party to another expressed as a percentage. It is normally measured against the last general election. If swing were uniform across the country then a 1% swing from one party to another would see all of the seats with less than a 1% majority change hands. In reality we see differential swing, with different constituencies behaving differently. This, coupled to the fact that there are third and minor parties involved, is why the 'swingometer' often used in election broadcasts is a flawed device. In the last election there was only a 1.8% swing from Labour to the Conservatives.

12.4 Models of voting behaviour

Introduction
Numerous models have been advanced to explain the dynamics of voting behaviour. While all have their merits, it is important to remember that they are not necessarily mutually exclusive. It might be possible, for example, to argue that 'social structures' position an individual politically, but that the 'context' or issues that are unique to a particular election might moderate their behaviour and make them more likely to vote against their 'natural party'.

Do we need voting models?
Voting models attempt to make a science out of human behaviour and are therefore bound to be flawed to a greater or lesser extent. What such models do offer us is a way of approaching what is a complex topic in a relatively structured way. If nothing else, they provide something to argue against.

Social structures model

This model emphasises the importance of certain social structures in shaping individuals' voting habits. Factors such as social class, ethnicity, occupation, education, geographical location and gender are, it is argued, important in this process. For example ...

Gender
Commentators once spoke of a gender gap: women being more likely to vote Conservative, perhaps due to traditional female roles. This gender gap appears to have closed. Why might this be?

% voting Conservative		
1987	Men 44%	Women 44%
1992	Men 38%	Women 44%
1997	Men 31%	Women 32%

Ethnicity
All 12 of the ethnic minority MPs currently in the House of Commons represent the Labour Party. In 1997, 70% of Asian voters voted Labour (25% voted Conservative) and 86% of Black voters voted Labour (8% voted Conservative). Many would therefore argue that ethnicity is a major determinant of voting behaviour.

Party identification model

Strong party identification or 'partisan alignment' was often said to go hand in hand with class alignment. People identified with a particular party and stuck with it. In the 1950s over 90% of voters voted for either the Labour Party or the Conservatives. In 1997 this figure was down to 74%, and up to 11 million voters changed their minds. Up to 10% of the electorate were said to have voted tactically rather than for any party they identified with. An ICM/BBC poll in 1997 showed that 50% of those 'likely' to vote felt that it didn't matter which party got into power because things would end up much the same. Amongst 'unlikely voters' the proportion agreeing with this view was 70%.

Class and voting
The 1950s and 1960s were decades of high class alignment – that is to say that the party one voted for was most often the party of one's class. Pulzer, in the 1960s, went as far as to suggest that 'class is the basis of British party politics; all else is embellishment and detail'. Put simply, the working class was expected to vote Labour and the middle classes were supposed to vote Conservative.

Class dealignment
Since those days, many commentators have charted what they have described as a process of class dealignment. For some, this is a result of **embourgeoisement** – working class people feeling more middle class (due to material possessions and changes in occupational structure, for example) and therefore voting for the party of the middle classes – the Conservatives. Others have written of **deferential voters** who, despite being working class, vote for the Conservatives because they see them as the natural party of government, a party of leaders. Ivor Crewe has put forward the idea that we are now faced with a **new working class** (occupied in new industries – particularly the service sector) who do not act politically in the same way as the **old working class** (who were heavily unionised). For David Denver, the 1997 election, with its 10% swing, underlined the validity of the dealignment thesis. The Alford Index (calculated by subtracting the percentage of non-manual voters voting Labour from the percentage of manual voters voting Labour) went down from 42% in 1964 to only 22% in 1997. In his article 'General Election 2001 Repeat or Revolution' (*Politics Review* Vol. 11 no 1), John Curtice provided a voting breakdown by class for the 2001 general election. What conclusions can we draw from these figures (shown below)? How can we account for the changes since 1997?

Rational choice model

In the rational choice or judgmental model, voters make rational and considered judgements taking on board factors such as current issues, party leaders and perceived competence. The latter might be a judgement on past performance (retrospective) or a perception of how the party might do if given the chance (prospective). In the 1992 general election Neil Kinnock was regarded as an electoral liability and was criticised following the triumphalist Sheffield Rally. In 1997 the Conservatives were suffering from the fact that they had lost their reputation for economic competence in the wake of Black Wednesday in 1992.

Dominant ideology model

This model takes the view that there is a dominant ideology amongst the elite that controls key institutions such as business, the media and political parties. This elite uses its influence to orchestrate elections in order to serve its own interests. For 'The media' see Ch 12.5.

Voting context model

This model raises the possibility that voting behaviour is affected by factors such as by the nature of the election being contested, the importance of the resulting institution and the workings of the electoral system employed in the election. Thus, voters might be more likely to vote in general elections than local elections if they have a low opinion of local government. They might choose to vote tactically or cast a protest vote if such a vote suits the situation. In a European election under a PR system, a LibDem voter might vote LibDem, whereas under the first past the post system they might vote tactically or not vote at all. **Why?**

Class	Con	Lab	LibDem
AB	40 (−3)	33 (+3)	21 (0)
C^1	33 (−2)	40 (+3)	21 (+2)
C^2	29 (+1)	47 (−5)	17 (+4)
DE	28 (+7)	49 (−9)	17 (+2)

Figures in brackets show change from 1997

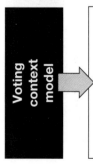

12.5 The media

Introduction

Studies of elections and voting behaviour often see the media as having a significant influence on both the course of elections and, in a broader sense, the formation of the political agenda. This page considers a number of different theories concerning the operation of the media, and attempts to assess the extent of media influence in the political sphere.

Daily newspaper circulation, November 2001

Sun 3 377 393	Mirror 2 078 107	Star 713 355	
Record 574 614	Mail 2 382 462	Express 859 366	
Telegraph 965 607	Times 669 003	FT 452 616	
Guardian 400 542	Independent 197 529		

Media theory

Manipulative theory

The mass media is controlled by an elite that uses it with the sole purpose of preserving the status quo and, therefore, its own position. It submerges a radical agenda in meaningless trivia. As Billy Bragg wrote in his song 'It says here':

'...If this does not reflect your view you should understand that those who own the papers also own this land and they'd rather you believe in Coronation Street capers in the war for circulation, it sells newspapers. Could it be an infringement of the freedom of the press to print pictures of women in states of undress.'

Under this theory, New Labour's re-branding under Blair might have had the effect of making it more acceptable to the dominant elite and, therefore, worthy of support in the face of a divided and unstable Conservative Party.

Hegemonic theory

The people who edit and write in newspapers and those involved in broadcast journalism have a particular view due to their education, age, social class etc. They write, therefore, from a particular perspective – however unconscious their bias might be.

Pluralist theory

There is a range of media output, and individuals choose what to read and what to watch based upon their own outlook and interests. The media, therefore, reflects opinion rather than shaping it. At best the media probably only reinforces views that the reader already has.

Media bias?

The press

Newspapers are not legally required to be impartial and most, if not all, take up clear party positions during election campaigns. *The Sun* was particularly vocal in support of the Conservatives in the 1992 general election, coming up with such memorable headlines as 'Will the last person to leave Britain please turn out the lights?' when a Labour victory appeared likely. Both Neil Kinnock (the then Labour leader) and Norman Tebbit (a former leading Conservative) believed that the tabloid press had been crucial in achieving the surprise Conservative victory in that year. The paper's owner, Rupert Murdoch, was courted by New Labour in the run-up to the 1997 general election and *The Sun* eventually backed Labour. Paul Whiteley has estimated that this switch in support cost the Conservatives around 500 000 votes in the election and this might well have made the difference in key marginals.

Broadcasting

The BBC and the ITC (Independent Television Commission) control broadcasting. The former controls public channels (for example, BBC1, BBC2, and Radio 1, 2, 3 and 4) the latter controls private stations. Under the terms of the BBC's Royal Charter and the Television and Broadcasting Acts, the BBC and ITC are supposed to remain politically impartial. This partly reflects the influence credited to broadcast material as opposed material published in the press. What this impartiality means in practice is that the various channels have to ensure that they are giving fair coverage. They should give the major parties a right to reply when running stories or interviewing ministers and should not give one party or another a disproportionate share of the air-time. Channels are also required to broadcast quality news coverage and provide slots for party political broadcasts. These are demands not made of the press. Despite all of this there are almost constant allegations of bias in the media from one party or another. BBC Radio 4's Today Programme, for example, is often criticised for the vehemence of its presenters' attacks on government ministers. It is also important to remember that while legislation might outlaw bias against a party, it does not account for the perhaps unconscious bias towards a particular class or region.

Press ownership

Despite the strengthening of anti-monopoly legislation in the 1990s, media moguls such as Rupert Murdoch still have massive concentrations of media power. Murdoch himself for example controls *The Sun*, the *News of the World* and *The Times*, as well as the BSkyB network.

How influential is the media?

Writers such as the American psychologist Festinger (in the 1950s) and David Denver (in the 1980s) argued that media influence was limited by three processes:

Selective exposure

Individuals generally choose to expose themselves to newspapers and television programmes that reflect rather than challenge their outlook.

Selective perception

Individuals mentally edit the media that they are exposed to, filtering out content that doesn't fit in with their own ideas.

Selective retention

People tend to forget programme and newspaper content that challenges the views that they hold, while retaining material that can be used to justify their position.

'Filters'

Individuals, it is argued, view media output through filters – different filters being applied to different types of material. Some argue that television is so powerful because people believe what they see – their filters are effectively down when watching television. When reading newspapers, however, they are expecting bias and their filters are up.

12.6 Opinion polls

What are opinion polls?

Opinion polls are surveys of public opinion on specific issues. They are most visible at elections times when the major polling companies (Gallup, Harris, ICM, MORI and NOP) question the voting intentions of sample groups. These sample groups are selected with the aim of creating a cross-section of the electorate in a sample of perhaps 1000 individuals. The sampling methods used are critical because errors in sampling can greatly reduce the accuracy of the poll. Even with a reasonable sample of 1000, pollsters normally allow a margin of error of plus or minus 3%. In 1997 ten out of 15 final polls were within the margin of error and in 2001 some of the companies produced extremely accurate results. According to Duncan Watts, ICM (for *The Guardian*) had an average error of only 0.55%. Errors **up to** 1992 are shown below – poor polling accuracy **in** 1992 is explained to the right.

Polling error in elections 1979–2001			
1979	1983	1987	1992
2.4%	3.6%	4%	8.9%

'Bandwagons' and 'boomerangs'

In some countries (France, for example) opinion polls are banned in the days leading up to elections for fear that they might influence voting intentions. Some believe that voters are more likely to vote for parties that are doing well in the polls (the co-called 'bandwagon effect'); others argue that there is in fact a 'boomerang effect'. This is where people vote for parties that are doing badly in the polls because they see them as the underdogs or, more likely, don't turn out to vote because the polls show their party well ahead.

Party polls and focus groups

Part of the remodelling of Labour under Blair was the opening of the new campaign and media centre at Millbank Tower. Millbank became synonymous with all that was spin and control during the first term of the Labour Administration. A lot of the work of those working in and around Millbank was informed by findings from Party-organised polls. Millbank organised specialised task forces to bring together the polling data upon which decisions and presentational approaches could be based. Focus groups were also central to the new strategy. Focus groups consist of a small number of individuals brought together to consider particular issues. Sometimes these groups are asked to respond to certain policies. In the US such groups are used extensively in pre-screenings of party election broadcasts and this is now becoming more common practice in Britain.

Exit polls

Exit polls are different from the ordinary polls conducted during the election campaigns. Rather than asking people how they intend to vote, exit polls ask people how they have voted. In theory, this should make them more accurate and this accuracy should be augmented by the fact that exit polls often use a far larger sample and, therefore, have a far smaller margin of error. This said, it is not necessarily the case that voters are prepared to tell the truth in such circumstances.

Tactical voting

Many have argued that opinion poll findings can cause an increase in tactical voting. Where polls, for example, show the Liberal Democrats a distant third and the Labour candidate in with a reasonable chance of unseating a Conservative MP, a LibDem voter might be more inclined to vote Labour tactically. Michael Portillo believed that his loss in Enfield in 1997 was partly the result of poll findings.

Opinion polls and the 1992 general election

The 1992 general election was a low point for most of the polling companies. For whatever reason, they got it very wrong indeed. The average predicted lead for Labour of 1.3% was not even close to the eventual 7.6% Conservative lead. Given the cost of commissioning such opinion polls (Harris claimed £200 000 from ITN alone during the 1992 campaign), such inaccuracy was a major disappointment and brought into question the very worth of such polls.

What went wrong?

Respondents not registered
Part of the problem in 1992 was that some of those being asked the questions (the 'respondents') were not registered to vote. This was made worse by the fact that such non-registration might have been more prevalent amongst potential Labour voters. Some Labour supporters had not registered to vote for fear of being tracked down and forced to pay the 'Poll Tax'.

Respondents lying
For whatever reason, some respondents were clearly not telling the truth. When asked which policies were the priorities, the majority offered health care. When asked which party would deal most effectively with problems in health care, the majority said Labour – yet the majority did not vote Labour. It has been suggested that people were too embarrassed to admit publicly that they were going to vote Conservative.

Respondents unrepresentative
Sampling errors, and samples that were too small or inappropriate, meant that some surveys were doomed from the start.

Respondents 'floating'
There was clearly a 'late swing' to the Conservatives. Was this perhaps due to a large number of floating/undecided voters?

12.7 Recent general elections

Introduction
Some have argued that the similarity in the general election results of 1997 and 2001 demonstrates the underlying stability in voting behaviour. The headline figures, given below, would certainly appear to support such a view. Others, however, maintain that both class and party dealignment remain the norm and that the similarity in the headline results masks enormous volatility amongst the electorate with millions of voters switching their allegiances and many more simply staying at home in 2001.

The 1997 general election

Context
By 1997 there had been 18 consecutive years of Conservative government and, therefore, 18 years of the Labour Party in opposition. During that time massive changes had taken place in society, the economy and the political landscape. The power of the unions had been challenged, and there had been changes in employment patterns and a massive programme of privatisation. Following Tony Blair's election as leader in 1994 the Party had entered an extended period of constitutional reform and re-branding.

Issues and events
The Conservatives were said to have lost their reputation for economic competence following Black Wednesday in 1992. Labour fought hard on economic policy in the 1997 campaign, promising to match Conservative spending plans and avoid increases in income tax. Whereas the Labour Party had undergone a massive image change, the Conservatives were still dogged by allegations of sleaze and scandal, in part stemming from the 'cash for questions' revelations. This was kept in the media spotlight by Martin Bell's 'anti-corruption' candidature in Tatton. The Referendum Party's involvement in the election also highlighted Tory divisions over Europe.

Voting behaviour
Some saw 1997 as a return to the norm after the class dealignment of the 1980s. In reality, however, the Conservatives did poorly amongst all classes compared to 1992 (see figures below – change from 1992 in brackets). Tactical voting was the key to the outcome in many areas. Many newspapers provided advice and lists of seats in where tactical voting might work.

Social grade	Con	Lab	LibDem
AB	42 (−15)	31 (+11)	21 (0)
C1	26 (−15)	47 (+14)	19 (−5)
C2	25 (−13)	54 (+13)	14 (−4)
DE	21 (−16)	61 (+14)	13 (−2)

Media coverage
The Sun, crucially, switched sides (see Ch 12.5). On Election Day it ran the headline 'It Must be You', a far cry from its 1992 campaign against Kinnock. Even solid Tory papers such as *The Times* fell short of backing Major, advising readers to vote 'Eurosceptic'.

Results

Party	% UK votes	Seats won
Conservative	30.7	165
Labour	43.3	419
Liberal Democrat	16.8	46
Nationalists	2.5	10
Others	6.8	19*
Turnout (UK)	71.2%	

* Northern Ireland Parties + Martin Bell (Indep)

The 2001 general election

Context
Having won a landslide victory in 1997, the 2001 general election offered the promise, failing a massive swing to the Conservatives, of a second consecutive term in office for Labour. The Government had faced problems in the run up to the election – with the fuel protests and the foot and mouth crisis – but the Conservative Party was still well behind in the polls by the time of the election. Though those on the left criticised the Labour Government for failing to deliver a radical agenda, it was difficult to see where else their votes could be cast to good effect.

Issues and events
As a whole, the campaign was lacklustre. The Conservatives characterised the vote as the 'last chance to save the pound' and were widely adjudged to have overestimated the electorate's interest in the issue – particularly in light of the referendum on the currency promised by all major parties prior to any UK entry into the euro-zone. The enduring images of the campaign were of Tony Blair being confronted outside a hospital by the angry partner of a patient and of the scuffle between the Deputy Prime Minister and a farm worker that led to *The Sun* updating John Prescott's nickname from 'two jags' to 'two jabs'.

Voting behaviour
There was some movement in terms of class support (see below and left) and the high levels of tactical voting seen in 1997 were repeated. Indeed, some MPs who were only just elected in 1997 were returned with far larger majorities in 2001 as a result of the campaign to 'keep the Tories out'. A key feature of the election was the low turnout – the lowest since 1918.

Social grade	Con	Lab	LibDem
AB	40	33	21
C1	33	40	21
C2	29	47	17
DE	28	49	17

Results

Party	% UK votes	Seats won
Conservative	31.7	166
Labour	40.7	413
Liberal Democrat	18.3	52
Nationalists	2.5	9
Others	6.8	19*
Turnout (UK)	59.4%	

* Northern Ireland Parties + Dr Richard Taylor (Indep)

Media coverage
Many newspapers, including *The Independent*, offered advice on how and where to vote tactically. New media, in the form of vote-swapping websites, also made an impression, though more as a discussion point than in terms of seats won or lost.

13.1 Definitions and classification

What are pressure groups?

Pressure groups are groups of like-minded individuals who campaign for their own interests and/or to achieve goals or pursue common causes. Pressure groups are significantly more numerous than political parties because they often fragment opinion whereas political parties tend to aggregate and accommodate with a view to being elected. Pressure groups do not generally seek election, but some groups do so as a way of raising public awareness, even though they have little realistic chance of being elected. In recent years such groups have included the Referendum Party and the ProLife Alliance. One exception to this rule is, perhaps, the election of a single-issue candidate in each of the last two general elections – Martin Bell as an anti-corruption candidate in Tatton in 1997, and Dr Richard Taylor as the Kidderminster Hospital and Health Concern candidate in Wyre Forrest in 2001.

Classifying pressure groups

Classification by aims

Sectional and cause groups

Early attempts to classify groups focused on who or what causes they represented.

Sectional groups...

represent the interests of a particular section of society. They are, therefore, sometimes referred to as sectoral, interest or protectionist groups. Membership of such groups is normally restricted to the groups whose interests they serve – for example, a teachers' union such as the NASUWT or the NUT will represent the interests of its members who will, for the most part, be practising teachers. The BMA, another good example of a sectional group, promotes the interest of the medical profession.

Cause groups...

campaign for a particular cause or objective. They are sometimes referred to as promotional groups. Unlike most sectional groups they seek a broader membership and do not necessarily stand to benefit individually from their campaigns.

Sectional cause groups...

protect a section of society. Shelter, for example, works on behalf of the homeless but its members are not all homeless.

Attitude cause groups...

aim to change people's attitudes on a particular issue. Greenpeace, for example, seeks to change attitudes on the environment (see Ch 13.4).

Political cause groups...

aim to achieve certain political goals. The Chartists, for example, put forward their People's Charter in the nineteenth century.

Classification by strategy or status

Insider and outsider groups

Writers such as Wyn Grant have suggested that it is more helpful to classify groups according to their status in relation to the government.

Insider groups

Core insiders...

are those who have close two-way relationships with policy-makers over a broad range of issues (e.g. BMA, NFU).

Specialist insiders...

are more focused but have a large input within their area of expertise. They are trusted by government and provide reliable and authoritative expertise (e.g. WWF).

Peripheral insiders...

have insider status but have little real influence, due to the nature of their interest/cause. They are only rarely needed by government (e.g. the Canine Defence League).

Outsider groups

Potential insiders...

are groups that would ultimately like to attain insider status but have not achieved it due to, for example, the nature of their cause (e.g. Charter 88 before 1997) or inexperience.

Outsiders by necessity...

include single-issue and local groups who do not seek insider status, and those not afforded insider status; therefore outsider by necessity (e.g. CND).

Ideological outsiders...

do not want to become part of 'the system' because their objectives require outside status and with it full independence and freedom of action (e.g. anti-globalisation groups).

Problems with classifications

Both types of classification carry with them their problems. In attempting to distinguish between those that campaign for their own interests and those that campaign for a cause, the first model ignores the fact that many pressure groups do both. The teaching unions, for example, aim not only to serve their members' interests but also to support developments in education policy. The model also fails to consider the scale or status of groups. The insider/outsider model addresses some of these weaknesses but ignores the fact that many groups can operate both as insiders and outsiders to some extent, and that groups can move very quickly from outside to inside and vice versa, for example following elections. Charter 88 was clearly outside the political loop before the 1997 general election but has assumed more influence since Labour's victory. Wyn Grant suggests that the NFU's insider status is under threat.

13.2   Methods

'Traditional methods' (?)

There was a time when discussion of pressure group activity focused on letter-writing campaigns, petitions and marches. Such activities are clearly still worthy of note. The anti-abortion LIFE organisation, for example, compiled a petition of more than 2 000 000 names in the mid-1980s, organised a 'Mail MPs a Mountain' campaign in 1987 and employed postcard campaigns in 1989 and 1990 against the Human Fertilisation and Embryology Act. Marches against the 'Poll Tax' in the early 1990s and in support of the Countryside Alliance in recent years have also been influential. Clearly, however, we need to move beyond the anecdotal and impose some kind of structure on the discussion.

Pressure group tactics

Most major modern pressure groups adopt a variety of strategies in pursuit of their aims. There are, however, a number of obvious approaches.

Influencing the legislative process directly

Some groups have regular contact with government over a broad range of related issues. These 'core insider groups' have the ability to influence the formation of policy at an early stage through meetings with ministers, civil servants and government-appointed bodies working on legislative proposals. Beyond these core insiders are other groups who might be called in to give specialist information on a particular issue. This will normally take place where the group has a relevant expertise and information not readily available elsewhere and/or where the group represents a particular viewpoint or section of society likely to be directly affected by the measure. Consultation might take the form of informal discussions, or be more structured around a Green Paper. Many larger groups employ lobbyists to pursue their legislative goals and the richest groups maintain permanent offices close to Westminster.

Influencing political parties

Pressure groups can cultivate links with political parties with a view to influencing the formation of policy (see pages on individual parties for detail on policy formation). When a party is in government this is likely to be harder to achieve because the government is likely to be subject to far greater demands on its time, and policy formation is likely to be more 'top-down'. The easiest time for pressure groups to gain a foothold within parties is when they are in opposition. At such a time the party will normally be looking to ground itself, take on board a variety of ideas, build up a broader base of support and formulate new policy. During Labour's lengthy period in opposition, groups such as Charter 88 and the Electoral Reform Society cultivated links with the Party. Such links have been important since the Labour victory in 1997.

Embarking on legal action

British courts do not have the same powers of judicial review open to the US Supreme Court. Legal action can still, however, be an effective pressure group tactic – if an expensive one. Such action can work on two levels. Firstly, where the court finds that the government has acted in a manner beyond the authority granted it, the court could find against that government. Secondly, such action raises public awareness of a particular issue and may, therefore, have positive outcomes for the group even where ithey loses the case. Bruno Quintsvalle's Pro-Life Alliance, for example, has taken legal action on a number of occasions recently; for example, using the Human Rights Act to try and prevent the separation of the Siamese twins Jodie and Mary, when it was clear that one of them (Mary) would die as a result of the procedure, and using legal action to highlight loopholes in the Human Fertilisation and Embryology Act that could allow reproductive human cloning. In both cases the group gained considerable press coverage.

Mobilising public pressure

Media manipulation

The media can often be used to good effect. Groups can employ **paid media**, taking out whole-page adverts in the national press, by using direct mail or by producing and airing adverts. During the 1997 general election the Referendum Party used newspaper advertisements to good effect and also produced a video, which it sent free of charge to millions of households. Established 'caring' charities have also made use of such tactics. Barnardo's has recently run a series of controversial magazine adverts depicting the fate of children that they might not be able to help. The NSPCC has used television advertising in its 'Full Stop' campaign against violence aimed at children. All of this said, there are even greater opportunities in **unpaid media**. By placing stories in the news (see Brent Spa, Ch 13.4) groups can get free air time and newspaper coverage. Organising stunts, marches or employing direct action techniques (see right) can attract such coverage.

Direct action

Direct action is an increasingly popular form of pressure group action. It starts from the premise that conventional methods of influencing policy are flawed and that more visible and direct protests – often involving illegal methods or violence – offer the best opportunity of success because they make the politicians take notice and can broaden public support. The anti-roads protests of recent years, the campaign against live animal exports, the campaigns against fox hunting and vivisection, and the fuel protest have all been seen to have some effect on policy or opinion.

Effectiveness

The effectiveness of pressure group activity is hard to gauge because if – as most people accept – insider groups have more influence than outsider groups, such groups are not likely to publicise the extent of their influence for fear of alienating the government and losing it. Equally, high-profile protests and stunts might appear impressive but only rarely succeed in changing policy. Even at the time of the fuel protests the Government chose to speak more to the Road Hauliers' Association than to those organising the protest.

13.3 The European dimension

Introduction

Many pressure groups, faced with national governments that are unsympathetic to their causes or interests, turn to the European arena. Under the European Communities Act that came into force in the UK in 1973, European law and regulations take precedence over national laws where the two are in conflict. In theory, therefore, pressure groups can force change on their national governments by effectively going over their heads. This route has proven particularly effective for groups whose causes or interests are heavily regulated by or affected by the European Union. In the broad areas of economic environmental policy, for example, the proliferation of Europe-wide regulation provides an opportunity for real influence not often afforded pressure groups at a national level. As the EU becomes more involved in aspects of common social policy and foreign and security policy, a greater range of UK pressure groups are likely to turn to Europe, when their resources allow it.

Environmental pressure groups and Europe

Environmental pressure groups have two good reasons to focus their attentions on Europe rather than solely on their national governments

- Environmental issues by definition do not respect national boundaries. It therefore makes more sense to deal with environmental issues at a European or international level than simply at a national level.

- The EU is already committed to environmental action and is therefore more sympathetic to the aims and objectives of many environmental pressure groups than are national governments.

On issues such as the improvement of water quality, environmental groups have made great progress. Many beaches in England, previously categorised as unfit for bathing due to sewage pollution, have been improved under pressure from the EU. The policy of awarding blue flags for clean beaches has also raised the public profile of the EU.

Environmental groups do, however, face major problems in getting to the root of the problem. Though environmental groups often come together as a **Eurogroup** (see right) to increase their 'punch', business interests remain better funded and better equipped to put their case than most environmentalists.

Qualified majority voting

QMV was brought in under the terms of the Single European Act (1986). Under QMV a single country is no longer able to veto (block) most measures alone. Before QMV, pressure groups were able to focus their attentions entirely on the domestic front in the knowledge that, if they convinced their national government, they would be able to block any European measures that affected the group's interests. Under QMV, however, it is necessary to build up a broader European support in order to block or indeed pass any measure. Under the Treaty of Nice (2001) QMV is to be extended into new areas.

Though QMV makes life more complicated, it does bring with it some real advantages. A group can, for example, now campaign for a measure affecting the UK in the knowledge that the UK government alone cannot prevent it from happening.

The practicalities of lobbying in Europe

Though lobbying in Europe provides clear benefits, it is not an avenue open to all groups. The scale of the EU means that there are many points of leverage where pressure can be applied. The most successful groups will, therefore, need the resources to make the most of these opportunities. A permanent EU office is the ideal, but not all groups can afford a permanent office in Brussels.

Eurogroups

The European Union consists of 15 member states, though at the time of writing 12 more are in negotiations over entry and a thirteenth (Turkey) has been accepted as a candidate. If pressure groups in each of these countries were to conduct their efforts in the European sphere independently, their voices might well be lost. As a result, like-minded pressure groups often aggregate their efforts, forming Eurogroups possessing sufficient resources and representing a large enough 'constituency' for their views to be heard. Having said this, the efforts of such Eurogroups are often hampered by internal divisions and difficulty in obtaining and deploying sufficient resources.

Eurogroups and the European Commission

As we have already seen, the Commission has a role initiating legislation, making proposals upon which the other EU institutions can act. As a result, the Commission has a massive appetite for information and recognises Eurogroups as a legitimate source of information.

13.4 Case studies: environmental groups and trade unions

Trade unions

The unions had been crucial in the formation of the Labour Party in 1900 and retained a massive influence within the Party, both in terms of decision-making at Conference (through the 'block vote') and in terms of Party funding (particularly in the form of contributions coming from union members' subscriptions). In the 1960s and 1970s, in a time of relatively low unemployment, unions also had significant power in society as a whole. The miners were widely credited with bringing down Heath's Conservative Government and the so-called 'Winter of Discontent' (1978–79) was also a key factor in the fall of Callaghan's Labour Government in 1979. This was a period in which levels of union membership were high and unions were militant in support of their goals.

Changing occupational structure and patterns of union membership

Between 1955 and 1996 employment in the service sector increased from 36% to almost 76%, while manufacturing employment fell from 43% to 18%. By 1996 only 0.9% worked in heavy industry compared even to the 1991 figure of 1.7%. This change in employment led to a decline of what Ivor Crewe called the 'traditional' or 'old' working class in favour of the 'new' working class that was less cohesive and less likely to be heavily unionised or militant.

'Anti-union' legislation in the 1980s

A raft of legislation pushed through by the Thatcher administration in the 1980s severely limited the unions' ability to act quickly and freely. The Employment Acts of 1980, 1982, 1988 and 1989 as well as the Trade Union Act of 1984 had a massive cumulative effect. Unions were no longer allowed to organise secondary or sympathy action, or secondary or mass picketing. Unions had to organise secret ballots before strike action and could face sequestration (freezing of union funds) if they engaged in illegal action. Unions were also prevented from organising national strikes without gaining approval for action in each place of work through a secret ballot and there was even to be a trade union commissioner to help finance court cases against unions. The defeat of the National Union of Mineworkers (NUM) in 1985, following a year-long strike, marked a watershed in union power. The union that had brought down the Conservatives in the 1970s had been brought down by the Conservatives in the 1980s.

1990s Labour Party reform and the role of the unions

Up until the 1990s the unions had unrivalled power within the Labour Party. They provided close to 80% of the Party's funding through political affiliations and took a similar share of power in the Party through the block votes that they wielded at the annual Party Conference. The 1990s, however, saw changes in both areas. The introduction of OMOV in 1993 marked a significant step in moving away from the power of the block vote, as has the move towards ongoing policy forums and away from truly policy-making Conferences. The unions' power in selecting the Party leader has also been diminished through an electoral college system that leaves unions only as part of the Affiliated Organisations section carrying one-third of the votes, while members carry a further one-third and the Parliamentary Labour Party takes the final third. In funding, too, the Party has become less reliant on the unions. The 1980s legislation limited the use of union political funds and the Party has also attracted major business donors.

Environmental groups

While political parties have seen their membership fall significantly since the 1950s, many pressure groups have seen rising levels of membership and, more importantly perhaps, participation in campaigns. As we have seen, Greenpeace's membership rose from 30 000 in 1981 to over 400 000 in 1992, whereas the Conservative Party's membership fell from 2.8 million in the 1950s to 780 000 in 1992 and 335 000 by the end of 2000.

Range of environmental groups

Environmental pressure groups come in a bewildering range of shapes and sizes from massive international groups such as Greenpeace down to small local groups such as those campaigning against the removal of trees from local parks. Some groups are clearly insider groups, though not always powerful core insiders. The World Wide Fund for Nature (WWF), the Royal Society for the Protection of Birds (RSPB) and the Royal Society for the Prevention of Cruelty to Animals (RSPCA), for example, will all find themselves consulted by the government from time to time (as was the case with the RSPCA and the Dangerous Dogs Act). Others groups such as the road protesters or the Animal Liberation Front (ALF) are firmly outside the political loop; the former because their aims run contrary to government policy and the latter because their extreme tactics result in the government regarding them more as animal rights terrorists than a legitimate pressure group. The key development in the late 1990s and early years of the twenty-first century has been the rise of direct action campaigns.

Case studies

Brent Spar

In 1995 Shell gained permission from the Government to dump the 14 500-ton Brent Spar oil platform in the North Atlantic. Greenpeace was looking for a symbol to focus attention on the forthcoming European environmental summit. Its members therefore boarded the Spar and made it secure using specialised climbers, set up a floating TV station with satellite communications and began broadcasting live to European news programmes. They flew in reporters to film Shell's attempts to remove them from the platform, organised boycotts and protests at Shell petrol stations in Germany and Holland, and put out detailed scientific data concerning the residues inside the Spar which – though not always accurate – effectively won the propaganda war. While John Major defended the dumping plans in Parliament during Prime Minister's Questions, Shell UK was being forced into a climbdown by its European divisions. Greenpeace had achieved its twin goals of raising the profile of the summit and preventing the dumping of the Spar.

'Swampy'

'Swampy' (Daniel Hooper) gained his 15 minutes of fame in direct action anti-road protests in which he dug himself into tunnels. Protests such as these resulted in massive delays in projects and multi-million pound security bills. Many argue that this forced the Government to rethink its road-building strategy.

14.1 Rights

Introduction

As is often stated, the UK does not have a formal 'Bill of Rights' in the US sense – that is, a codified and entrenched (i.e. not easily amended or repealed) document setting out the various rights afforded to citizens. Citizens' rights in the UK have traditionally been protected by a combination of existing statutes, common law and case law. Many saw the Human Rights Act (see Ch 14.4) as a step towards a more formal declaration of rights, but it falls short of allowing courts to void conflicting statute and – as we have seen with the recent anti-terrorism legislation – is too easily brushed aside by government in times of apparent crisis.

What are rights?

Natural rights

Philosophers such as John Locke have identified so-called natural rights; universal God-given and inalienable rights including life, liberty and property. Such ideas are echoed in documents such as the US Declaration of Independence (1776). A belief in 'natural rights' rests on the concept of a 'natural human state' (pre-dating political structures and society).

Citizens' rights

More commonly when we refer to rights, we are referring to those rights granted to citizens by the state. Such **positive rights** should, in theory, be more tangible because they have been set out and recorded by an institution rather than being part of an attempt philosophically to reconstruct pre-history.

The rights of British citizens (?)

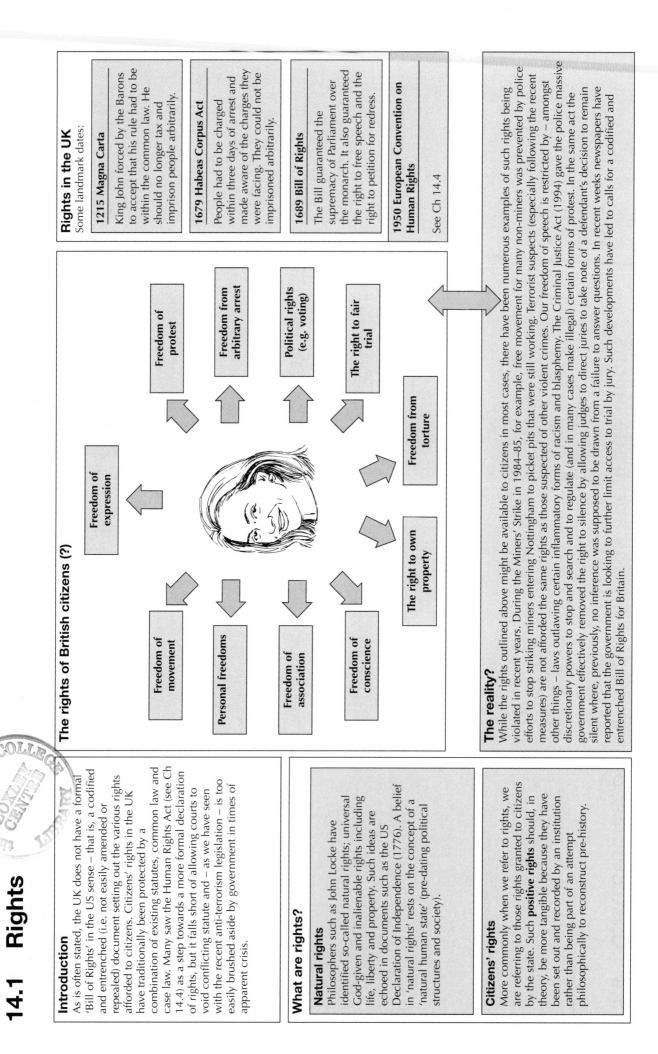

- Freedom of expression
- Freedom of movement
- Personal freedoms
- Freedom of association
- Freedom of conscience
- Freedom of protest
- Freedom from arbitrary arrest
- Political rights (e.g. voting)
- The right to fair trial
- The right to own property
- Freedom from torture

The reality?

While the rights outlined above might be available to citizens in most cases, there have been numerous examples of such rights being violated in recent years. During the Miners' Strike in 1984–85, for example, free movement for many non-miners was prevented by police efforts to stop striking miners entering Nottingham to picket pits that were still working. Terrorist suspects (especially following the recent measures) are not afforded the same rights as those suspected of other violent crimes. Our freedom of speech is restricted by – amongst other things – laws outlawing certain inflammatory forms of racism and blasphemy. The Criminal Justice Act (1994) gave the police massive discretionary powers to stop and search and to regulate (and in many cases make illegal) certain forms of protest. In the same act the government effectively removed the right to silence by allowing judges to direct juries to take note of a defendant's decision to remain silent where, previously, no inference was supposed to be drawn from a failure to answer questions. In recent weeks newspapers have reported that the government is looking to further limit access to trial by jury. Such developments have led to calls for a codified and entrenched Bill of Rights for Britain.

Rights in the UK
Some landmark dates:

1215 Magna Carta

King John forced by the Barons to accept that his rule had to be within the common law. He should no longer tax and imprison people arbitrarily.

1679 Habeas Corpus Act

People had to be charged within three days of arrest and made aware of the charges they were facing. They could not be imprisoned arbitrarily.

1689 Bill of Rights

The Bill guaranteed the supremacy of Parliament over the monarch. It also guaranteed the right to free speech and the right to petition for redress.

1950 European Convention on Human Rights

See Ch 14.4

14.2 Law and the courts

Criminal and civil law

We have already considered the nature and origin of laws. In this section we draw a distinction between civil and criminal law.

Civil law...

is concerned with interrelationships between different individuals and groups. Civil cases generally involve matters such as wills or contracts. Successful civil cases generally result in compensation awards in favour of the victor and against those losing the case.

Criminal law...

is that dealing with crimes by an individual or group against the state. Criminal cases include those concerning violent behaviour, serious fraud or burglary. These prosecutions are normally conducted by the state and result in a variety of punishments including fines and imprisonment.

The courts in Scotland

Scotland has a different legal history and, accordingly, different legal structures and procedures than those operating in England and Wales. Those interested in the Scottish system should refer to a core textbook, *British Politics in Focus* edited by David Roberts (Causeway Press, 1999) provides a clear summary (p589).

The structure of the courts in England and Wales

The House of Lords

The House of Lords is positioned at the very apex of both the civil and the criminal court hierarchies. It is the ultimate appeal court. The Law Lords (normally numbering around 12) are experienced judges who have been made life peers in order that they might consider appeals referred to them by the Court of Appeal (Civil and Criminal Divisions). Usually, five Law Lords will consider a case. Only the European Court of Justice has the power to overrule the House of Lords, and then only in matters concerning EU law.

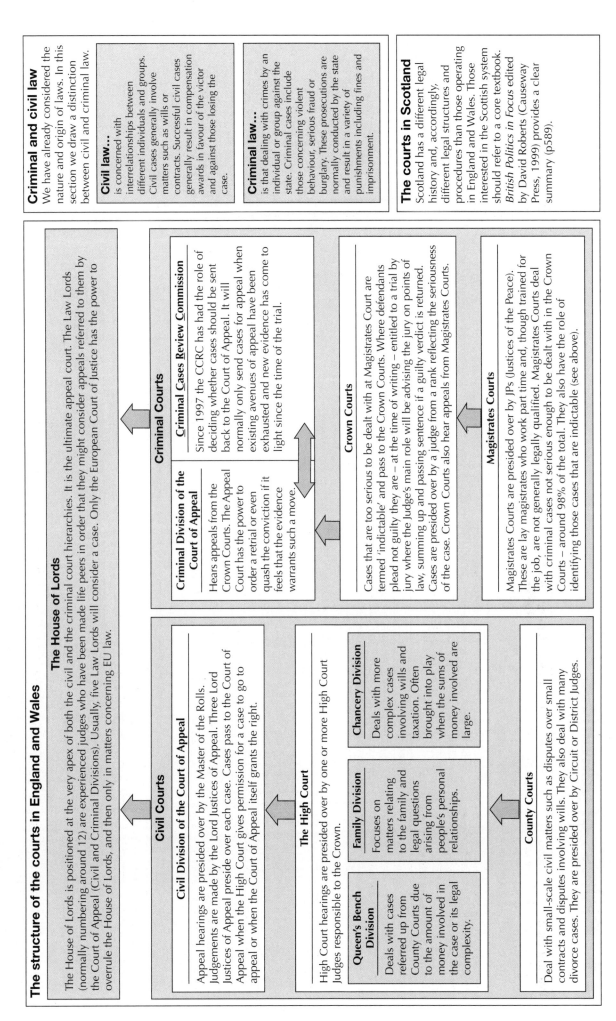

Civil Courts

Civil Division of the Court of Appeal

Appeal hearings are presided over by the Master of the Rolls. Judgements are made by the Lord Justices of Appeal. Three Lord Justices of Appeal preside over each case. Cases pass to the Court of Appeal when the High Court gives permission for a case to go to appeal or when the Court of Appeal itself grants the right.

The High Court

High Court hearings are presided over by one or more High Court Judges responsible to the Crown.

Queen's Bench Division	Family Division	Chancery Division
Deals with cases referred up from County Courts due to the amount of money involved in the case or its legal complexity.	Focuses on matters relating to the family and legal questions arising from people's personal relationships.	Deals with more complex cases involving wills and taxation. Often brought into play when the sums of money involved are large.

County Courts

Deal with small-scale civil matters such as disputes over small contracts and disputes involving wills. They also deal with many divorce cases. They are presided over by Circuit or District Judges.

Criminal Courts

Criminal Cases Review Commission

Since 1997 the CCRC has had the role of deciding whether cases should be sent back to the Court of Appeal. It will normally only send cases for appeal when existing avenues of appeal have been exhausted and new evidence has come to light since the time of the trial.

Criminal Division of the Court of Appeal

Hears appeals from the Crown Courts. The Appeal Court has the power to order a retrial or even quash the conviction if it feels that the evidence warrants such a move.

Crown Courts

Cases that are too serious to be dealt with at Magistrates Court are termed 'indictable' and pass to the Crown Courts. Where defendants plead not guilty they are – at the time of writing – entitled to a trial by jury where the Judge's main role will be advising the jury on points of law, summing up and passing sentence if a guilty verdict is returned. Cases are presided over by a judge from a rank reflecting the seriousness of the case. Crown Courts also hear appeals from Magistrates Courts.

Magistrates Courts

Magistrates Courts are presided over by JPs (Justices of the Peace). These are lay magistrates who work part time and, though trained for the job, are not generally legally qualified. Magistrates Courts deal with criminal cases not serious enough to be dealt with in the Crown Courts – around 98% of the total. They also have the role of identifying those cases that are indictable (see above).

14.3   Redress of grievances

The nature of grievances

Government is an imprecise science and it is inevitable that many individuals will find themselves in a position where they feel that they have a justifiable grievance against some agency or tier of government. An individual might feel that their planning application has been dealt with unfairly, or that their tax allowances have been calculated incorrectly. They may feel that they are being victimised by a government agency or that a local authority is failing to discharge a particular aspect of its duties effectively. Any number of serious grievances might motivate a citizen to seek redress. What avenues are open to them?

Channels for redressing grievances

Tribunals

Tribunals sometimes offer a source of redress where there is no real remedy through the courts, whether because the complainant does not have the ability (perhaps the money) to pursue the case legally or because they have been denied the right to judicial review. Tribunals offer a relatively cheap and easy way of having a grievance considered. Hundreds of different types of tribunals exist to mediate in disputes not only between citizens and the various agencies of the state but also between employers and employees.

Inquiries

Public inquiries exist to take in views about proposed projects or to investigate particular events (e.g. the 'arms for Iraq' inquiry). Inquiries are often very long and expensive. The Heathrow Terminal 5 inquiry, for example, ran from 1995 to 1999 costing taxpayers £80 million. Some feel that inquiries are often PR exercises and that governments generally pick and choose which, if any, inquiry recommendations to accept. At the time of writing the government is planning to do away with inquiries for airport and roads projects.

The courts

The courts do not generally deal with the merits of particular act or decision. They tend to look more at the way in which the decision was taken – whether the correct procedures were followed or whether the minister was acting within their authority when making a decision. Judicial review in the UK is not, therefore, the same as that in the US where courts can strike down acts and regulations. Access to the legal system is also limited by the cost of embarking on such actions and on the difficulty of being granted judicial review in your case.

Judicial review

In the UK judicial review normally takes place where unreasonableness, illegality or procedural impropriety can be found. The High Court, for example, found that the Foreign Office had illegally decided to spend £34 million on the Malaysian Pergau Dam project. It ordered that a further £65.6 million set aside for similar projects should be paid back into the overseas aid budget.

The European Court of Human Rights

The Court was set up in 1950 to enforce the various guarantees set out in the European Convention on Human Rights (EHCR). Cases from Britain could be taken to the Court where the domestic appeals procedures had been exhausted. Up to 1998 the European Commission on Human Rights received about 800 cases each year from British citizens and, by 1997, the Court had found violations of human rights in 50 out of the 98 cases referred to it. Under the Human Rights Act (1998) which came into force in October 2000 many of the protections set out in the ECHR are now available to citizens in British courts. This act is dealt with more fully in Ch 14.4.

Elected representatives

Individuals can approach their elected representatives for help in redressing their grievances. MPs can speak or write to ministers and civil servants, ask parliamentary questions and seek to initiate debates in the House on behalf of their constituents. Local representatives might also be able to address grievances and facilitate some remedy. In many ways, working through one's elected representatives was the traditional way of having one's concerns addressed. In recent years, however, many citizens have come to see MPs as too controlled by their party and special interests to provide effective help. Such feelings were brought in to focus by the 'cash for questions' scandal and the subsequent activities and findings of the Parliamentary Commissioner for Standards (Gordon Downey and later Elizabeth Filkin).

The Citizen's Charter

The Citizen's Charter – John Major's 'big idea' – was launched in 1991. Charters were to be drawn up setting out the levels of service citizens could expect from public bodies. Such bodies would be expected to meet these target levels. Citizens were, therefore, presented with something concrete to measure services against. The Citizen's Charter also gave the service providers something to aim at – an aspect of the policy enhanced by the issuing of Charter Marks for excellence in public service.

Ombudsmen (see ombudsman.org.uk)

An ombudsman ('people's friend') has the role of investigating complaints made by the public and suggesting possible redress where they find maladministration. Though ombudsmen have little real power, they do have a certain authority and the ability to shame. At the time of writing Michael Buckley is the Parliamentary and the Health Service Ombudsman.

Example: On November 1, 2001 Michael Buckley in his capacity as Health Service Ombudsman found in favour of a woman who had complained about the way in which she had been treated by St Mary's NHS Trust following a miscarriage. He was particularly critical of the Hospital's 'insensitive disposal of the foetus'.

14.4 The Human Rights Act

Context

The European Convention on Human Rights, signed in 1950, set up a Commission of Human Rights and a European Court of Human Rights (not to be confused with the European Court of Justice) to enforce the Articles of the Convention (some of which are now incorporated into the Human Rights Act. This Act was passed in 1998 and came into force in October 2000.

The European Court of Human Rights (ECHR)

The ECHR sits in Strasbourg and was established by the Convention to hear cases where governments were accused of violating the Convention's terms. Appeals by individuals could only take place when the national appeals process had been exhausted and when the Commission of Rights declared cases admissible. This was an extremely long process. The passing of the HRA has allowed individuals the opportunity of using the Articles in the British courts.

The Human Rights Act

The Act itself does not bring all of the rights or protocols of the Convention into British law – though those areas left out can be added later if necessary. If acts of Parliament conflict with the HRA then the courts can make a 'declaration of incompatibility'. Government and Parliament then have to consider whether the law needs changing and in the meantime the courts have to enforce the law as it stands.

Protocols … are parts of the Convention that have been added since the Convention was first drafted. Some, though not all, of these are incorporated into the HRA. Others are already catered for in existing laws. Protocol 1 includes the right to protection of property, free elections and education. Protocol 6 abolishes the death penalty.

Mini case studies

The treatment of Thompson and Venables (the killers of Jamie Bulger)

The courts granted a lifetime ban on revealing the new identities of the two boys. This ban was granted on the grounds that identifying them might threaten their life (Article 2) and possibly subject them to inhuman and degrading treatment (Article 3). It was also argued that such a ban might help protect their right to a private and family life (Article 8). Newspapers had argued that Article 10 gave them the right to publish details but the court disagreed.

The 1997 'Two strikes and you're out' legislation

Four individuals serving life sentences challenged the legislation that gave mandatory life sentences for second-time serious offences. They argued that it constituted a violation of their right to liberty (Article 5), constituted inhuman and degrading treatment (Article 3) and compromised the ban on making law retrospective (Article 7). The appeal court in effect disabled the law by allowing judges to use their discretion when sentencing (as had been the case before the Act was passed).

Treatment of mental patients

A paranoid schizophrenic killer being held in Broadmoor argued that the onus should not be on him to prove that he was no longer suffering from the condition before he could be released, but on the authorities to prove that he was still dangerous enough for them to detain him against his will. In requiring him to prove his health, the Mental Health Act of 1983 reversed the burden of proof (protected by Article 6) and infringed his liberty (Article 5). The appeal court agreed and ruled the Act incompatible with the Convention.

The right to remain silent

A woman, Margaret Brown, who was charged after admitting being drunk in charge of a vehicle, argued that section 172 of the Road Traffic Act (1988), which makes it an offence not to name the driver of a vehicle, violated her right against self-incrimination – i.e. her right to silence (Article 6). This section also applied to vehicles caught on speed cameras. Scotland's High Court threw out the prosecution against her on the grounds that section 172 violated her right to a fair trial (Article 6). The Privy Council later reversed this decision.

The Convention Rights

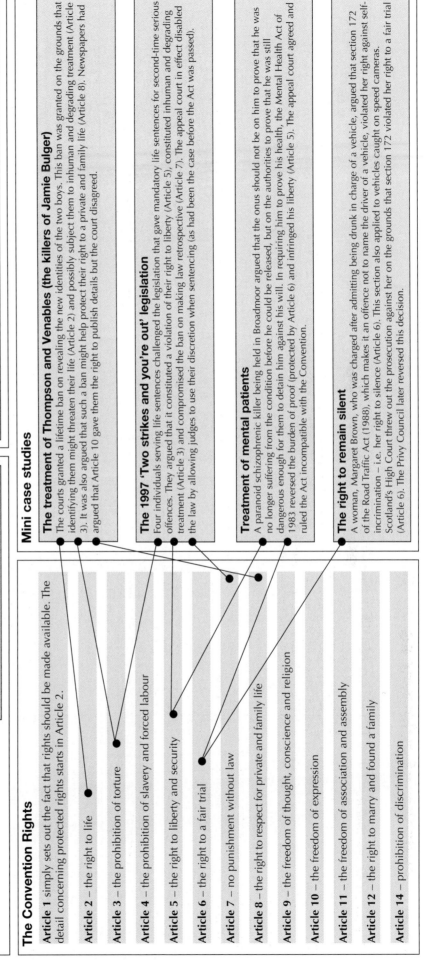

Article 1 simply sets out the fact that rights should be made available. The detail concerning protected rights starts in Article 2.

Article 2 – the right to life

Article 3 – the prohibition of torture

Article 4 – the prohibition of slavery and forced labour

Article 5 – the right to liberty and security

Article 6 – the right to a fair trial

Article 7 – no punishment without law

Article 8 – the right to respect for private and family life

Article 9 – the freedom of thought, conscience and religion

Article 10 – the freedom of expression

Article 11 – the freedom of association and assembly

Article 12 – the right to marry and found a family

Article 14 – prohibition of discrimination

14.5 Justice – some key debates

Do we need a codified and entrenched Bill of Rights?

Y E S	N O
(1) Bringing together all of our rights in a single codified document would empower citizens and make protection of rights easier. (2) An entrenched Bill would prevent governments making changes easily. (3) A Bill would properly limit government power. (4) It would finish the job started by the passing of the HRA in 1998.	(1) Our rights are already protected in other statutes (including the HRA). (2) Codifying rights in a document might limit rights, by devaluing anything that is not included. (3) What should we include? (4) An entrenched Bill would not allow governments sufficient flexibility to act in emergencies.

Are judges biased?

Y E S	N O
(1) The fact that many are ultimately chosen by the Lord Chancellor means that they may be untypical of the population as a whole, sharing his outlook. (2) Judges are biased due to their social background (e.g. over 80% of senior judges are public school and Oxbridge educated.) (3) The increasingly political nature of judicial review means that judges are no longer the umpires. They are becoming political players.	(1) Any method of appointment brings with it problems, and elections don't necessarily ensure a great degree of social representation (look at Parliament). The US Supreme Court is appointed and works well. (2) Judges are never going to be socially representative because they need to be highly qualified and experienced. Inequalities will diminish as other social groups work their way up through the legal hierarchy.

Key debates

Is the Police Complaints Authority (PCA) worthwhile?

Y E S	N O
(1) The police are the best people to investigate complaints because they have the resources and experience to do it. (2) The results suggest that it is working. Complaints are down from 18 354 in 1997–98 to 17 248 in 2000–01. Deaths in custody are down from a high of 65 (1998–99) to 32 (2000–01). (3) The police have tried to crack down on officers avoiding investigation by claiming ill health.	(1) It is bizarre that the police should be investigating complaints against the police. (2) The process is far too slow. (3) In the past officers have been able to avoid action too easily by leaving the force on 'ill health'. (4) Officers are too often given the benefit of the doubt. Too few officers are found guilty.

Should we have elected judges?

Y E S	N O
(1) Many judges are out of touch, not least due to their socio-economic backgrounds. Elections would address this. (2) It would make judges accountable. (3) The extension of judicial review brings judges into the realm of policy-making. They are no longer simply umpires. We therefore need some control.	(1) Elected judges might act in pursuit of popularity rather than justice. (2) The demands of elections might lead to candidates setting out 'manifestos' making promises on sentencing etc. that might tie their hands once elected. (3) Elections will not necessarily result in those with the best legal minds being chosen.

Should we have a right to 'trial by jury' in Crown Court Cases?

Y E S	N O
(1) Trial by jury is fairer because juries are drawn from all ranks of society. (2) Juries can make decisions that are legally wrong but 'just' (in the Clive Ponting case for example). (3) It is the 'start of a slippery slope'. Eventually all trial by jury will be ended.	(1) Magistrates have a better knowledge of the law than most jurors do. (2) Removing juries will save money (probably more than £10 000 per case). (3) It will save time. Justice will be more immediate for defendants and for the victims of crime.

15.1 Before Philadelphia

The historical context

The Declaration of Independence

In 1776 the 13 colonies on the east coast of North America issued the Declaration of Independence. This act resulted from a deterioration in relations between the colonies and Britain that had seen such landmark historical events as the Boston Tea Party in 1773. The key issue for many in the colonies was the British insistence on demanding taxation without granting any meaningful representation. The Declaration, drafted by Thomas Jefferson, formally put into words the colonies' justification for their rejection of British rule as well as setting out some of the principles upon which a new government could be formed.

'We hold these truths to be self-evident, that all Men are created equal, that they are endowed by their Creator with certain unalienable Rights, that among these are Life, Liberty and the Pursuit of Happiness. That to secure these Rights, Governments are instituted among Men, deriving their just Powers from the Consent of the Governed that whenever any Form of Government becomes destructive of these Ends, it is the Rights of the People to alter or to abolish it, and to constitute new Government, laying its foundation on such principles, and organising its powers in such form, as to them shall seem most likely to effect their safety and happiness.'

The American War of Independence (1776–83)

The War of Independence, or American Revolution as it is sometimes referred to, dates back to at least 1775 when fighting broke out between colonial militia and the British. In 1774 the various colonial assemblies had sent delegates to a first national 'Continental Congress'. In 1775 the 'Second Continental Congress' appointed George Washington to command their army and, in July, adopted the Declaration of Independence. After seven years the War was over and the Treaty of Paris was signed in 1783. In this Treaty Britain recognised American independence.

The Articles of the Confederation (1781)

In 1781 the former American colonies formed a loose confederacy. Under this system there was to be no national executive (such as a president) or any national judiciary. There would simply be a Congress consisting of representatives from each state. Under the Articles of the Confederation this 'central government' only had power over the following areas:

| Foreign policy and defence | Territorial disputes between states | Coinage |
| Weights and measures | Postal services | Relations with Indians |

All other matters were left to the states

Preparations for the Philadelphia Convention

By 1786 there was widespread disillusionment with the form of government created by the Articles of the Confederation. Many, including Hamilton (see below), called for a convention to discuss reform of the Articles. This Convention was eventually called in 1787. Fifty-five representatives, out of the 74 who were invited from the various states, turned up at the Constitutional Convention in Philadelphia. Only one state, Rhode Island, sent no representatives. Many of the leading figures present were from Virginia, at that time the largest of the states. George Washington, a unifying figurehead following his leadership in the Revolution, was asked to preside over the meetings, but individuals such as James Madison provided the real driving force.

Key participants

George Washington (1732–99)
Washington had represented Virginia in the First (1774) and Second (1775) Continental Congress. In 1775 the Congress had given him control of American forces and in 1787 he presided over the Philadelphia Convention. He was the first US President (1789–97).

James Madison (1751–1836)
Madison had been involved in Virginia politics since 1776 and became a real driving force at the Convention. He collaborated with Hamilton in the writing of the Federalist Papers, supporting the ratification of the finished Constitution. He was a strong advocate of a Bill of Rights.

Thomas Jefferson (1743–1826)
Jefferson was another Virginian. He had served on the Second Continental Congress in 1775 and then drafted the Declaration of Independence issued in July 1776. He was a keen advocate of the separation of powers and limited government.

Alexander Hamilton (1755–1804)
Hamilton was Washington's aide-de-camp in the American Revolution (between 1777 and 1781). He co-authored the Federalist Papers (with Madison) and was the founder and the leader of the Federalist Party until the time of his death in a duel in 1804. Hamilton was a firm believer in a strong federal government. He believed, however, that pure democracy would lead to mob-rule.

15.2 Framing the Constitution

The Philadelphia Convention, 1787

Who were the Founding Fathers?

The Founding Fathers were the 55 delegates who wrote the new Constitution in 1787. Most of them were fairly young, wealthy landowners, lawyers and businessmen with a good level of education. When they met at Philadelphia in 1787 they were supposed to discuss reforms to the Articles of the Confederation that had been in force since 1781. In the event, they decided to go beyond this remit and start afresh on a new constitutional settlement.. Throughout the summer of 1787 the delegates debated and argued the detail of the new arrangements. No small difficulty was the need to balance the need for strong and effective central government with the need to protect the rights of states and individual citizens. Under British rule, the remoteness and unitary nature of government had been seen to impinge upon individual rights. The confederacy arising from the Articles of the Confederation had been to the other extreme – weak and ineffective.

Conflicting interests and compromise

The Virginia Plan

This plan set out the interests of most of the larger states. There would be a bicameral legislature, with representatives in each house apportioned to each state in relation to the state's population. There would be an elected national executive and national courts. The central (federal) government would have power to declare acts of state governments invalid and could use the federal army to quell problems within states.

The New Jersey Plan

This placed a greater emphasis on the needs of the smaller states who feared that their voices might be lost amongst the larger states. The plan provided greater detail on the power of the legislature. This legislature would, for example, appoint the President, and its laws would be the supreme law in the land. The real sticking point, however, came over the way in which seats in the legislature would be apportioned between states.

The Connecticut Compromise

One of the main barriers to reaching an agreement during the summer of 1787 was the conflicting views of larger and smaller states concerning the apportionment of seats in the legislature. The larger states, reasonably perhaps, believed that seats in both chambers of the bicameral system should be apportioned between states in proportion to state populations. The smaller states in contrast were worried that this would see their voices lost in the new Congress and were unwilling to agree to a constitution that would result in such a situation. The so-called Connecticut Compromise, proposed by Connecticut delegate Roger Sherman, offered a solution. One chamber (the House) would be apportioned in relation to a state's population and the other (the Senate) would comprise two representatives from each state regardless of state population. Thus, the deadlock was broken.

Key issues at Philadelphia

Centralisation or fragmentation?

As we have seen, by 1786 it was clear that a more effective balance had to be struck between the need for effective government and the need for the protection of state rights and individual liberties. Under the British (King George III), the colonies had experienced a particularly centralised 'unitary' system of government. Under the Articles of the Confederation they had experienced an unusually loose and disparate form of government with a 'confederal' system. Both had proven unacceptable for different reasons. The key was, therefore, to create a truly 'federal' system where the powers of federal (central) and state governments would be clearly defined and in balance.

Democracy or 'mobocracy'?

As we have seen the majority of the delegates at the Convention – the Founding Fathers – were relatively well educated and wealthy. Many were landowners, all were white men. Many of them – Hamilton included – feared that democracy, unchecked, could reel out of control and become the rule of the uneducated, politically ignorant mob – 'mobocracy'. As a result they put in place mechanisms to avoid such an eventuality, including the electoral college which is dealt with in Ch 22.

The end product

After four months of deliberations the final draft of the new Constitution was signed by 39 of the 55 delegates who had attended the Convention. As George Washington wrote to Partick Henry in 1787:

'I wish the Constitution, which is offered, had been made more perfect, but I sincerely believe it is the best that could be obtained at this time.'

The new Constitution established a federal government with a bicameral Congress (composition, conditions of office and powers were set out in Article 1), a President (Article 2) and a Supreme Court (Article 3). The constitutional positions of each of these institutions and other aspects of the political process are dealt with in context on their respective pages.

15.3 Principles

Introduction

As we have seen, the Founding Fathers were – for the most part – well-educated men. In such circles the influence of the social contract theorists such as Locke and Rousseau spread, along with the ideas of other writers such as Thomas Paine and the French writer Baron Montesquieu. They developed an understanding of natural rights, limited government and the separation of powers, taking such ideas with them when they attended the Constitutional Convention in Philadelphia in 1787.

Federalism

The key issue at the 1787 Philadelphia Convention was the role that the central government was to play in relation to the state governments. Some would have preferred to retain something closer to the loose confederation created by the Articles of the Confederation; others would have wanted the amalgamation of all of the states into a single unitary national government. As was so often the case at the Convention, a compromise was reached. Certain powers (**the enumerated powers**) were given to the federal government. Others were **inherent** or **implied** because the federal government would not have been able to discharge its enumerated powers without them. Some powers were **denied** the federal government. In addition, the Tenth Amendment to the Constitution stated that 'the powers not delegated to the United States by the Constitution, nor prohibited by it to the States, are reserved to the States respectively, or to the people.' These then are the **reserved** or **residual** powers. Finally, some powers were to be held jointly – the **concurrent** powers.

Dual federalism (1780s–1920s)

Under this manifestation of federalism, the federal (central) and various state governments each had separate spheres of authority. Within their own areas they were sovereign and they were, therefore, equal in status. This system operated fairly well as long as the federal government was small and was not interventionist. In the 1930s, however, things changed significantly.

Co-operative federalism or intergovernmentalism (1930s–1960s)

Until the end of the 1920s the various states were reasonably powerful and the federal government's powers to intervene were fairly narrowly interpreted. Following the Wall Street Crash (1929), however, the federal government was forced to become more involved in the co-ordinating the effort to get the economy moving again. Franklin D Roosevelt's New Deal policy brought the federal government into Americans' lives, wherever they lived in the US. Truman's 'Fair Deal', Kennedy's 'New Frontier' and Johnson's 'Great Society' continued this interventionist trend, particularly in their use of targeted grants.

New Federalism (1970s–present)

Criticism of federal government intervention/interference led to calls for 'smaller government'. Reagan's 'New Federalism' was a stated desire to return power to the states. Reagan was critical of the way in which the Tenth Amendment's guarantee of state rights had been ignored since the 1930s. Republican domination of the White House in the period 1970–93 led to plans to reduce federal grants as part of the budget-balancing programme The Supreme Court also took the lead by, for example, allowing states to pass statutes undermining Roe v. Wade locally, by limiting access to abortion (e.g. Webster v. Reproductive Health Services, 1989).

Republicanism

Their experiences under British rule had led many Founding Fathers to oppose the idea of establishing a US monarchy in principle. For them, the tyranny visited on the 13 colonies by George III was reason enough to establish a republic. Though some, Hamilton for example, felt that a monarchy could work in the US, the republicans won the day. Congress was also prevented from granting other titles of nobility in Article 1, Section 8.

Separation of powers

This was the principle outlined by the French writer Baron Montesquieu. Essentially, Montesquieu argued that a concentration of the three key elements of state power could lead to tyranny. These three elements (see right) should, therefore, be separated in the three branches of government. In the US this principle means, for example, that no individual can hold office in more than one of the three branches simultaneously. This is a far cry from the situation in the UK where the Prime Minister is head of the executive and sits in the legislature, and the Lord Chancellor is part of the government (executive), the House of Lords (legislature) and at the apex of the legal system (judiciary).

Executive

The executive branch has the role of executing – putting the laws into effect.

Legislature

The legislature has the role of legislating – this means that it makes the laws.

Judiciary

The judiciary has the role of enforcing and interpreting the laws. The US Supreme Court has to interpret the meaning of the Constitution – the supreme law of the land.

Checks and balances

A total separation of power and an absence of co-operation between branches would lead to 'gridlock' in government. As a result, the Constitution forces co-operation between the three separated branches by instituting checks and balances. Those in each branch know that they can achieve little without the other branches but, by negotiation, can go some way towards achieving their goals. In order to avoid the dangers of branches co-operating too much or simply capitulating, the Founding Fathers also staggered the length of terms of office for President (four years), Supreme Court (life), House of Representatives (two years) and Senate (six years with one-third elected every two years). This means that those in different branches often have different ideological perspectives.

15.4 Checks and balances

Introduction

The separation of powers was central to the Constitution framed at Philadelphia but, as we saw on the last page, a total separation of the powers to make laws, to execute laws and to enforce laws would have left government permanently gridlocked and unworkable. As a result interconnections, 'checks and balances', were built into the system of government. These checks and balances provided enough linkage for the government to be effective while, at the same time, providing barriers to any one branch dominating the political process.

What checks exist between the three branches of the federal government?

President

Checks on Congress

(1) The President effectively recommends/proposes legislation though the 'State of the Union Message'.
(2) The President can veto legislation and also has a 'pocket veto' in certain circumstances (see Ch 16.2).
(3) The President can call special sessions of Congress.

Checks on Supreme Court (and the federal judiciary)

(1) The President can appoint top federal judges including Supreme Court Justices.
(2) The President can issue pardons, thus reversing judicial action.

Congress

Checks on President

(1) Congress can reject, amend or delay the President's legislative proposals.
(2) The President's Budget has to be approved by Congress.
(3) Congress can override the President's veto (with a two-thirds majority in each house).
(4) Many Presidential appointments have to be approved by a majority vote in the Senate.
(5) A two-thirds majority is required in the Senate for treaties to be ratified.
(6) Congress retains the War Power and can, in theory, prevent the President entering a war or force him into one against his will.
(7) Congress can initiate impeachment proceedings against the President as it did in the case of Bill Clinton.

Checks on Supreme Court

(1) Congress (the Senate) confirms Supreme Court appointments by majority vote.
(2) Congress controls the size and appellate jurisdiction of the Court and can set up inferior courts as it sees fit.
(3) Congress can initiate constitutional amendments with a view to changing the passages of the Constitution upon which the Court is basing the judgements that Congress disapproves of.

Supreme Court

Checks on President

(1) Through judicial review, the Supreme Court can declare the actions of the President unconstitutional.

Checks on Congress

(1) Through judicial review, the Court can declare acts of Congress unconstitutional, thus making them void.
(2) The Court can also interpret the meaning of acts, affecting the way in which they are implemented.

15.5 The Bill of Rights

Introduction

The first ten amendments to the Constitution are referred to collectively as the Bill of Rights. They were ratified in 1791 as part of the deal that ensured some states accepted the Constitution itself.

The Bill of Rights outlines a number of key constitutional guarantees and the majority, if not all, of these ten amendments still have a direct relevance to the lives of Americans today. The important thing to remember is that although many of the protected rights appear unambiguous and clear cut (**absolute**), in reality the Supreme Court and inferior courts have had to **balance** the rights of one individual against another and balance the rights of all individuals against the legitimate interests of the state in regulating human activity.

The Bill of Rights

1. Protects the freedom of religion, the press, speech and assembly (see right)
2. Protects the right to bear arms
3. Protects the privacy of property owners
4. Guarantees freedom from unreasonable searches and seizures
5. Guarantees the rights of the accused and includes the 'due process clause'
6. Sets out rights for those standing trial
7. Deals with common law suits
8. Bans excessive bail and 'cruel and unusual' punishments
9. Deals with rights reserved to the people
10. Deals with rights reserved to the states

NB This page focuses on the First Amendment but you should also make yourself familiar with other key elements of the Bill of Rights. See Appendix I.

Case study: the First Amendment

Introduction

The majority of Americans are familiar with the First Amendment; if not 'word-for-word', then for what it represents. This first plank of the Bill of Rights has become, as Lee C Bollinger noted, 'one of the nation's foremost normative and cultural symbols' because it 'reflects the vital attributes of the American character'. What, then, is the basis of this 'cultural symbol'? For all of the heat it generates, the First Amendment is a remarkably compact piece of prose:

'Congress shall make no law respecting an establishment of religion, or prohibiting the free exercise thereof; or abridging the **freedom of speech**, or of the press; or the right of the people peaceably to assembly and to petition the Government for a redress of grievances.'

To the reader many of these guarantees appear absolute. What the Supreme Court has had to do, however, is to 'draw a line between constitutionally and legally appropriate application of the quintet of First Amendment guarantees' (Henry Abraham) in order to decide whether they should be taken as absolute or subject to some 'balancing' (against the rights of others and the interests of the state).

The limits of speech

The free-speech clause has been used to defend a wide range of practices. Though the decision that upheld the right to burn the US flag (Texas v. Johnson, 1989) is still considered significant, the protection of free speech has gone far further. The Court has ruled, for example, that the guarantee of free speech protects the right of women to strip (expressive conduct), though they allow some regulation of this non-pure form of 'speech'!

CITY OF ERIE et al. v. PAP's A.M, tdba 'Kandyland' (2000)	
Controversy:	**Decision:**
Dancers in Erie were supposed to wear G-strings and 'pasties' (fake jewel – 'paste' – nipple tassels). PAP's A.M, however, operated 'Kandyland', an establishment offering *totally* nude erotic dancing by women.	The Court argued that the overall loss of expression (in wearing G-strings and 'pasties') was insignificant, and that small losses of expression could not be used to justify invalidating Erie's otherwise constitutional measure. Erie's regulation was therefore upheld.

Freedom of speech

In protecting this right, the US Supreme Court has had to consider what precisely constitutes speech.

Protected speech

The Court has identified two types of speech which are protected by the First Amendment. The first is **pure speech** – the right of people to say or write things. The second is what is known as **expressive conduct**. Expressive conduct generally consists of non-verbal communication (burning the flag, for example) that is expressing a view. Expressive conduct is not granted the same protection as pure speech but it is, in the Court's eyes worthy of some protection.

Unprotected speech

The Court sees some forms of speech as unprotected. Justice Frank Murphy explained that obscenity, libel and fighting words are unprotected under the First Amendment because 'such utterances are no essential part of an exposition of ideas, and are of such slight social value as a step to truth that any benefit that may be derived from them is clearly outweighed by the social interest in order and morality.'

In many cases the line between expressive conduct worthy of some protection and unprotected speech is a fine one. This is particularly true over the question of what constitutes obscenity.

Conclusions

Barbara Jordan observed in 1990 that 'The Bill of Rights was not ordained by nature or God. It's very human, very fragile'. If this were true, we might expect the First Amendment, given its language and scope, to be particularly vulnerable to attack. In reality, however, the 45 words that constitute these five key guarantees have proven incredibly resilient; providing threads of continuity, yet leaving enough flexibility for the Supreme Court to shape the Amendment to the demands of each new age. This is crucial. While 'the great thing about the First Amendment' may well be 'that it extends its rights to everyone. The wise and the foolish' (Samuel J Ervin), no state can protect the rights of *all* individuals, at *all* costs, at *all* times. The Court has to find a balance between the *liberal* interest of individual freedom and the *democratic* need to regulate some activities.

15.6 The living Constitution

Introduction

The fact that the US Constitution is **codified** often leads people to suggest that it is **rigid** rather than **flexible**. However, while the amendment process is tortuous, the Constitution is anything but rigid. Indeed, it has shown itself to be incredibly flexible and adaptable in the 214 years since it was framed. This flexibility has been provided not only by the possibility of amendment but also by the ability of the Courts – ultimately the US Supreme Court – to interpret the document and apply it to each new age. The legality of practices never dreamt of at the time that the Constitution was written has been assessed through this process of interpretation and – at the same time – the Supreme Court has been able to update its own interpretations of the same constitutional passage over a period of time. In this sense the Constitution is a truly living document.

Amending the Constitution

Amendment proposed by		Amendment ratified by
Congress Two-thirds majority in both houses necessary	**All bar 21st** →	**State legislatures** Three-quarters of state legislatures vote to ratify amendment, normally within a certain time.
O R	**21st only** →	O R
National Constitutional Convention Called by at least two-thirds of states (never used)		**State Constitutional Conventions** Three-quarters of states call conventions and ratify (used only for the 21st Amendment)

The 27 Amendments

There have only been 27 Amendments to the Constitution since it was framed and the first ten of those, the 'Bill of Rights' were ratified together in 1791 (see Ch 15.5 and Appendix I).

Updating the Constitution through judicial action

The Supreme Court updating interpretations over time

Arthur J Goldberg stated that 'the Supreme Court, when it decides a new legal question, does not make illegal what was previously legal; it gives a final authoritative determination of whether an action was legal when it took place'. However, while in theory the Court is only interpreting the Constitution, in practice the differences between interpretations of the same constitutional passage over as short a time as 60 years (Plessy v. Ferguson, 1896 to Brown v. Board of Education, Topeka, 1954) may often appear tantamount to legislative action (see below). Indeed, James F Byrnes referring to just that transformation in interpretation took a radically different view of the Court's role to that taken by Goldberg, remarking that 'the Court did not interpret the Constitution – the Court amended it'.

PLESSY v. FERGUSON, 1896 (MAJORITY 7:1)

Controversy:	Decision:
Whether the 13th and 14th Amendments allowed the segregation of races on trains.	The Court argued that for there to be a violation of the 13th Amendment, there would have had to be some attempt to reintroduce slavery and that this had not occurred. Under the 14th Amendment segregation was acceptable as long as the result was 'separate but equal'.

BROWN v. BOARD OF EDUCATION, TOPEKA (KANSAS), 1954 (MAJORITY (9:0)

Controversy:	Decision:
Was it a violation of the 14th Amendment to prevent a black girl (Linda Brown) from attending a white school?	Looked at the merits of the case and used (then) controversial sociological research to show that the separation of races created inequalities. Separate was, therefore, always unequal and unacceptable under the 14th Amendment. 'In the field of public education, separate but equal has no place.' Plessy was thus out of date.

The Supreme Court addressing a new phenomenon (in this case, the internet)

RENO v. AMERICAN CIVIL LIBERTIES UNION, 1997 (MAJORITY 7:2)

The Supreme Court struck down two provisions of the 1996 Communications Decency Act, which sought to protect minors from harmful material available on the internet. The Court maintained that these sections violated the First Amendment protection of freedom of speech.

The majority:	The dissent:
Stevens, Scalia, Kennedy, Souter, Thomas, Ginsburg, Breyer	O'Connor, Rehnquist
'At issue is the constitutionality of two statutory provisions enacted to protect minors from 'indecent' and 'patently offensive' communications on the Internet. Not withstanding the legitimacy and importance of the congressional goal of protecting children from harmful materials, we agree with the three judge District Court that the statute abridges "the freedom of speech" protected by the First Amendment.' (Stevens)	'I write separately to explain why I view the Communications Decency Act of 1996 (CDA) as little more than an attempt by Congress to create 'adult zones' on the Internet. Our precedent indicates that the creation of such zones can be constitutionally sound. Despite the soundness of its purpose, however, portions of the CDA are unconstitutional because they stray from the blueprint our prior cases have developed for constructing a "zoning law" that passes constitutional muster.' (O'Connor)

16.1 An outline of the role and power of the presidency

The intentions of the Founding Fathers

Some have questioned the merit of looking at the intent of the Founding Fathers at all. Arthur Schlesinger (see below) argues that such an endeavour is flawed in two ways:

1. The Constitution's meaning should be determined not by the original intentions of those who drew up the paper but by the exigencies and new aspects of life itself.
2. Assessment of original intent is difficult because, while the role of the President in domestic affairs is reasonably well set out, in foreign policy the division of power was 'ambiguous and unclear'.

Clearly some of the Founding Fathers wanted a strong President. 'Energy in the Executive,' stated Alexander Hamilton, 'is a leading character in the definition of good government.' Others, however, were concerned that the President could become too powerful and become, effectively, a monarch – particularly in times of emergency (see below).

Constitutional position (de jure)

A number of formal presidential powers are set out in Article 2.

Domestic	Foreign
Can make proposals through the 'State of the Union Message', signs or vetoes legislation, acts as chief executive, nominates executive branch domestic policy officials and top judges, can issue pardons.	Acts as Commander in Chief, can negotiate treaties, can appoint executive branch foreign policy staff and foreign ambassadors and envoys.

Emergency powers

Locke had stated that 'in emergency responsible leaders could resort to exceptional power' but this was not included in the Constitution because, as Congressman White of the First Congress noted, it would be better 'to extend his power on some extraordinary occasion, even where he is not strictly justified by the Constitution than the Legislature should grant him an improper power to be exercised at all times'.

Reasons for the growth in presidential power

Several factors have led to an expansion in the role of the President:

1. Congress has been all too willing to delegate unconstitutional powers to the President in times of crisis when public opinion is against it and the President can 'wrap himself in the flag'. It shows a tendency to allow the President to make decisions which they themselves are not prepared to make (see Ch 16.6).

2. The expansion of the federal government: The federal government has grown and is growing. The decline of 'laissez faire' government means that everything is legislated for. A lot of this dates from the time of the New Deal.

3. The Supreme Court has failed to make decisions on critical areas (e.g. Vietnam) and has been scared into submission in other areas (e.g. over the New Deal's Industrial Recovery Act and Agricultural Adjustment Act).

4. The role of head of state has expanded. The international role of the US has increased massively since the time of the Constitution and, as a result, the President has become the representative of the nation, rather than just one part of the tripartite government. This has been emphasised by
   i) the US's superpower status (the 'black box') – even more so since the collapse of the USSR
   ii) the rise of the mass media

Actual position (de facto)

The result of these pressures has been a significant increase in the potential power available to modern Presidents. The President is now not only chief executive, chief diplomat, and commander in chief, but also chief legislator, chief war and peacemaker, head of state and head of his party. Some of these areas are dealt with in the pages that follow.

The imperial presidency

In his book 'The Imperial Presidency (1973), Arthur Schlesinger outlined what he saw as the monumental increase in presidential power since the framing of the Constitution. Crucially, however, Schlesinger showed that this was not a sudden change but a gradual process that had begun almost as soon as the ink was dry on the Constitution and had accelerated significantly in the 40 years up to the time that the book was published. Schlesinger wrote from a position of some knowledge. As an advisor to President Kennedy he had experienced at first hand the nature of presidential power. Following the fall of Nixon in 1974 and the relatively ineffectual presidencies of Ford and Carter, many felt that talk of 'imperial presidencies' was somewhat overstated. Others suggested that it was more sensible to look on the presidency as carrying with it a potential for power that effective incumbents could tap to great effect if they had the abilities.

Perceptions of presidential power

Other views

'The Power of the Presidency is awesome.' Thomas ('Tip') O'Neill (former Speaker of the House, 1986)

'When the President does it, that means that it is not illegal.' (Richard Nixon, 1977)

'The Buck stops here.' (Harry S Truman)

'I sit here all day saying do this and do that and nothing ever gets done. Christ! What a job!' (Harry S Truman)

'All Presidents start out to run a crusade but after a couple of years they find they are running something less heroic and much more intractable: namely a Presidency. The people are well cured by then of election fever, during which they think they are choosing Moses. In the third year, they look on the man as a sinner and a bumbler and begin to poke around for rumours of another Messiah.' Alistair Cooke (1968)

'Weakness is still what I see; weakness in the sense of a great gap between what is expected of a man (or someday woman) and assured capacity to carry through.' Richard Neustadt.

16.2 The Domestic Policy President

Two presidencies (?)

As H G Nicholas remarked in his book *The Nature of American Politics* (OUP, 1992), that 'the power of the President in foreign affairs has received such striking demonstration in the era of the Cold War that it has seemed to some observers that there are, in effect, two Presidencies. Presidents who have been thwarted or defeated by Congress in their domestic programmes have succeeded time and again in persuading Congress to acquiesce in their foreign policy'. In setting out this view Nicholas was, therefore, echoing Aaron Wildavsky (*The Two Presidencies*, 1969) in identifying a 'Domestic Policy President' and a 'Foreign Policy President'. Such a distinction should come as no surprise:

Firstly, the Constitution divided domestic legislative powers between legislature and executive far more clearly than it divides foreign policy powers;

Secondly, members of Congress are far more likely to be concerned about domestic policy because their re-election is more likely to depend upon it;

Thirdly, successful modern foreign policy is, by its very nature, difficult to formulate in a Congress numbering 535 individuals.

Domestic policy powers

Legislative powers
Given the Founding Fathers' interest in the separation of powers, it is surprising that we should be calling the President chief legislator. The societal changes outlined on the previous page have, however, demanded a greater role of the chief executive.

To sign or to veto
The Constitution grants the President the power of veto over legislation passed by Congress. The President must veto the whole bill, returning it to the house in which it was initiated within ten days of his receiving it. He is also required to include a written explanation of why the veto has been issued. If he does not send it back within ten days then it becomes law. However, if Congress is adjourned within the ten-day period then the President can pocket the bill – killing it. This is known as the pocket veto.

Proposing legislation
The Constitution grants the President the right to address Congress on the State of the Union. This has, in effect, become an agenda-setting exercise. Presidents can then enlist the help of their friends in Congress to introduce legislation.

The 'line-item' veto
In 1997 a law came into effect granting the President a 'line-item' veto. In effect this meant that the President could delete the amounts allocated to specific items in spending bills within five days of the bill being signed. Clinton first used this power in August 1997, and by June 1988 had used the measure on 82 occasions, cutting over $300 million from the federal budget. In June 1998 the Supreme Court ruled the line-item veto unconstitutional (6:3).

The budget
The President has taken on the role of formulating the annual budget proposals; a task completed in the Office of Management and Budget (OMB) see Ch 17.2.

Powers as chief executive
The Constitution gives the President the role of chief executive. In this role he has the responsibility of ensuring that 'the laws be faithfully executed (Article II, section 3). As chief executive he also has the role of appointing executive branch officials. He also appoints top federal judges (including Supreme Court Justices). These individuals are dealt with more fully in later pages.

Head of state
In the US the head of the executive is also, de facto, head of state. This role can bring with it significant influence because the President can mobilise patriotic feeling in support of his measures by 'wrapping himself in the flag'.

Important note
Because this page focuses on the President, it tends to rather overstate the degree of freedom that the President has to act in domestic policy. You should use this page in conjunction with the pages on 'Recent presidencies' and 'Checks and balances', as well as the chapters on Congress.

Case study
Many Presidents have come into office with visionary domestic policy programmes (see Ch. 15.3). For example:

FDR and the 'New Deal'
The Wall Street Crash of 1929 devastated the US economy, and state governments found that they could not deal with the hardship which the Depression brought to their localities. In the Presidential election of 1932 therefore, the electorate looked for a candidate who would bring the federal government in to deal with the economic problems on a national level. The result, was the election of Franklin D Roosevelt and the introduction of the policies known collectively as the New Deal.

In 1935 three major Acts were passed:
1) The Social Security Act, which gave assistance to the aged, blind, dependent children and unemployed.

> 'The Act provided a solid, enduring, legal foundation for the Federal grant-in-aid system to reach into almost any are of public concern.'
> C E Barfield (*Rethinking Federalism* 1981)

2) The National Industrial Recovery Act
3) The Agricultural Adjustment Act

The Supreme Court ruled that these acts were invalid (e.g. United States v. Butler,1936, which said that the Agricultural Programme was invalid) but when Roosevelt was re-elected with a landslide victory in 1936 he threatened to use Congress to 'pack the Court' with an additional six members (from nine to 15) who would support his policies.

Faced with such opposition the Court thought again and one Justice changed his mind, resulting in the *New York Times* reporting the next day that 'a switch in time' had 'saved nine'.

NB: more recent presidencies are dealt with in Ch 16.5.

16.3 The Foreign Policy President

Introduction

Modern foreign policy is, by its very nature, more effective when directed by a relatively small number of individuals because:

Firstly, it demands a degree of secrecy that would be hard to achieve if every detail were discussed on the floor of the House;
Secondly, it requires a speed of response not suited to careful congressional deliberations and amendment;
Thirdly, it requires a unified and determined approach – difficult to maintain in a group of 535.

It was partly for this reason, and the need for the President to be able to act in emergencies, that the Founding Fathers left foreign policy powers deliberately vague and overlapping when framing the Constitution. They wanted to provide the potential for speed of action and flexibility while at the same time avoiding some permanent grant of major military power into the hands of one man – the President.

The growth of foreign policy powers

War-maker

The power to declare war was placed firmly and clearly in the hands of Congress but – as we have seen – the Founding Fathers were fully aware that emergencies might require the President to take independent action and return to Congress later. It was in the area of war-making that Schlesinger thought the most marked growth of presidential power had occurred, with the rise of so-called presidential wars – wars in all but name that were never formally declared by Congress but justified, most often, on the grounds of emergency or self-defence. The problem was, as Schlesinger recognised, that allowing Presidents the power to defend the US was 'to imply unilateral authority to conduct defences so aggressively that … those on the receiving end may well be pardoned if they mistook it for aggression'.

Examples

Schlesinger charted abuses of the war-making power back to the early 1800s but saw the major growth as having taken place in 1950s, 1960s and early 1970s. US involvement in Cuba and particularly in Vietnam eventually under the Gulf of Tonkin Resolution (1964) marked a real shift in power from Congress to the President. The secret US air-war against Cambodia (1969–71) was the final insult to a Congress that didn't even know it had been happening.

Peacemaker

The power to ratify treaties was, like the power to declare war, also given to Congress – more specifically, the Senate. Though the President had the right to negotiate treaties, he had to gain the ratification of the Senate (two-thirds support needed) in order for them to come into force legally. This ratification has been no mere formality. For example, the Senate refused to ratify any meaningful treaty between 1871 and 1898 and in 1919 it had refused to ratify the Versailles Peace Treaty that was supposed to ensure long-term peace in Europe. Faced with such opposition, Presidents had begun to make treaties by other names. These so-called executive agreements had the same legal standing as treaties (as underlined in the 1942 Supreme Court case US v. Pink) but – because they were not called treaties – they circumvented the rules, not needing the customary two-thirds Senate majority. Such executive agreements proliferated in the years following the Second World War

Expansion of executive agreements

Between 1850 and 1900 there were 215 treaties and 238 executive agreements. Between 1889 and 1939 there were 524 treaties and 917 executive agreements. Under Nixon things deteriorated further. In 1971 there were only 17 treaties compared to 214 executive agreements. Since then there have been an average of 30 treaties + 250 executive agreements per year.

The Symington Committee

The Senate Foreign Relations Committee set up this special committee in February 1969 under the chairmanship of Stuart Symington of Missouri. It was charged with the task of investigating secret US security agreements and commitments abroad. Amongst other things, the Committee discovered that:

In 1971 the US had seven air bases, seven generals and 82 000 men in Thailand without congressional authorisation or detailed knowledge; The executive had been fighting a secret war in support of the Vientiane Government against Pathet Lao in Northern Laos since 1964, yet Congress believed that American bombing over Laos was against North Vietnamese troops passing along South East Laos; Since 1953 the US had been subsidising the Ethiopian Army for an electronic communication base at Kagnew. Congress did not know until 1969.

The War Powers Act (War Powers Resolution) of 1973

In 1971 Senator Barry Goldwater remarked that 'we [the US] have only been in five declared wars out of over 150 that we have fought'. In 1973 the War Powers Act was passed. It said that the President could only send troops into battle for 60 days without congressional approval. Congress intended this as a measure limiting presidential power, yet in reality it granted the President unconstitutional powers.

The Case Act of 1972

Like the War Powers Act, the Case Act was designed to limit the power of the President to make executive agreements, while in reality recognising a presidential power not intended by the Constitution. Under the Act, Presidents were free to make such agreements but had to tell Congress within 60 days. This gave Congress the opportunity to vote to cancel such agreement or withhold funding, thus stopping their implementation. In 1977 the time limit was reduced by Congress from 60 to 20 days.

Foreign policy in the 1970s and 1980s

The War Powers Act and the Case Act were not particularly effective in limiting presidential activity in the foreign policy arena. Both measures were more symbolic than anything, not dealing with the fact that the nature of secret wars and secret treaties made it hard for Congress to know whether or not the two acts had, in fact, been broken. Presidents also became adept at completing military engagements within the 60 days or ignored the restrictions: Reagan in Grenada (1983), for example, or Bush in Panama (1989), or when deploying troops in Kuwait (1990). Executive agreements have also continued as 'arrangements' or 'accords'; for example, Nixon with South Vietnam, Ford with regard to Sinai, and Carter over disarmament.

16.4 Presidential persuasion

The 'power to persuade'

President Harry S Truman is generally credited with coining this phrase. 'I sit here all day,' he lamented, 'trying to persuade people to do things they ought to have sense enough to do without my persuading them. That's all the powers of the president amount to.' Truman's frustration in the face of what he saw as massive practical limitations on the power of his office was obvious, though not unique. Other recent Presidents, Ford for example, have voiced similar concerns. The central problem that any President faces is that, regardless of the apparent growth in the powers of his office, he needs the help of others to achieve his objectives – and this help is not always forthcoming. The art of persuasion is, therefore, an art that all new Presidents need to master rapidly.

Limitations on presidential power

The sheer scale and complexity of government

As we have already seen, the expansion of the federal government in the last 70 years has been incredible. The very scale of federal operations, however, presents the President with a real problem of co-ordination and overview. He must – by necessity – have a massive staff and he must inevitably delegate a great deal.

The power of Congress

We have already identified many of the congressional checks and balances that operate upon the President. The President can do little that is dramatic and lasting without the agreement of Congress.

The vigilance of the US Supreme Court

The Supreme Court has not been afraid to declare the acts of Presidents unconstitutional. In the case of United States v. Nixon (1974), for example, the Court found that Nixon had acted unconstitutionally in refusing to hand over the so-called 'White House Tapes' to the authorities investigating 'Watergate'.

Public opinion, pressure groups and the media

Public opinion is unlikely to bring down a President, though some argue that Johnson's decision not to run for a second term in 1968 was largely a result of the public reaction to his pursuit of the war in Vietnam ('LBJ, LBJ, how many kids did you kill today?' to quote the anti-war protesters). Pressure groups can aggregate and amplify public concern, and the importance of media coverage is underlined by the numbers of presidential staff permanently assigned to 'media management'.

Means of persuasion

1. Using his friends
   - The **Vice-President, party leaders** in Congress, the **Chief of Staff** can put the President's case.
2. Personal persuasion
   - **Telephone calls** – Johnson is said to have called Congressmen late at night, prior to key votes. 'You might need some time and I'll remember you if you do this thing for me now.'
   - **Entertaining** – Reagan, for example, invited key Congressmen to breakfast at the White House before important votes.
   - **Offering 'pork'** (see above right) or **help in their election campaign.**

'Pork-barrelling' and 'log-rolling'

1. **Pork-barrelling** is where Congressmen appropriate money by adding 'riders' to bills. These riders provide funds for 'pet projects' back in their states. The 'rider' will normally have little to do with the bill that it is riding on (see example below). As such 'rider' amendments would be difficult to effect alone, Congressmen generally have to engage in log-rolling.

2. **Log-rolling** is where groups of Congressmen help each other to add clauses to bills that will benefit each other's constituents. They do this by voting for each other's amendments in a reciprocal fashion.

Some Presidents have been extremely adept at manipulating Congressmen with the lure of 'pork':

- John F Kennedy, facing problems with his tax legislation, gained the support of Senator Robert Kerr by promising Kerr, in return, his support for the Arkansas River Project;
- Gerald Ford found Congressman Mitchel supportive on his jobs bill when he told Mitchel that he would not allow the closure of an air base in his constituency.

Individual Congressmen in key positions can also reap great rewards for their constituents. L. Mendel Rivers, Chairman of the Armed Services Committee 1965–70, gained 11 major new naval installations for his state (ship yards, missile bases, hospitals and training camps). In addition, the Bureau of Naval Personnel and the Naval Reserve Headquarters were all moved to his state (South Carolina) and he had a complex of buildings named after himself. According to David S. Sorenson, 'it was said of L. Mendel Rivers that if he located one more base near Charleston, the whole district would sink into the sea.'

Case study

On March 20, 1986 the House rejected a bill sponsored by President Reagan, which was designed to provide aid to the 'Contras' fighting against the Communist Sandinistas in Nicaragua. On April 16 the House had to reconsider the bill, as the Senate had been persuaded to support it. The House Rules Committee supported the bill, but added a 'rider' worth $1.1 billion of supplementary spending to it. That is to say, if Reagan wanted to send the aid to the Contras, which the bill offered, he would have had to pay 170 times the value of the aid to the pet projects of Congressmen. The President had no 'line-item veto'. He could not choose which bits of the bill to accept and which to reject. He had to accept the whole bill or none of it. Reagan's aides described the rider as a 'rancid barrel of pork', a 'shabby and shameful trick': but there was little that could be done in the time available.

16.5 Recent presidencies

The presidency of Bill Clinton (1993–2001)

Context

The election of Bill Clinton as the 42nd President of the United States in November 1992 was something of a surprise, as a year before the election few would have given Clinton a chance. At that time George Bush (senior) was riding high in the polls following the success in the Gulf War. By the time of the 1992 presidential election, however, the Gulf War effect had worn off and voters were beginning to turn their attention to domestic policy where Bush had failed to keep to his 1988 'No New Taxes' pledge. Against this background Clinton was able to win even though allegations of affairs (Gennifer Flowers), student drug use, and draft-dodging (Vietnam) followed him everywhere.

Personality and character

Though Clinton proved adept at capturing the public mood – keeping the public largely on-side throughout his two terms – the ongoing scandals did little to enhance the institution of the presidency. The accusations of an affair with Gennifer Flowers paled into insignificance when set against the legal action initiated by Paula Jones and the whole Monica Lewinsky affair. Though Clinton remained President, the fallout from the impeachment investigations that followed certainly lessened the President's chances maintaining effective legislative coalitions within Congress.

Popularity

Even at his lowest rating (38% in 1994) Clinton was more popular than Carter, Reagan or Bush were at their low points. During the impeachment crisis his approval ratings remained above 70%, an incredible figure, given the circumstances.

Clinton's legislative programme

Clinton secured some significant pieces of legislation. The North American Free Trade Agreement (NAFTA) was in place within the first two years, as was the Brady Bill regulating purchasing of guns. The Budget Deficit Elimination Agreement of 1997 – which aimed to get rid of the deficit by 2002 – was also a significant measure. In other areas, healthcare reform for example, Clinton found progress more difficult, particularly after the Republicans took control of the House (230/204) and the Senate (54/46) from 1995. From that point the House, under the Speakership of Newt Gingrich pursued its 'Contract with America'. Ironically, Congress's decision to grant the President a 'line-item veto' at this time could have benefited Clinton's Presidency significantly, had not the Supreme Court declared it unconstitutional.

Foreign policy

Clinton's foreign policy was fairly modest. The US intervention in Somalia was a failure but Clinton had more success in Haiti, reinstating the legitimate government. He was ineffective in addressing the Rwandan crisis but highly visible as mediator in other conflicts and disputes (e.g. the Middle East).

The presidency of George W Bush (2001–present)

Context

Bush became President at a time when Clinton achieved record opinion poll ratings for an outgoing President. Moreover, the traumatic nature of the November 2000 presidential election appeared to cast a massive shadow over the Bush presidency:

Partly because of the fact that Bush had entered the White House with a smaller proportion of the popular vote than Al Gore;

Partly because his victory came as a result of a Supreme Court decision handed down by a Court containing four Reagan appointees (including Rehnquist as Chief Justice), made while George Bush senior was Vice-President, and two of Bush senior's own appointees.

Domestic policy

Bush entered the White House committed to a programme of tax cuts that would stave off the fears of recession. Bush, widely regarded as a friend of business has:

relaxed federal orders protecting union rights, encouraged non-union contracts in federal projects, committed himself to stopping all airline strikes, and moved to cut corporation tax.

As Steve Rosenthal of the AFL-CIO commented, 'George Bush makes Ronald Reagan look like Mother Jones'. Bush has also blocked some health reforms and rejected the CO_2 emissions targets set at Kyoto, the latter causing some embarrassment to his Environmental Protection Agency Director, Christie Todd Whitman.

Foreign policy context

As Doris Kearns Goodwin notes 'crisis provides the opportunity for larger deeds, an opportunity to walk on a different stage' (*Time Magazine*, December 31, 2001). Bush, surrounded by an extremely experienced group of foreign policy advisors, has gained significantly in terms of his approval rating (80% in January 2002) from his handling of the 'war against terrorism' launched in the wake of the September 11 attacks. Though, as David Kennedy notes, 'Bush has had the gift of a crisis that automatically creates a consensus in public opinion about the necessity, the morality and the justice of what we are doing', one should not underestimate the manner in which Bush has ridden the crisis following an uncertain start.

Image and spin

Bush's tax-cutting measures were not as well received in Congress as had been expected and the Kyoto farce opened the President up to international as well as domestic criticism. Since then Bush's media team has done a lot to pull the situation around. Key figures include Larry Lindsey (economic policy), Karen Hughes (according to *Time Magazine*, Bush's 'alter ego' who runs the 'message machine') and Ari Fleischer (Bush's Press Secretary, who manages the briefing room). At present (February 2002) they are pushing the 'Two E's' (education and the economy) to revive the domestic agenda; as witnessed by the recent imposition of US import duties on foreign steel.

16.6 Presidential power since September 11, 2001

Outline

In times of national crisis the role of the President becomes more crucial, not least because the President acts as a national figurehead (a head of state) as well as a chief executive.

Faced with national emergency, the other two branches of the federal government (legislature and judiciary) normally allow the President more freedom to act. At such times, therefore, the President's powers are normally significantly greater than in the normal course of events.

Faced with the terrorist threat demonstrated on September 11, the country united behind George W Bush – a man who only ten months previously had failed to win a majority of the popular vote in the presidential election. Bush was able to 'wrap himself in the flag', demanding patriotic support for his 'war on terrorism'. In response, Congress granted the President extraordinary powers to deal with the crisis.

Foreign policy

As Commander in Chief of the Armed Forces, George W Bush was able to launch the attacks on Afghanistan as an emergency act of self-defence, without a formal declaration of war by Congress. This demonstrates the power of the US President to commit US troops and incur massive costs in such circumstances, without the need for the normal authorisations.

Domestic policy

One of George W Bush's first moves following the attacks of September 11 was to create a new executive department, the Office of Homeland Security:

The Office of Homeland Security

Bush's executive order created an Office of Homeland Security and a Homeland Security Council that could develop and co-ordinate a national counter-terrorism strategy. This Council consists of the President and the Vice-President, the heads of a number of executive departments (for example, defense, treasury, and transportation) plus key security officials (including the directors of the FBI and the CIA)

Tom Ridge, former Governor of Pennsylvania and a decorated combat veteran, was appointed as head of the Office of Homeland Security. He is also a member of the Homeland Security Council. His brief is to address issues of:

detection, preparedness, prevention, protection, response and recovery, and incident management.

The President also:

1. Froze the bank accounts of suspected terrorists; and
2. Put in place additional security, including air-patrols over major cities by US Air Force F16 combat aircraft and restrictions on private flights.

Eventually, Congress passed formal legislation empowering the President to act against terrorists. This legislation is known as the **USA Patriot Bill** and it was passed by 357 votes to 66 in the House and by 98 votes to 1 in the Senate. The law, amongst other things, authorises the FBI to access computer files and e-mails, as well as allowing the arrest and holding of terrorist prisoners for seven days without charge.

In February 2002, *The Guardian* reported that Bush was also taking the opportunity to slash corporation tax while Congress was on his side.

September 11 and the Supreme Court

From an early stage in the crisis, sources close to the Supreme Court reported that it would look sympathetically at any violations of constitutional rights that were clearly in the public interest. One month after the attacks, the suspects arrested in the days that followed September 11 had, according to *Time Magazine*, still not spoken to those interrogating them. It was suggested that a 'truth drug' might be used on the prisoners (without their consent) in order to gain information that might prevent further attacks. Once again it was said that the Supreme Court might effectively 'turn a blind eye' to such a violation of constitutional protections, in the interest of public safety. Though the US Supreme Court has not yet been called to address such issues, leading civil rights lawyers in the US led by Stephen Yagman have, at the time of writing, just filed a petition for habeas corpus on behalf of the 110 al-Qaida suspects being held at Guantanamo Bay, Cuba (on the grounds that they are being held in violation of the Constitution and the Geneva Convention).

'Like father, like son?'

As the 'war against terrorism' dragged on, many US commentators started to draw parallels between George W Bush's presidency and that of his father. In 1991 George Bush senior had seemed assured of election victory in 1992. Operation Desert Storm against Iraqi forces in Kuwait was widely regarded as a success. Casualties had been kept low on the American side and Bush was achieving impressive approval ratings in the polls. At the same time, however, attention was returning to the domestic front where many felt that the economy was in trouble. In the election campaign that followed Bush senior lost the initiative and Clinton took the White House by highlighting Bush's failure to address domestic issues ('It's the economy, stupid!', as the Clinton slogan read).

George W Bush is facing similar problems. Though the 'war on terrorism' has been well received at home, the attention of many Americans is once again returning to domestic issues and, in particular, the economy. Bush, eager to avoid making the same mistakes as his father, has tried to revive the economy by pushing through large tax cuts. He has also sought to take the initiative on the domestic front by launching a campaign to address what he calls the 'two Es' (education and the economy).

17.1 The Vice-President and Cabinet

The Vice-President

Introduction

In 1789 the first US Vice-President, John Adams, wrote to his wife reporting that 'My Country has, in its wisdom contrived for me the most insignificant office that ever the invention of man or his imagination conceived'. This quotation has, until recently perhaps, continued to be the common view of the vice-presidency. Though, as James Baker noted, the Vice-President is only 'a heartbeat away from the big office', commentators have often struggled to identify a meaningful role for the Vice-President not linked to the demise of the President. As the US humorist Will Rogers remarked, 'the man with the best job in the Country is the Vice-President. All he has to do is get up every day and say, "How's the President?"'.

How Vice-Presidents are chosen

Since the 1950s vice-presidential candidates have been chosen by each party's presidential candidate following their nomination. As Bob Dole remarked in 1991, 'It only takes one vote to win the vice-presidential nomination'. The vice-presidential candidate is often chosen with a view to 'balancing the ticket' and gaining the broadest possible support from within the party and beyond. The relatively inexperienced Bush, therefore, went for the political heavyweight Cheney. This was clearly an astute move. Since the pair were elected many have argued that Cheney has been the real power behind the throne – the 'Prime Minister' to Bush's 'head of state'.

The main functions of the Vice-President

The Vice-President has a number of constitutional functions:

(1) Acting as the President of the Senate, having the right to chair debates and cast the deciding vote when the Senate is tied. Cheney cast such a deciding vote in April 2001 in support of Bush's tax-cutting measures.

(2) Becoming President in the event of the death, resignation or impeachment leading to removal from office of the President (e.g. Johnson taking over from Kennedy, or Ford from Nixon).

(3) Taking on the role of Acting President where the President declares himself or is declared disabled (e.g. following the shooting of Reagan in 1985, George Bush took over temporarily).

Informed opinions on the office

'Handmade for ridicule and for dismissal. In the nature of it if you always look like a beggar, a person on a string.' (Walter Mondale, 1984)

'Can the Vice-President be Useful' (title of an article by FDR in 1920)

'The vice-presidency ain't worth a pitcher of warm spit... I gave up the second most important job in the government [Speaker] for one that didn't amount to a hill of beans. I spent eight years as Mr Roosevelt's spare tyre.' (John Nance Garner, 1948 and 1963)

Where a vacancy occurs

The 25th Amendment (1967) gives the President the power to fill vice-presidential vacancies. These will most often occur when the elected Vice-President has had to take on the role of President. Before the 25th Amendment, the office was often left empty in such circumstances.

Training ground?

(Vice-Presidents who became Presidents)

John Adams
Thomas Jefferson
Martin van Buren
John Tyler
Millard Fillmore
Andrew Johnson
Chester A Arthur
Theodore Roosevelt
Calvin Coolidge
Harry S Truman
Richard M Nixon
Gerald Ford*
George Bush

*Ford became Vice-President in 1973 when Spiro Agnew resigned the post. Ford then became President following Nixon's resignation in 1974.

The Cabinet

Introduction

The US Cabinet shares little in common with the UK Cabinet beyond its name. Whereas in Britain the Cabinet is drawn from the legislature (in a large part the Commons), the separation of powers prevents members of the executive branch simultaneously holding office in legislature or the judiciary. US Cabinet members are, therefore, not elected but appointed by the President and this means that they are dependent upon him far more than members of the UK Cabinet who, if all else fails, can return to the back benches and wait for their moment.

Composition

Whereas in Britain Cabinet Ministers are normally generalists who move between departments as a result of reshuffles, US Cabinet members are most often specialists in their field. Anthony Principi, for example, the Veterans' Affairs Secretary, is a Vietnam War veteran. In reality only about one in five Cabinet members have any experience in Congress, the rest being drawn from state and local government and academia. Presidents tend to try and appoint a Cabinet which reflects the US society in terms of race, age, gender, ideology, religion and geography. Clinton certainly spoke of his desire to appoint a Cabinet that 'looked like America'. George W. Bush followed suit by appointing two Afro-Americans (Colin Powell and Rod Paige) and members from other ethnic minorities (e.g. Elaine Chao and Norman Mineta). Ultimately, however, Presidents have a free hand as long as they can persuade the Senate to approve their nominees. As Harry S Truman remarked in 1945, 'Everyone is telling me who I should have on my staff and in my cabinet. No S.O.B is going to dictate to me who I am going to have.'

Roles

The scale of work undertaken normally means that Cabinet members work fairly independently of one another. The President is easily able to divide and rule, and the fact that they are competing for the President's attention tends to make the Cabinet, as Richard Fenno noted, 'a schizophrenic body'. Cabinet meetings are still important however because the allow:

• members a chance to see one other
• members a chance to see the President
• the collection and dissemination of information
• the resolution of interdepartmental conflicts and the focusing of collective effort

Constitutional importance

Ultimately, the Constitution makes no mention of the Cabinet and so the institution is totally in the hands of the President. The Cabinet is divided and members must compete for the ear of the President. There is no real idea of collective responsibility based upon discussions in Cabinet. As George Bush told his Cabinet nominees in 1989, 'when I make a call, we move as a team'.

Informed opinions on the institution

'Seven noes, one aye – and the ayes have it.' (President Lincoln, having voted 'aye' in Cabinet)

'You can't have 15 people coming together to give the President advice in a Cabinet session. They're all arguing with each other for their own interests and he gets confused. What he decides has to come to him in an orderly way.' (John Erlichman – Nixon's aide – 1974)

'It is significant that no President has ever left the Office extolling the virtues of Cabinet Government.' (Hugh Heclo, 1983)

'When I've heard enough of a debate to satisfy my needs about knowing, then I make a decision.' (Ronald Reagan, 1982)

17.2 The Executive Office of the President (EXOP)

What is the EXOP?

In 1937 the Brownlow Committee famously reported that 'the President needs help'. Their comments reflected the massive expansion in the role of presidency that had taken place since the time of the Constitution. The problem facing the modern President as he grapples with the gargantuan federal bureaucracy is a considerable one: as Truman complained, 'I sit here all day saying do this, do that and nothing ever gets done. Christ! What a job!' Essentially, EXOP has the role of helping the President to cope with such enormous demands. What, then, does it consist of?

The Brownlow Committee, 1937

The Brownlow Committee was reporting against the background of the Wall Street Crash, the Depression that followed and the New Deal that FDR had brought in to address the economic crisis. This New Deal gave the federal government a far greater role in the states, particularly through the use of grants. An expansion of the federal government's role inevitably led to an expansion in the role of the presidency and the workload associated with it.

Key elements of the EXOP

The White House staff

Origins and history

In the wake of the Brownlow Committee's comments came a massive expansion in the role in the size of the White House staff (the closest advisors and aides to the President.).

President	Number of staff
Franklin D Roosevelt	51
Harry S Truman	243
Richard M Nixon	606

Though subsequent Presidents have invariably come into office promising swinging cuts in staff, few have been able to deliver faced with the job at hand. Such an enormous staff can, however, cause more problems than it solves unless the President has a very good Chief of Staff (as it is clearly impossible for the President to know exactly what 600+ individuals are doing at any one time). Nixon certainly had problems keeping tabs on what was going on in his administration, and his increasing reliance on Haldeman and Erlichman (the so-called 'Berlin Wall') was less than healthy. Haldeman, in particular, insulated the President from reality to an alarming degree, seeing him seven times more than any other official. All phone calls, information and requests for meetings with the President had to pass through Haldeman. As Haldeman himself explained, 'Rather than the President telling someone to do something, I'll tell the guy. If he wants to find out something from somebody, I'll do it. ... every President needs an S.O.B and I'm Nixon's'.

Composition

The White House staff includes the President's closest aides and confidants working beneath them. Whereas Cabinet members are focused on the work of their own departments and have to consider the demands of Congress (who assign their budgets) as well as the President, those in the White House staff are the President's true policy advisors. As in Britain, the role of the Press Secretary (currently Ari Fleischer) is significant. The role of Chief of Staff (currently Andrew Card) is even more crucial.

The Chief of Staff

Unless the President has a good Chief of Staff, who can decide objectively what the President needs to deal with personally and what can be dealt with without wasting the President's valuable time, the President will be smothered by an avalanche of paperwork and telephone calls.

Roles

1. **Policy advice** – the White House staff are the main source for policy advice, particularly in times of crisis.

2. **Liaison** – the staff have the job of co-ordinating efforts with the federal bureaucracy (see Ch 18.1) and with Congress.

3. **Administration** – the staff organise the White House, scheduling events and meetings and managing staff.

The Office of Management and Budget

The OMB was created in 1970 under the control of an OMB Director. It has three clear roles:

1. Organising the budget, balancing the demands of the various departments and deciding where to wield the axe.

2. Overseeing departmental and agency spending.

3. Providing on-tap specialist financial backup and advice for the President.

The National Security Council

Created in 1947, the NSC has the role of co-ordinating policy relating to national security, both domestic and foreign. It is headed by the National Security Advisor (NSA) and includes the President, the Vice-President, and the Secretaries of State and Defense, with occasional visits from the CIA head and the Chiefs of Staff. Kissinger was a key figure in expanding the role of the NSC under Nixon. (Kissinger kept the title of National Security Advisor even when he became the Secretary of State.)

In the past there has often been conflict between the Secretary of State and the President's National Security Advisor. Kissinger (NSA) effectively excluded William Rogers (Secretary of State) from foreign policy matters during Nixon's presidency, and under Carter there were problems between Zbigniew Brzezinski (NSA) and Secretary of State Cyrus Vance.

George W Bush's NSA is Condoleezza Rice.

18.1 The federal bureaucracy

Introduction

The federal bureaucracy employs some 3000 staff, working throughout the country in federal offices. Many of those staff work for one of the 14 executive departments, but others work within executive agencies or independent regulatory commissions (see right).

Executive departments

There are currently 14 executive departments, each headed by a member of the Bush Cabinet. The expansion in the number of executive departments mirrored the expansion in the role of the federal government dealt with in earlier pages. Names are correct as of January 7, 2002.

Department	Created	Current head
State	1789	Colin Powell
Treasury	1789	Paul O'Neill
War (now Defense)	1789 (1949)	Donald Rumsfeld
Interior	1849	Gale Norton
Justice	1870	John Ashcroft
Agriculture	1889	Ann M Veneman
Commerce	1903	Don Evans
Labour	1903	Elaine Chao
Health and Human Services	1953	Tommy Thompson
Housing and Urban Development	1965	Mel Martinez
Transportation	1966	Norman Mineta
Energy	1977	Spencer Abraham
Education	1979	Rod Paige
Veterans' Affairs	1989	Anthony Principi

Independent executive agencies (IEAs)

IEAs were set up to provide a greater degree of focus and control in specific areas of policy. They act independently of executive departments and are funded separately, making their budget requests direct to the OMB. Prominent IEAs include the Environmental Protection Agency (EPA) and the Central Intelligence Agency (CIA). Agencies are normally headed by an individual ('director') who directs their efforts. The EPA, for example, is headed by Christie Todd Whitman.

Independent regulatory commissions (IRCs)

What are they?

Congress passes acts which set up regulatory commissions in many areas of industrial and commercial life. Naturally, as the federal government has expanded, this role has become more significant. Each commission is headed by a board which averages five members, each of whom have been appointed by a President for a fixed length of time. The appointments are ratified by the Senate. The President has no legitimate right to sack board members – this was tested by Humphrey's Executor v. US, which stated that the President could not dismiss a member of the Federal Trade Commission.

The reason for creating IRCs

Independent regulatory commissions were designed to be non-political agencies organising certain aspects of administration and they were aimed at limiting the sort of presidential power demonstrated during the New Deal. As Ernest S Griffith noted, 'It was hoped that they would function with a high degree of specialised competence and independence, free from partisan and Presidential pressure'.

IRCs are given powers by Congress, but they make 'laws' and 'judge' themselves. Therefore they are quasi-legislative and quasi-judicial. M J C Vile described them as a 'headless fourth branch' of the US Government, but in reality Congress and the President do have influence over them. Eisenhower's assistant, Sherman Adams, admitted to secretly asking commissioners to resign and there are close informal links between the IRCs and the presidential staff.

IRCs 'good'	IRCs 'bad'
a) Congress wanted IRCs to limit presidential power over the bureaucracy.	a) Presidents control IRCs (by appointments and informally through links between commissioners and presidential staff).
b) IRCs meet the public demand for regulation of certain industries and services.	b) IRCs become oriented towards their clientele rather than serving the public they were designed to protect. Pressure groups can get 'inside'.
c) As IRCs are theoretically independent from political control, they should therefore be able to be objective.	c) Congress controls IRCs

Examples of IRCs

IRCs operate in a wide range of areas, most often where there is a need for visibly independent regulation and scrutiny. For example:

Federal Trade Commission (1914)
Formed to deal with –
i) unfair competition
ii) price-fixing (cartels)
iii) misleading advertising

Securities and Exchange Commission (1934)
Formed to –
i) regulate the stock exchange
ii) register stock brokers
iii) protect the public

Other examples include the Federal Reserve Board (controlling aspects of monetary policy) and the Civil Aeronautics Board (licensing and regulating airlines).

House of Representatives

Composition

Size

There are 435 members in the House. Each state has a number of Representatives in proportion to its population.

Election and term

The term of office is two years. The whole House is re-elected every two years. Candidates must be 25+, a citizen of the US for 7+ years and resident in the state for which they are standing.

Background of Representatives

14% women, 13% Black or Hispanic, 36% lawyers.

Powers exclusive to House

1. To consider all 'money bills' first

This power was originally given to the House because it was the only directly elected chamber (until the 17th Amendment, 1913).

2. To impeach ...

any member of the federal government, executive or judicial branches

3. To choose a President ...

in the event that no candidate has received a majority in the electoral college.

Key figures

The Speaker (see below) is *the* key figure in the House of Representatives. There is also a Majority and a Minority Leader, elected by their respective party groups. These individuals play a key role of co-ordinating the day to day activities of the House as well as representing the views of the Chamber in meetings with the President.

The Speaker

The role of the Speaker of the House is compared to the role of British Prime Minister more often than it is to the role of the Speaker in the House of Commons. This is because the US Speaker is a partisan player rather than an umpire. Speaker Newt Gingrich, for example, – with his party's 'Contract with America' – took a real lead in politics from 1995.

Roles: refers bills to committee, appoints select committee and conference committee chairs while influencing the appointment of standing committee chairs, appoints majority party contingent on the House Rules Committee (see Ch 19.4), and presides over the House, enforcing the rules.

Power held by Congress (as a whole)

1. To pass laws
2. To pass the budget
3. To undertake investigations into the actions of the executive branch
4. To start constitutional amendments by a two-thirds majority in each House
5. To declare war
6. To confirm the appointment of a newly elected Vice-President

Senate

Composition

Size

There are 100 members in the Senate. Each state has two Senators.

Election and term

The term of office is six years. One-third of the Senate is elected every two years. Candidates must be 30+, a citizen of the US for 9+ years and a resident in the state for which they are standing.

Background of Senators

13% women, 0% Black or Hispanic, 53% lawyers.

Powers exclusive to Senate

1. To ratify treaties by a two-thirds majority

2. To confirm many federal appointments

... by simple majority (e.g. Supreme Court Justices)

3. To try cases of impeachment

... brought by Congress (two-thirds majority needed for conviction)

4. To elect a Vice-President

... where two or more candidates are tied

Key figures

The Vice-President is the President of the Senate and has the right to preside over the chamber and control the casting vote in the event of a tie. Normally, however, the Senates elect a President pro tempore – a senior figure of the majority party – to chair the chamber in the Vice-President's absence. Majority and Minority Leaders are also important (see above). In the Senate – in the absence of a 'Rules Committee' – it timetables bills though **unanimous consent agreements**.

'Filibustering'

The right of Senators to speak freely throws up the curious spectacle of the filibuster – a unique brand of procrastination. Through this practice of talking at length on virtually any subject, a single-minded minority – indeed one – can succeed in 'talking a bill' out of time and therefore out of existence. Senator Strom Thurmond of South Carolina, for example, spoke for 24 hours and 18 minutes against the 1957 Civil Rights Act, and a group of Southern Democrats conducted an 83-day group filibuster against the 1964 Civil Rights Act. A filibuster can be ended by a cloture motion, requiring the support of three-fifths of the entire Senate (60).

19.2 The passage of legislation

Introduction

The legislative process in the US is not vastly different from that in the UK. One difference, however, is that both houses have equal legislative power. One feature of this is that bills pass through the House and Senate at the same time. As a result, conference committees are sometimes needed at the end of the third reading stage in order to iron out any differences that exist between the House and Senate versions of a bill.

Presidential action

1. **Sign** – If the President signs the bill then it can become law.

2. **Veto** – The President can veto the **entire bill** within ten days of receiving it as long as he sends it back with note explaining his reasons for using the veto.

3. **Pocket veto** – If the congressional session ends before the end of the ten days, the President can 'pocket' the bill, killing it.

The line-item veto – In 1997 Congress passed a law granting the President the right to delete individual parts of a bill (see Ch 16.2). This was declared unconstitutional in 1998. The President, therefore, has no line-item veto.

The passage of legislation

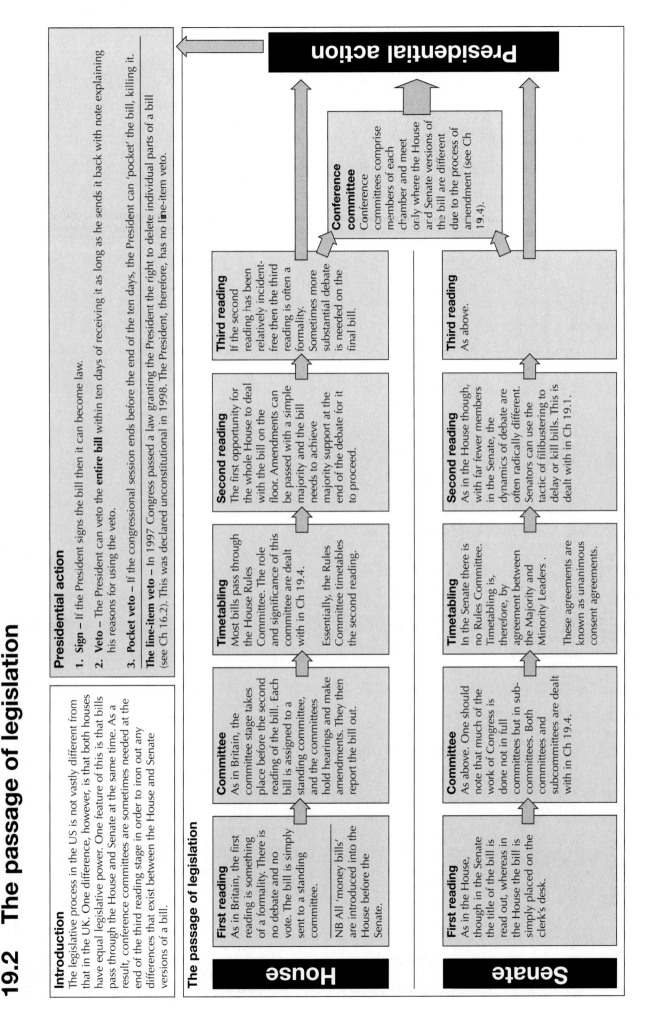

Presidential action

House

First reading
As in Britain, the first reading is something of a formality. There is no debate and no vote. The bill is simply sent to a standing committee.

NB All 'money bills' are introduced into the House before the Senate.

Committee
As in Britain, the committee stage takes place before the second reading of the bill. Each bill is assigned to a standing committee, and the committees hold hearings and make amendments. They then report the bill out.

Timetabling
Most bills pass through the House Rules Committee. The role and significance of this committee are dealt with in Ch 19.4.

Essentially, the Rules Committee timetables the second reading.

Second reading
The first opportunity for the whole House to deal with the bill on the floor. Amendments can be passed with a simple majority and the bill needs to achieve majority support at the end of the debate for it to proceed.

Third reading
If the second reading has been relatively incident-free then the third reading is often a formality.
Sometimes more substantial debate is needed on the final bill.

Conference committee
Conference committees comprise members of each chamber and meet only where the House and Senate versions of the bill are different due to the process of amendment (see Ch 19.4).

Senate

First reading
As in the House, though in the Senate the title of the bill is read out, whereas in the House the bill is simply placed on the clerk's desk.

Committee
As above. One should note that much of the work of Congress is done not in full committees but in sub-committees. Both committees and subcommittees are dealt with in Ch 19.4.

Timetabling
In the Senate there is no Rules Committee. Timetabling is, therefore, by agreement between the Majority and Minority Leaders .

These agreements are known as unanimous consent agreements.

Second reading
As in the House though, with far fewer members in the Senate, the dynamics of debate are often radically different. Senators can use the tactic of filibustering to delay or kill bills. This is dealt with in Ch 19.1.

Third reading
As above.

19.3 Pressures acting upon members of Congress

What factors are the most important in determining outcomes in Congress?

Pressure group action

The issue of abortion provides an excellent illustration of pressure group influence on Congressmen. Though Kay Orr remarked that '[it would be] a disservice to our political system if we allow … [abortion] to be the test of every candidate', the 'pro-life' lobby has tried to make it just that. During the 1980s groups such as Jerry Falwell's 'Moral Majority' undertook a series of campaigns not only to raise public awareness, but also to back sympathetic candidates and attack unsympathetic ones. Several liberal Senators – Birch Bayle, George McGovern and Frank Church among them – came under attack for their positions on issues such as abortion, while candidates who backed such groups, it was argued, gained significantly.

By forming Political Action Committees (PACs), pressure groups can maximise their financial contributions to candidates' campaigns, circumventing the 1974 Campaign Finance Act.

Constituency pressure

Members of Congress have to take a good deal more notice of their constituents than most MPs in the UK. This is in part because …

1. It is constituents who select candidates through congressional primaries.
2. Representatives in the House face election every two years, as do one-third of Senators.

This said, the vast majority of those Members of Congress who seek re-election are successful:

House

Year	% re-elected*
1998	98.3
2000	97.8

Senate

Year	% re-elected*
1998	89.6
2000	82.8

Do these re-election rates suggest that incumbents are re-elected whatever they do, or do they reflect how attentive incumbents are to the needs of their constituents?

* NB % of those seeking re-election

Party pressure

Those comparing the influence of US 'party whips' and their namesakes in the UK have often concluded that in the US the whips have no 'sting'. This is partly because of the fact that…

parties cannot threaten to deselect candidates (because constituents have control of this through congressional primaries) and they can't offer promotion to the executive, due to the separation of powers.

Members of Congress, it is argued, are under so much pressure from their constituents that they cannot maintain as slavish an obedience to the party line as MPs generally do in Britain. In addition it should be remembered that…

parties are ideologically weak and decentralised compared to their counterparts in Britain – they are truly 'broad-churches'.

If we take a 'party vote' to be a vote where the majority of one party votes for a measure and the majority of the other party votes against, then only 43% of House and 49% of Senate votes were 'party votes' in 2000.

Executive pressure

The President can have significant influence over individual members of Congress. We have outlined this influence in earlier pages. To recap:

1. The President can use his friends

The **Vice-President**, **party leaders** in Congress, the **Chief of Staff** can put the President's case.

2. The President can use personal persuasion

- **Telephone calls** – Johnson is said to have called a Congressman at the time of a crucial vote. 'You might need me some time and I'll remember you if you do this thing for me now'.
- **Entertaining** – Reagan, for example, used to invite key Congressmen to breakfast at the White House before important votes.
- **Offering 'pork'** (for example federal contracts or financial help for local projects) or **help in the election campaign.**

Conscience?

Some members of Congress have views on particular issues that will not allow them to follow the party line. On the issue of abortion, for example, some Democrats are committed 'pro-lifers' even though their party has explicitly endorsed a 'pro-choice' position since the 1992 presidential election.

That said, Democrats uneasy over abortion have increasingly been forced to 'toe the line' and it is noticeable that Al Gore, Jesse Jackson and Representative Richard A Gephardt have, as the *New York Times* noted, 'jettisoned their previous reservations about abortion'. As the paper went on to conclude, 'no Democrat with pretensions to national leadership can afford not to be strictly in favor of abortion rights'.

19.4 Congressional committees

Standing committees

Introduction

There are a variety of committees in Congress: standing committees (meaning they are always present), select or special committees (being set up for more limited and more specific purposes), and conference committees. This box deals with standing committees; select and conference committees are dealt with below.

There are 17 permanent standing committees in the House and a further 17 in the Senate. Each committee is normally divided into sub-committees dealing with more specific areas of legislation and then reporting back to the full committee.

Composition and membership

The composition of committees in both houses is in proportion to each party's strength in the relevant chamber. Each party produces a list of prospective committee members and these lists are then voted on by each party and then by the House as a whole. In January 2001 the Republicans had 221 members in the House compared to the Democrats' 212. This meant that they had a majority of members in each committee. In the Senate the parties were split 50–50 so they decided to split the membership of each standing committee 50–50. The decision of Senator James Jeffords of Vermont to switch from Republican to Independent left the Democrats with a 50–49 majority. As of June 2001, therefore, Democrats controlled all committees and all committee chairmanships in the Senate.

Decisions over who gets which committee jobs is largely governed by issues such as seniority, partisan regularity, regional dispersion, suitability (perhaps specialism) and, in the Senate, the fact that every Senator is required to be in at least one committee.

Role and powers

At the beginning of each session, each committee has a number of executive meetings to discuss a possible agenda for the session and try to work out a possible order in which the committee will look at the bills presented to it. Committee chairmen (see right) play a key role in prioritising bills. Many bills are simply pigeon-holed (put to one side and effectively killed). Those bills that avoid pigeon-holing are then subject to hearings (see right). Following hearings, the bill is amended (if necessary) in light of the evidence. This is called the marking-up session. It is then reported out of the committee back to the chamber. Committees can be forced to report out a bill that they have 'sat on', but this is rare.

Committee hearings

Once underway, the committee will organise hearings relating to bills. Many Congressmen and women are trained lawyers (36% in the House, 56% in the Senate in 2001) and as a result the committee hearings are similar in format to a trial, with evidence being brought forward by specialists and interested parties alike in the belief that, as Ernest S Griffith observed, 'truth customarily emerges from a battle of protagonists'. Pressure groups with an interest in a particular piece of legislation will send professional lobbyists to the committee hearings and to meet the committee members who they feel might be sympathetic to their case.

Committees also spend a considerable amount of time, and money, conducting independent research. For example, 200 investigators were sent to Europe after the Second World War to check the Marshall Plan. Only after such hearings will the committee consider the fate of the bill being considered.

Importance of committee chairs

The chairmen of committees and sub-committees wield considerable power over the agenda and procedure of the committees and, as a result, committee chairmen can exert a great deal of influence in the House and the Senate. This is particularly true of those chairing major committees.

In the past, committee chairs were filled largely on the basis of seniority – where the member with the longest continuous period of service on the committee became its chair. In the 1960s this resulted in many of the top committee chairmen jobs being permanently occupied by a handful of old, white southern Democrats. During the 1970s, however, the Democrats made some major changes to the committee system including the effective abolition of the old seniority system (1971) and an agreement that if 20% of a committee's members so desired, the committee chair would be elected by the committee.

The House Rules Committee

The Rules Committee is one of the most important committees (along with the Ways and Means Committee, which deals with legislation which requires the raising of new taxes, and the Appropriations Committee, which appropriates the necessary money from federal funds to pay for authorised programmes).

Once reported back to the House of Representatives, the bill must be placed on the calendar for its second reading. Most bills are passed to the Rules Committee to be given a rule which stipulates the date on which they are to be heard and the degree of debate and amendment that they will be subject to. The committee can place a bill under one of three types of 'rule':

an **open rule**, which allows the bill to be amended without limits (i.e. 'to death');
a **closed rule** (which restricts the amendments which can be passed);
and a **special rule** (which demands the House considers the bill immediately).

Like other standing committees, the Rules Committee has the power to pigeon-hole a bill, but the House can force it to release a bill by passing a 'discharge petition' with a simple majority.

Professor William H Riker described the Rules Committee as 'a toll bridge attendant who argues and bargains with each prospective customer: who lets his friends go free, who will not let his enemies pass at any price'.

Select committees

Where investigations fall outside of the normal scope of an existing standing committee or are likely to be on such a large scale as to affect the committee's normal work, a select or special committee may be formed on an ad hoc basis to deal with the issue. A good example is the Joint Select Committee on the Iran–Contra affair.

Conference committees

Once both chambers have considered a bill there is a fair chance that the two finished versions will be slightly different. As a result, the Speaker of the House and the President pro tempore from the Senate choose people from each chamber to sit on a conference committee that can iron out the differences. The compromise bill is then re-entered into both chambers and they must accept it, refer it back again, or kill it.

The Sheffield College
Hillsborough LRC
Telephone: 0114 260 2254

20.1 The structure of the US courts system

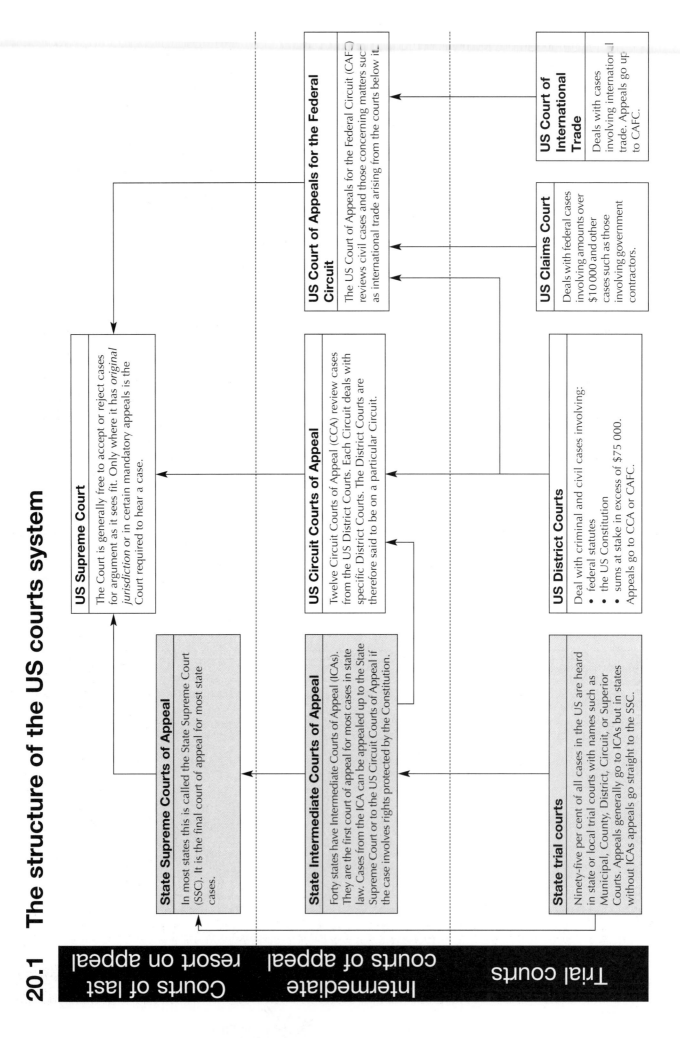

US Supreme Court

The Court is generally free to accept or reject cases for argument as it sees fit. Only where it has *original jurisdiction* or in certain mandatory appeals is the Court required to hear a case.

US Court of Appeals for the Federal Circuit

The US Court of Appeals for the Federal Circuit (CAFC) reviews civil cases and those concerning matters such as international trade arising from the courts below it.

US Court of International Trade

Deals with cases involving international trade. Appeals go up to CAFC.

State Supreme Courts of Appeal

In most states this is called the State Supreme Court (SSC). It is the final court of appeal for most state cases.

US Circuit Courts of Appeal

Twelve Circuit Courts of Appeal (CCA) review cases from the US District Courts. Each Circuit deals with specific District Courts. The District Courts are therefore said to be on a particular Circuit.

US Claims Court

Deals with federal cases involving amounts over $10 000 and other cases such as those involving government contractors.

State Intermediate Courts of Appeal

Forty states have Intermediate Courts of Appeal (ICAs). They are the first court of appeal for most cases in state law. Cases from the ICA can be appealed up to the State Supreme Court or to the US Circuit Courts of Appeal if the case involves rights protected by the Constitution.

US District Courts

Deal with criminal and civil cases involving:
- federal statutes
- the US Constitution
- sums at stake in excess of $75 000.

Appeals go to CCA or CAFC.

State trial courts

Ninety-five per cent of all cases in the US are heard in state or local trial courts with names such as Municipal, County, District, Circuit, or Superior Courts. Appeals generally go to ICAs but in states without ICAs appeals go straight to the SSC.

Courts of last resort on appeal

Intermediate courts of appeal

Trial courts

20.2 Composition and power

Size of the Court

Constitutionally, Congress has control over the size of the Court. The present Court numbers nine but this has not always been the case: 1789 = six; 1801 = five; 1802 = six; 1807 = seven; 1837 = eight/nine; 1863 = ten. The Judiciary Act of 1866 reduced the size of the court from ten to seven (to be achieved through attrition); The Act of 1869 re-established the Court at nine.

Trivia

The youngest serving Justice was Joseph Story (32). The oldest was Oliver W Holmes (90). The average age of current Court is 67. The shortest term of office was John Rutledge's (16 months). The longest term was Willaim O Douglas's (36 years, 7 months).

Who qualifies?

There are no formal requirements for office. However, As John R Schmidhauser noted, 'with exceedingly few exceptions, Supreme Court Justices have been white males chosen past middle age from socially and economically advantaged families: Protestant by religion and high status by denomination, descendants of natives of the British isles, and recipients of undergraduate education at schools of national reputation.'

The current Supreme Court

Justice	Born	Appoint.	Oath	Alignment
*William Rehnquist	1/10/24	Nixon (R) / Reagan (R)*	1972 / 1986*	right
John Paul Stevens	20/4/20	Ford (R)	1975	left centre
Sandra D O'Connor	26/3/30	Reagan (R)	1981	centre
Antonin Scalia	11/3/36	Reagan (R)	1986	right
Anthony Kennedy	23/7/36	Reagan (R)	1988	right
David Souter	17/9/39	Bush (R)	1990	right centre
Clarence Thomas	28/6/48	Bush (R)	1991	right
Ruth Bader Ginsburg	15/3/33	Clinton (D)	1993	left
Stephen Breyer	15/8/38	Clinton (D)	1994	left

NB: 1) '*' = Chief Justice. 2) The 'Alignment' column only offers the crudest assessment of political orientation.

The appointment process

A *vacancy occurs* (through death, disability, resignation, retirement or impeachment). The last ten Justices to leave the Court have done so as a result of resignation or retirement, though in the earlier days of the Court it was common for Justices to remain in office until death. Only one Justice, Samuel Chase, was ever impeached and he was not convicted (he eventually died in office in 1811).

President nominates replacement

Constitutionally, Presidents have a free hand in nominating replacements, though the Attorney General and the American Bar Association provide extensive advice. Not all Justices work in legal practice immediately prior to their appointment; Earl Warren, for example, was Governor of California before being appointed Chief Justice by Eisenhower. Most members of the current Court, however, do have considerable legal experience and Presidents nominate in the knowledge that Senate approval is required.

The Senate Judicial Committee conducts hearings ...

to assess the suitability of the candidate. This is a serious business. During the appointment of Clarence Thomas, for example, the Senate took a good deal of time investigating allegations of sexual harassment made against Thomas by a former colleague, Anita Hill. Sometimes candidates will withdraw or be withdrawn at this stage if the findings are unfavourable. Generally, however, the Senate will proceed to vote on the nomination, a candidate needing 50%+ of the votes to be successful. Most appointments gain Senate approval, though Ronald Reagan had Robert Bork rejected (by 42 votes to 58) and Nixon had two nominees, Clement Haynsworth Jr and G Harold Carswell, rejected.

Constitutional position

Article III section 2 gives the Court the power to hear directly (have *original jurisdiction* over) cases involving public officials or where a state is a party. In all other cases it acts as the highest court of appeal (its *appellate jurisdiction*). The Court normally accepts for consideration cases that are the subject of debate or confusion in the lower courts, and such confusion generally arises from areas of the Constitution that are more open to interpretation. These areas include: the 'Interstate Commerce Clause'; the 'General Welfare Clause' and the 14th Amendment; The War Power; The Treaty Power; the 1st, 4th and 5th Amendments; and the 'Necessary and Proper Clause'. Justices adopt a variety of different approaches when interpreting the Constitution. Right-wing conservative Justices such as Rehnquist and Scalia, for example, tend to favour a more literal interpretation of the Constitution and are, therefore, often referred to as **strict constructionists**. Left-wing or liberal Justices (**loose constructionists**) such as Breyer, in contrast, favour 'reading between the lines' a little, looking for things that are not written (explicit) but implied by the Constitution (*penumbras* or shadows).

Judicial Review

As early as 1832 Andrew Jackson had voiced his belief that 'the opinion of the Supreme Court ... ought not to control ... this government. The Congress, the Executive, and the Court' he asserted, 'must each be guided by its own opinion of the Constitution.' By then however, the foundations of judicial review had been established through the Marbury v. Madison case of 1803. Judicial review is the convention by which the Court may void any actions or statutes, whether by state or federal government, where the Court determines that such actions or statutes come into conflict with the Constitution. The development of such authority was ground-breaking, because it meant that the Supreme Court had begun to establish itself as a body which could hold other branches of government to its interpretation of the Constitution. An excellent recent example of judicial review in action is the case of George Bush v. Al Gore (2000) where the Court reviewed the judgement of the Florida Supreme Court and overturned it; effectively making Bush the 43rd US President.

Judicial activism

While in theory the Court is only interpreting the Constitution, in practice the differences between interpretations of the same constitutional passage over as short a time as 60 years (Plessy v. Fergusson, 1896 to Brown v. Board of Education, Topeka, 1954) may often appear tantamount to legislative action. Between those dates the Court moved from a position where it saw racial segregation on trains as acceptable (as long as separate accommodation was equal) to a position where all segregation caused inequality and was, therefore, unconstitutional. In the wake of this change, James F Byrnes remarked that 'the Court did not interpret the Constitution – the Court amended it'. Under the leadership of Earl Warren from 1954, the Court began to make massive use of its powers of judicial review, often in sensitive areas. The way in which the Court pushed back the frontiers of society at that time, in cases such as 'Brown', led some to hail the advent of judicial activism. 'The Supreme Court of the United States [had],' as John W Brocker noted, 'assumed quasi legislative authority', dragging the other branches behind it.

Judicial restraint

Despite this, the Court tends to follow precedent rather than make excessively showy use of its powers. Where precedent is challenged and changed, the process often takes many years and is the result of several cases. In the case of abortion for example, the Roe v. Wade decision (1973) was based firmly in earlier cases which had established a right to privacy (e.g. Griswold v. Connecticut, 1965). Since the landmark Roe case, which upheld a woman's right to control over her own body and thus the right to have an abortion, a number of cases have limited access to abortions (e.g. Maher v. Roe, 1977; Webster v. Reproductive Health Services, 1989), but the Court has stopped short of totally overturning Roe. Thus, precedent is the norm and the Court moves slowly, if it moves at all. If the Court were to test the patience of the other two branches by making excessive use of the power of 'review' it might find itself under attack. In any case, the Court has little power with which to enforce its decisions. Restraint therefore, is the norm.

20.3 Control and questions of democracy

Four limitations on the power of the court

1. Congressional control

Congress can:

- control the appellate jurisdiction of the Court;
- control the number of Justices (i.e. the size of the Court); and
- control the times when the Court can sit.

But these are controls that Congress **threatens** to use only rarely and **uses** even less.

2. Presidential control

The President can:

- nominate Justices to fill vacancies in the Court (although these appointments must be agreed by the Senate); and
- work with Congress to reform or 'pack the Court'.

In reality however, the President's power is strictly circumvented.

(a) He can only nominate Justices where vacancies occur

Different Presidents have had significantly different levels of input into the appointment process. Carter, for example, appointed no Justices whereas Washington appointed 11 and Franklin D Roosevelt appointed nine.

(b) He needs the confirmation of the Senate for his nominations and this is not always forthcoming

Nixon had two nominees rejected – Clement Haynsworth Jr (rejected by 45 votes to 55) and G Harold Carswell (by 45 votes to 51). Reagan also failed in his attempt to get Robert H Bork onto the Court.

(c) Once installed, the Justices do not always live up to the President's expectations

Eisenhower described his nomination of Chief Justice Earl Warren as 'the biggest damn fool mistake I ever made' and Nixon found that a Court including four of his nominees was still prepared to hand over his White House tapes to the Watergate investigation (US v. Nixon, 1974).

(d) 'Packing' the Court is neither quick, nor guaranteed of success (though the threat of it can move minds)

Franklin D Roosevelt's court-packing bill failed in 1937 but it did persuade one Justice, Owen Roberts, to change his position and back the New Deal programme's constitutionality. Roosevelt thus carried the Court by 5:4 and his threats had, the *New York Times* reported, precipitated the 'switch in time that saved nine'.

3. Public opinion

Though the Court is free from the pressure of re-election, there has always been a feeling amongst US political commentators that the Court is receptive to public opinion. As Finley Peter Dunne commented in *Mr Dooly's Opinion*, 'No matter whether th' Constitution follows th' flag or not, the Supreme Court follows th' election returns.' Public pressure was certainly present, and influential at the time that the Court backed down over the New Deal and even the Brown v. Board of Education Decision (1954) was handed down with a fairly strong public support in the North, despite a certain amount of inertia elsewhere on the issue of race relations.

The Court would be unlikely to survive long unchanged if it persistently acted in a manner diametrically opposed to the wishes of the people, Congress and the President. After all, with the Congress having control of Court size and oversight of appellate jurisdiction, and the President's power of appointment checked only by the Senate, the executive and the legislative branches could easily rein in a wayward Court.

4. Difficulty in enforcing decisions

Students of Politics will be familiar with the distinction between power and authority, and the US Supreme Court is an excellent case in point. As Felix Frankfurter noted,

'the Court's authority – possessed neither of the purse nor the sword – ultimately rests on sustained public confidence in its moral sanction. Such feeling must be nourished by the Court's complete detachment, in fact and appearance, from political entanglements and by abstention from injecting itself into the clash of political forces and political settlements.'

What the Court has, therefore, is prestige, moral authority, and a fair amount of obedience from the lower courts. In addition, the Justices have the knowledge that they may from time to time call on Congress' *purse* and the President's *swords* where their *authority* fails to carry the day.

The Court and democracy

'Quis custodiet ipsos custodes? (Who is to guard the guards themselves?)'
    Decimus Iunius Iuvenal (c60–140)

The charge

Many feel that the Supreme Court has become an anti-democratic force. They argue that excessive use of judicial review is unacceptable in light of the fact that the Court consists of nine 'unelected and unaccountable' Justices. For them, the idea that such a narrow, and practically irremovable group could interpret the Constitution in such a way as to make void the legislation created by a democratically-elected Congress, is perverse.

Are these arguments realistic? Have the *umpires* really become the *players*?

The defence

In defence of the Supreme Court, we need only say that it has made the survival of the US Constitution as we know it possible. The Court has re-worked the Constitution to meet the demands of a developing society:

1. It has allowed flexibility through its willingness to change its interpretations on key issues through the passage of time, while at the same time allowing judicial precedent to be the norm;

2. It has given guidance to lower courts when they could not agree with one another and it has acted as the ultimate court of appeal for many wrongly convicted at lower, less impartial (often elected) levels of the judiciary;

3. It has led the reversal of anti-democratic practices (e.g. segregation), when elected bodies seemed unable or unwilling to act decisively; and, more than anything else

4. It has acted as a constant thread in US political society, underpinning the separation of powers (both in its verdicts and through its very existence) and remaining to foil the attempts of popularly-elected governments to curtail individual rights or threaten the spiritual heart of the constitution.

The Supreme Court has as Max Lerner concluded, 'acted as the final barricade against the assaults of democratic majorities'.

20.4 The Court in action

This table outlines **some** of the Court's key decisions and shows how interpretations have developed over time under different Chief Justices. See also 'Bill of Rights'.

Area	The Warren Court (1954–69)	The Burger Court (1969–86)	The Rehnquist Court (1986 –)
Segregation and the rights of ethnic minorities	**1954 Brown v. Board of Education, Topeka** Segregation was always unequal (reversed Plessy v. Ferguson, 1896). **1969 Alexander v. Holmes County Board of Education** Schools must be desegregated at once.	**1971 Swann v. Charlotte-Mecklenburg Board of Education** This case led to the introduction of 'bussing', where pupils of different ethnic backgrounds were taken to schools in such a way as to provide racially mixed schools in all areas. **1978 Regents of the University of California v. Bakke** There had been reverse discrimination due to quotas and Bakke – who was white – should be allowed into the University	**1989 Ward's Cove Packing Company v. Atonio** **1989 Richmond v. J A Croson Company** … two cases that saw a narrowing of affirmative action (this narrowing was later reversed following the 1991 Civil Rights Act). **1990 Metro Broadcasting Inc. v. Federal Communications Commission** FCC's affirmative action policy favouring minority broadcasters was justifiable. **1995 Ada-land Constructors v. Pena** The Court struck down a federal affirmative action programme in favour of minority workers.
Abortion	**1965 Griswold v. Connecticut** The last surviving laws against birth controls were removed, and a constitutional right to a protected 'zone of privacy' established. Roe (see right) was largely founded upon protections identified in this case.	**1973 Roe v. Wade** The Court established a right to abortion within the 'zone of privacy', but the right offered different protection at different stages of pregnancy. **1980 Harris v. McRae** The Court upheld the constitutionality of the 'Hyde Amendment', which limited Medicaid funding of abortions. **1983 City of Akron v. Akron Center for Reproductive Health Inc.** Local statutes were too restrictive of abortion and consequently struck down.	**1989 Webster v. Reproductive Health Services** The Court upheld Missouri's law that banned abortions from state facilities and banned state employees from doing them. **1990 Ohio v. Akron Center for Reproductive Health Inc.** Minors must inform their parents before abortion procedures.
The rights of the arrested/accused	**1963 Gideon v. Wainwright** States had to provide legal counsel for the poor. **1964 Escobedo v. Illinois** The accused had the right to have counsel before the trial. **1966 Miranda v. Arizona** Those arrested must be read their rights or the evidence gained will be invalid.	**1971 Harris v. New York** Confessions that had been taken in violation of Miranda rule could be used for limited purposes. **1974 Michigan v. Tucker** Miranda warnings were not in themselves rights protected by the Constitution. **1984 New York v. Quarles** The Court recognised a 'public safety exception' to Miranda.	**1984 Strickland v. Washington** Defendants have a right to a counsel whose performance is not defective to the point of altering the course of the trial. **1989 Duckworth v. Eagan** The exact wording from Miranda does not have to be used for a subsequent confession to be valid.
Religion	**1962 Engel v. Vitale** A non-denominational prayer was declared unconstitutional because it promoted religion. **1963 Abington v. Schempp** There should be no bible worship in state schools	**1985 Wallace v. Jafiree** The Court invalidated an Alabama law which allowed a moment's silence for voluntary prayer	**1987 Edwards v. Aquillard** Louisiana could not force teaching of the creation story alongside evolution. **1992 Lee v. Weisman** It was unconstitutional for a public school to include prayers at a graduation ceremony because this violated the establishment clause of the First Amendment.
Politics	**1962 Baker v. Carr** Gerrymandering was bad because apportionment should be equal. Gerrymandering violated 'equal protection'.		**1986 Davis v. Bandemer** 'Gerrymandering' was still wrong under 'equal protection', but Indiana State was not guilty of it.

21.1 State and local government

State government

Introduction

The United States operates under a federal system of government. Though most of the Constitution focuses on the powers given to the various branches of the federal (central) government (the so-called 'enumerated powers'), the Tenth Amendment crucially reserves powers for the various states.

> **AMENDMENT X**
>
> The powers not delegated to the United States by the Constitution, nor prohibited by it to the States, are reserved to the States respectively, or to the people.

These 'reserved powers' include the powers to regulate their own commerce, organise elections (as we saw in Florida in 2000) and put in place measures aimed at ensuring safety. In practice, however, the states have an enormous range of responsibilities including health, education and many aspects of welfare. States also control whether or not they make use of the death penalty, regulations concerning marriage and the age at which individuals can consume alcohol.

Structure

The structure of state government mirrors the structure of the federal government with executive, legislative and judicial branches.

State executive

An elected governor heads the executive branch in each state.

State governors

Most governors have a four-year term and can stand for re-election, but in some states the term can be shorter and governors are forbidden to succeed themselves. Though the power of the governor also varies from state to state, virtually all governors have a veto power and the vast majority have a line-item veto over appropriation bills. Most governors also have significant powers of patronage.

State legislature

All of the states apart from Nebraska have bicameral legislatures. The two chambers are most often referred to as the assembly and the senate. Though terms of office vary from state to state, the majority have a two-year term for the lower chamber and a four-year term for the upper chamber. That said, most state legislatures meet very infrequently.

State legislatures pass state laws and regulations governing those areas over which the state has jurisdiction. As in the federal Congress, the bulk of work is done in committees.

State judiciary

Each state has a state judiciary that enforces state laws and some federal laws. In most states judges are **elected** for fixed terms (most commonly between four and 15 years). Some feel that such elections are inappropriate because:

(1) Elected judges may act in pursuit of popularity rather than justice.
(2) The demands of elections can lead to candidates setting out 'manifestos' making promises on sentencing etc. that might tie their hands once elected.
(3) Elections do not necessarily result in those with the best legal minds being selected.

Role

In the 1990s state governments spent well over $1 000 000 000 000 (1 trillion) per year. Most of this money is spent providing services within states. Education (see right) is normally the biggest area of spending within a state, but states also provide a wide range of welfare services.

Finance

Such a massive expenditure requires a massive income. The federal government still provides financial grants in support of state programmes but these only make up between 10% and 15% of the total figure. The rest comes from state property taxes, sales taxes and income generated by public utilities and lotteries.

Managing education

State governments control the higher levels of educational provision within the state. This would include universities and higher education. On the whole, regular schools are run by local governments (see below).

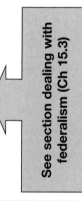

See section dealing with federalism (Ch 15.3)

Local government

Below state government there is local government. Local governments have their powers delegated to them by state governments. The emphasis in local government is on administering and delivering services. The 80 000 or so local government units that exist nationally can be broadly divided into municipal governments and county governments.

Municipal government

Municipal government operates at the level of a city, village or borough. In the case of a city the municipal government structure will normally involve an elected city council, with an elected mayor or city manager providing focus and direction.

County government

In rural areas county government is the norm. County governments vary enormously. Some focus around a board of supervisors, working alongside key elected representatives such as the local sheriff. Others have an elected commission, an assembly or, as is often the case in cities, a council with an elected administrator as chief executive.

22.1 The electorate

Extension of the franchise

In order to vote, Americans must be registered to vote in the state in which they live. Over the last 40 years, however, there have been many changes to the rules that govern who precisely may register.

The original constitutional document gave states the right to control many of the rules governing elections within their territory. Following their defeat in the Civil War, many southern states introduced complicated rules that prevented Blacks from voting in the elections. These rules could not be explicit (i.e. 'Blacks can't vote') because such measures would have fallen foul of the 14th Amendment's equal protection clause. Instead, many states introduced poll taxes (which most Blacks did not pay), literacy tests (which many Blacks could not pass) or introduced mechanisms such as the Grandfather Clause (which stated that you could only vote if your grandfather had been an American citizen). The federal government eventually moved to confront these restrictions with the 24th Amendment of 1964 (removing the various clauses and abolishing poll taxes) and the Voting Rights Act of 1965 (giving the federal government the power to register voters in states where literacy tests were used).

These reforms had a dramatic impact. For example:

State	% Blacks registered pre-1964	% Blacks registered 1968
Alabama	19.3%	51%
Mississippi	6.7%	59.8%

These measures were followed by:

1970	The Voting Rights Act which gave all 18-year-olds the vote in federal elections
1971	The 26th Amendment which extended the 18-year-old rule to all elections.

These two reforms increased the size of the electorate by 11 million.

Population profile

Population

According to the US Census in 2000 the population of the US was then 281.4 million. Since then, the US Government estimates that there has been an increase of some 3.4 million people to 284.8 million. California remains the most populous state with 34.5 million people (12.1% of the total US population) and Nevada has the fastest-growing population (5.4% between Census 2000 and July 2001). During the same period several states experienced falling populations: North Dakota (−1.2%) and West Virginia (−0.4%), for example. Such changes in population will eventually be reflected in changes in the states' seat allocation in the House of Representatives and, consequently, their vote allocation in the electoral college. In 2004, for example, California will have 55 votes (54 in 2000), Florida will have 27 (25 in 2000) and Pennsylvania will have 21 (23 in 2000).

Ethnicity

The US has often been described as a multi-variant or pluralist society. Wave after wave of immigration has led to an incredibly diverse population ethnically. Between 1820 and 1914 an effective 'open door policy' operated and around 30 million immigrants arrived in the US (48 million between 1820 and 1978). Even today, immigration is a significant feature. Since the 1980s over one million immigrants per year have arrived in the US. There is a clear correlation between ethnicity and voting patterns. This is dealt with in Ch 22.3.

Single race or mixed race (total 281 421 906)		
Single race	274 595 678	97.6%
Mixed race	6 826 228	2.4%

Population by race (total 281 421 906)		
White	211 460 626	75.1%
Black	34 419 434	12.9%
Asian	11 898 828	4.2%
Other	15 359 73	5.5%
NB all figures in this table include Hispanics and Latinos (White Hispanics, Black Hispanics etc.)		

Hispanic and Latino (including those of mixed race)		
Mexican	20 640 711	7.3%
Puerto Rican	3 406 178	1.2%
Cuban	1 241 685	0.4%
Other Hispanic and Latino	10 017 244	3.6%
Total Hispanic or Latino	35 305 818	12.5%

% population by geographical region

East	23%
Midwest	26%
South	31%
West	20%

For 'Geography and voting' see Ch 22.3

Gender

There have been some attempts by psephologists to link age with voting behaviour. This is dealt with in Ch 22.4.

Male	138 053 563	49.1%
Female	143 368 343	50.9%

Age

As is the case with gender, age has often been linked to voting behaviour.

Age group as % of population		
Under 5	19 175 798	6.8%
5 to 9	20 549 505	7.3%
10 to 14	20 528 072	7.3%
15 to 19	20 219 890	7.2%
20 to 24	18 964 001	6.7%
25 to 34	39 891 724	14.2%
35 to 44	45 148 527	16.0%
45 to 54	37 677 952	13.4%
55 to 59	13 469 237	4.8%
60 to 64	10 805 447	3.8%
65 to 74	18 390 180	6.5%
75 to 84	12 361 180	4.4%
Over 84	4 239 587	1.5%

Potential electorate (18+) as % of population		
Male	100 994 367	35.9%
Female	108 133 727	38.4%
Total	209 128 094	74.3%

22.2   How elections work

Presidential elections

Introduction

The quadrennial presidential election is a constant and invariable restating of democratic values. In the UK, during times of extreme national crisis (e.g. during the Second World War) elections are cancelled and the parties work together against the common enemy. In the US, however, little has got in the way of the presidential election since the framing of the Constitution. In November 1864, as the North fought the South in the American Civil War, Lincoln (then President) had to stand for re-election. As he later remarked,

> 'The Presidential Election, occurring in regular course during the rebellion added not a little to the strain, but the election was a necessity. We cannot have free government without election and if the rebellion could force us to forgo or postpone a national election it might fairly claim to have already conquered and ruined us.'

The race for the White House is divided into a number of distinct stages.

Primaries (the pre-nomination stage)

During this stage:

1. *Delegates are selected to go to the National Party Conventions;*
2. *The public are made aware of the candidates and in many cases get to have a say in which one will be chosen.*

Two broad types of system are used at this stage: **primaries** and **caucuses**

Primaries

Primaries give the broader public a chance to express a preference for one or more of the candidates seeking the party nominations for the presidential election race proper. In **'open primaries'** anyone can vote in either or both of the parties' primaries or but in recent years **'closed primaries'** – where only registered supporters of the party can have a say – have become more widely used.

Caucuses

Under this system the power to select delegates rests with party activists who meet first at local, then at county and finally at state level to make their choices. Most states have now moved away from caucuses towards primaries but some, including Iowa and North Dakota, persevere with caucuses.

Party Conventions (the nomination stage)

The Conventions are where the final decisions are taken regarding each party's **'ticket'** (its Presidential and Vice-Presidential candidate) and its **'platform'** (the policies on which the candidates will stand). The ticket is normally a foregone conclusion because most of the convention's delegates are committed to vote in a certain way, at least in the first ballot (supporters of Edward Kennedy tried to remove this first ballot pledge in 1980). If there is no winner after the first ballot, delegates are free to switch their support to one of the other candidates or vote for a new 'unity candidate' in order to ensure a speedy resolution to the impasse. In a situation where a second ballot occurs, a candidate running third or lower might 'trade' the support of their delegates in return for the assimilation of some of his/her policy ideas into the platform of the former. Jesse Jackson might have been in this position in 1988 had the result at the Democratic Convention been a little closer. It should be remembered, however, that no vote has gone beyond the first ballot since 1952 when the Democrats took three ballots to select Adlai Stevenson.

The other half of the ticket and the platform

Though the conventions theoretically also choose the other half of the ticket, the reality is that since the 1950s, in both parties, nominated presidential candidates have chosen their own running mates. In some cases there is an attempt to balance the ticket. Gerald Ford, for example, was believed to have been asked to be the running mate for the former actor Reagan in 1980, in order that he might add political weight; Cheney added experience and a certain authority to the George W Bush ticket in 2000 but other nominations are less easily explained. Some questioned whether Bush's choice of Dan Quayle as his running mate in 1988 wasn't simply 'impeachment insurance'.

The Convention's role in influencing the 'platform' is also limited by the fact that the winning candidate will often come ready with a set of policies of his own or be unwilling to be too specific about policies prior to election, for fear of alienating potential support.

The general election

The 'general election' itself puts the two parties' presidential candidates head to head, though often with the added distraction of 'third party' candidates (see Ch 23.3). The election takes place on the first Tuesday after the first Monday in November and is a public holiday. The election is indirect as voters are, in reality, voting for the people who will vote for the President as part of the electoral college.

The electoral college

The electoral college is a relic of the Founding Father's fear of popular power or 'mobocracy'. The candidate who wins the vote in each state receives all of the so-called electoral college votes assigned to that state. Each state has a number of electoral college votes equal to the number of Senators it has (two) plus the number of members of the House of Representatives it has (which will depend upon the population of the state). Three additional Electors represent Washington DC. The Electors (not the actual Congressmen and Senators) chosen to represent the state can then vote for the new President. There are 538 votes in the electoral college. The winning candidate needs to secure 270 votes in order to become President.

See Ch 22.8

Congressional elections

Members of the Senate (two from each state) represent the whole state. Members of the House of Representatives, in contrast, represent districts within states; each district having a population of around 500 000. The entire House is elected every two years, as is one-third of the Senate. As in presidential elections, hopefuls normally have to compete in primaries in order to be selected as their party's candidate.

In a leap year (1992, 1996, 2000 etc.), presidential elections coincide with congressional elections. Mid-term elections are those congressional elections that occur in the middle of the four-year presidential term (1994, 1998, and 2002). These mid-term elections can be very important because they can change the whole balance of the legislature in the middle of the four-year presidential term and, therefore, dramatically affect the President's chances of being able to secure favourable legislation. In 1994, for example, the mid-term elections saw the Republicans – fighting on the national platform of the 'Contract with America' – win control of both the House and the Senate. This signalled that start of a difficult period for Bill Clinton from 1995, with Newt Gingrich (the new Speaker of the House) providing a serious check on the President's agenda.

22.3 Influences on voting behaviour (part 1)

Introduction

A lot of what we said about voting behaviour theory in UK elections can also be applied to elections in the US. This page does not, therefore, aim to repeat this. Instead, it looks at a number of important factors, illustrating them with examples from the elections in 2000. You should use the material provided here and on the next page in conjunction with the page on 'The electorate' (Population profile).

Partisan alignment

In the UK we have seen a decline in partisan alignment. This has been attributed partly to the rise of a strong third party and partly to the tendency for major parties to compete for the centre ground; 'middle England'.

In the US we might also expect to see low levels of party identification and loyalty because of the nature of US society and the nature of American political parties (see Ch 23). In the 2000 presidential election, however, there appears to have been significant evidence of party identification.

% who identified with a party

Total	74%
Democrats	39%
Republicans	35%

% who voted in-line with their party identification

Democrats	86%
Republicans	91%

Split-ticket voting . . .

is where voters do not vote consistently for one party's candidates on election day. They may vote for a Democrat as President, a Republican as Senator and an independent as State Governor, where all three elections coincide. The result of split-ticket voting has been a situation where the President is often from one party whereas another controls one or both chambers in Congress. Sometimes, this leads to 'gridlock'. In the 1980s, in contrast, writers spoke of a 'coat-tails effect' where Reagan's massive popularity got Republican Congressmen elected 'on his coat-tails'. During this period Republicans controlled the White House and the Senate. Following the 2000 congressional elections (before the defection of Senator James Jeffords from Republican to Independent), the Republicans briefly held House, Senate (through the Vice-President's casting vote) and the White House. They had not done this since 1952.

Urban/rural residency and voting

% voting by residential type

Area	Bush (R)	Gore (D)
Rural	59%	37%
Suburbs	49%	47%
Cities (500 000+)	26%	71%

Commentary

The Democrats have, in recent years, achieved far greater success in urban areas than in rural areas and the suburbs. In rural areas in particular, the Republican Party appears to have a clear lead.

Many attribute this to the fact that urban areas tend to benefit from the kind of 'big government' social/welfare spending programmes favoured more by Democratic administrations than Republican ones. In contrast, the gun lobby has campaigned hard in rural areas in support of Republican candidates over the last ten years.

Ethnicity and voting

% voting by race

Race	Bush (R)	Gore (D)
White	54%	42%
Black	9%	90%
Hispanic	35%	62%
Asian	41%	55%
Other	39%	55%

Commentary

The figures above are largely self-explanatory and reflect broad and longstanding trends in the ethnic support for the two parties.

There has, however, been some movement in recent years. George W Bush, for example, campaigned hard in pursuit of the Hispanic vote and achieved an estimated 14% increase in support amongst this group for the Republicans compared to as to 1996.

Geography and voting

% voting by geographical area

Area	Bush (R)	Gore (D)
East	39%	56%
Midwest	49%	48%
South	55%	43%
West	46%	48%

Commentary

Well into the second half of the twentieth century it was possible to talk about the Democrats' control of the 'solid South'. This support had resulted largely from the fact that it had been a Republican – Lincoln – who had waged war against the Southern states and ended slavery.

As the figures show, the solid South appears more solid for the Republicans now than the Democrats, and they have now won majority support in the region in the last three presidential elections.

Religion and voting

% voting by religion

Religion	Bush (R)	Gore (D)
Protestant/Christian	54%	42%
Catholic	47%	50%
Jewish	19%	79%
Other	28%	62%
None	30%	61%

Commentary

The Democrats traditionally far better than Republicans amongst those in the 'other' or 'no' religion category. They also tend to do better amongst the Jewish community. Gore's choice of Jew Joe Lieberman as his vice-presidential candidate no doubt firmed up this support but Clinton had also achieved 78% support amongst Jews in 1992 and 1996.

As a rule, those who attended religious services weekly or daily tended to support Bush more than those who attended less frequently.

22.4 Influences on voting behaviour (part 2)

Issues, policies, events and voting

Issues, policies and events in the public eye in the months running up to the election can have a significant impact on voting behaviour. Commentators on both sides of the Atlantic in recent years have highlighted the increasing importance of short-term factors in elections and the increasing trend towards issue-led politics. The 2000 elections are dealt with in Ch 22.7. This box highlights some issues that were important in two previous elections.

Ford v. Carter in 1976

Ford was appointed Nixon's Vice-President in 1974 following Spiro Agnew's resignation, and then became President following Nixon's own resignation over the Watergate scandal in 1974.

In the 1976 election, Ford faced significant difficulties:

- *He was tainted by Watergate, however unfairly.*
- *He was seen as a rather ineffectual and weak President.*
- *He had previously said that he would not run in 1976.*

Carter, on the other hand, had advantages:

- *There was a desire for change.*
- *He was seen as a 'Washington outsider'.*
- *As a 'born-again Christian', he was seen as being morally sound.*

Bush v. Clinton in 1992

If the election had taken place in 1991, Bush would have been the likely winner because of the incredibly high opinion poll ratings he was achieving in the light of US action in the Gulf War.

By 1992, however, things had moved on but Bush was still trying to play the foreign policy card. This led Clinton famously to launch the slogan 'It's the economy, stupid!' Such sentiments were echoed in car bumper stickers seen at the time of the New Hampshire Primary. They read 'Saddam Hussein still has a job; do you?'.

Candidates and voting

The candidates themselves clearly have a role in affecting voting behaviour. A particularly effective or an inadequate candidate can swing the voters one way or the other. This importance is emphasised by factors such as:

- The relative weakness of the parties;
- The increasing importance of image rather than policy in elections;
- The role of the modern media.

See next page for 'image'

The importance of money

Candidates need an enormous amount of money for, amongst other things:

producing adverts and buying airtime; travelling (not just for them but for their campaign teams); acquiring office space and office staff (offices cost money and although some staff are volunteers, not all are); setting up phone-lines and administering donations; issuing mail-shots (sending out information to the voters); co-ordinating merchandising (shirts, banners, badges, mugs etc.)

Though candidates can take donations (subject to limits – see Ch 22.8) candidates need to be relatively wealthy themselves before embarking on the campaign trail. Even in 1992 the average incumbent in the House spent $580 000 on their re-election campaigns and, in the presidential campaign of the same year, the independent Ros Perot spent $23.9 million, nearly all his own money.

Spending money doesn't guarantee success. For example:

- Perot lost in 1992 and in 1996 when he spent more than the federal limit (over $50 million of his own money) and therefore received no matching funds;
- Michael Huffington spend $26 million trying to win a Senate seat (California) in 1994 and still lost to incumbent Dianne Feinstein

. . . but it nearly always helps raise a candidates profile and it is difficult for a candidate to stay on the campaign trail for over a year and hold down a job! As political consultant Raymond Strother noted, 'poor people can't be elected now'. This would appear to be born out by the fact that over one quarter of all Senators are said to be millionaires.

Income and union membership

% voting by income group

Family income	Bush (R)	Gore (D)
< $15 000	37%	57%
$15 000–$29 999	41%	54%
$30 000–$49 999	48%	49%
$50 000–$74 999	48%	48%
> $75 000	53%	44%

% voting by unionisation

	Bush (R)	Gore (D)
Union households	37%	59%

Commentary

Lower-income and more highly-unionised households are more likely to vote Democrat than Republican. This should come as no surprise. The Republicans have long been associated with business interests (think of the recent Enron scandal) whereas the Democrats have been seen as more the party of the common man. It should be remembered, of course, that there is also a strong correlation **between race and average income.**

Gender and voting

% voting by gender

Gender	Bush (R)	Gore (D)
Male	53%	42%
Female	43%	54%

Commentary

In Britain those studying electoral behaviour have charted the closing of the so-called 'gender gap'. In the US, however, it is alive and well. Some have attributed such massive differences in gender voting to candidate appeal or to the platforms of the two parties (the fact that the Democrats have been firmly pro-choice on abortion since 1992, for example).

NB The role of the media is dealt with separately in Ch 22.5.

22.5 Influences on voting behaviour (part 3): the media

What is the modern campaign like?

In the nineteenth century, candidates travelled around the country gaining support and exchanging ideas with opponents and audiences in a series of two-way public meetings. When Lincoln and Douglas spoke to audiences on the campaign trail in 1858, they were reinforcing one of the most important principles underlying American politics: that people need to be and feel involved. The modern election campaign is, however, much more of a one-way process; the candidate presenting himself or herself to the voters in contexts where the majority of those watching cannot have an input. For example:

- on **whistle-stop tours** of the country . . . where the focus is on 'population coverage' rather than engagement or dialogue; or
- on **television** . . . where, as H G Nicholas noted, 'a candidate draws no sustenance from his unseen millions; the millions meet not a man but an image'.

Such changes have resulted in a campaign where:

- **individuals feel less involved,** possibly even **disaffected**
- **candidates themselves become increasingly lightweight,** because their ideas are not as thoroughly tested as they might have been previously.
- there is a **focus on the image** and even the **physical appearance** of the candidate. As political consultant Raymond Strother noted, there are some 'people that are not electable. . . . Lincoln [due to his appearance] could not have been elected in today's politics'. In 1976 Walter Mondale withdrew from the Democratic Party primaries saying, 'Nationally it is more theatre than the politics I know. I kept getting constant suggestions that I needed to buy different clothes and go to speech instructors. I hated that.'

The press

There are no major national newspapers apart from *USA Today.* The *Washington Post* and the *New York Times* are, however, both widely read and have strong editorials. Local newspapers also back and attack particular candidates.

NB: Re-read Ch. 12.5. You can use a lot of the theory here as well.

Television broadcasting

Television time can be broadly divided into two types: paid and unpaid. Naturally, any candidate will want as much 'air-time' as possible, but with limited budgets it is important that the candidates get as much unpaid exposure as possible.

Unpaid coverage (standard programming)

Though unpaid coverage does not offer the candidate the same degree of control over programme content and tone, it is important that the candidate gets as much unpaid media coverage as possible due to the financial demands of any campaign. The candidate's campaign team is crucial in terms of locating and managing such opportunities.

1 Candidates might be pursued by camera crews to give their 'on-the-spot' feelings on given issues. This is fine if you are a candidate who can think on your feet but not if you are one who is used to having every word you say written for you. Reagan's communications advisor Michael Deaver certainly protected his candidate from this kind of exposure.

2 Presidential candidates are normally invited to take part in three major televised debates. This is a little better because you usually get a chance to reel off some pre-prepared sound-bites in response to a question.

3 Candidates might be the targets of investigative journalism. In 1992 Bill Clinton was constantly on the television being quizzed about his avoiding fighting in the Vietnam War, his smoking pot (though apparently 'not inhaling'!) at college and his supposed affair with Gennifer Flowers. Is it true that 'all publicity is good publicity'?

Paid coverage (commercial advertising)

If a candidate is paying for the airtime then obviously they have complete control over the content. Having said that, television time is so expensive that candidates normally have to cram the essence of what they want to say into a few seconds. When using paid media the candidate can adopt one of two broad strategies:

Positive advertising

Today's positive advertising can take a number of forms:

1. **Biographical ads** – ads that seek to tell the voter something about the candidate's life and put a face to a name. For example, the ad by Frank Greer that helped Gaston Caperton III become Governor of West Virginia in 1988, despite his obvious lack of political experience.

2. **Subliminal ads** – those that rarely mention the candidate but instead focus on creating a positive mood and allowing voters to make their own connections to a large extent. For example, the 'It's Morning in America' ads deployed by Reagan's team in 1984.

1. **Infomercials** – almost unique to Ros Perot, the man who spent $2 million a day in the latter stages of the campaign buying up 30-minute TV slots and then broadcasting lengthy party political programmes that he presented himself.

Negative campaigning

As Larry Sabato observed 'many advertisers have made the mistake of believing that in 30 to 60 seconds you can change someone's mind. What you can do is crystallise a feeling that is already there.'

It was in this belief that Tony Schwartz produced his infamous 'daisy ad' on behalf of Lyndon Johnson against Barry Goldwater in the 1964 presidential race. Goldwater was seen as an extremist and the ad showed a girl counting the petals of a daisy as she removed them, with her voice gradually being replaced by the countdown to a nuclear detonation. Johnson won a landslide victory and Goldwater at least felt that such negative propaganda had been crucial.

Following such ads, negative advertising became endemic in the US system. In recent years, however, there has been something of a public backlash against overtly negative ads and, as a result, some consultants have even started making negative ads that accuse the other side of making negative ads.

22.6 Voter turnout

How low is turnout?

Turnout in US elections is measured as a percentage of voting age population. According to the Federal Election Commission:

'The term Voting Age Population (VAP), refers to the total number of persons in the United States who are 18 years of age or older regardless of citizenship, military status, felony conviction, or mental state.'

This definition of turnout creates a number of problems:

- Firstly, not all of those who are voting age are entitled to vote. A large number are not US citizens.
- Secondly, many of those who are entitled to vote are not registered to vote.

These two factors mean that any measurement of turnout by voting age will be artificially low (see below)

Turnout as a % of VAP

Year	Presidential	Mid-term
1980	52.6	
1982		39.8
1984	53.1	
1986		36.4
1988	50.1	
1990		36.5
1992	55.1	
1994		38.8
1996	49.1	
1998		36.0
2000	51.3	

It is, however, also possible to measure levels of voter registration and then show turnout as a percentage of registered voters.

% of VAP registered (1980–2000)

Year	Presidential	Mid-term
1980	67	
1982		65
1984	71	
1986		66
1988	69	
1990		65
1992	71	
1994		67
1996	74	
1998		71
2000	76	

% of registered who voted (1980–2000)

Year	Presidential	Mid-term
1980	77	
1982		61
1984	75	
1986		55
1988	72	
1990		56
1992	78	
1994		58
1996	66	
1998		52
2000	68	

NB: Figures rounded.

Study these statistics carefully.

1. *What do they tell us about turnout in general?*
2. *What do they tell us about the differences in turnout in presidential and mid-term election years?*
3. *What do they tell us about registration?*

Focus on voter registration

Variation by region (2000)

Different states enforce different deadlines and procedures governing voter registration. Levels of voter registration also vary markedly from state to state.

State	% VAP Reg.	Registration deadline
Missouri	94%	28 days before
New York	81.6%	25 days before
Idaho	79.1%	25 days before by mail, 24 days before in person. On the day at the poll.
Alabama	75.9%	10 days before
Connecticut	75%	14 days before
California	63.2%	29 days before
Arizona	59%	29 days before

Variation by race and gender (1996)

The percentage of the population registering and voting can also vary significantly by race and gender

Race	% registration	% voting
White (not Hispanic)	73%	60.7%
Black (not Hispanic)	66.5%	53%
Hispanic	59%	44.3%
Other (not Hispanic)	58.1%	44.9%

Gender	% registration	% voting
Male	69.6%	57%
Female	72.2%	59.6%

Recent efforts to increase registration rates

The National Voter Registration Act (NVRA) passed in 1993 took effect in 1995. It aimed to extend voter registration across the board. Known as the 'motor voter', law it required states to make registration available at facilities more easily accessible to voters.

Forty-three states implemented 'motor voter' regulations, one (South Dakota) already had no registration requirements, and the six others either already had or chose to introduce election day registration for those that wanted to vote. Though the results have been far from clear-cut, states with more voter-friendly systems tend to achieve higher average turnout figures.

22.7 US elections 2000

The main candidates

Democrats	Republicans
Bill Bradley	George W Bush
Al Gore	Steve Forbes
	John McCain

The primaries

Though Bush had an early scare in New Hampshire (see below), both he and Gore had a relatively easy path through to nomination. The main Democrat challenger, Bill Bradley, fell away partly as a result of lack of campaign finance, and Bush's main rival, John McCain, suspended his campaign on March 9, two days after 'Super Tuesday' (see below). In the Super Tuesday primaries and caucuses Bush and Gore effectively ended their respective contests. Bush won 9 out of 13 Republican contests (Connecticut, Massachusetts, Rhode Island and Vermont went to McCain). Gore won all 15 Democratic contests.

The first five dates

State	Primary	Caucus
1. Iowa		January 24
2. New Hampshire	February 1	
3. Delaware (D)	February 5	
4. Delaware (R)	February 8	
5. South Carolina (R)	February 19	

Focus: New Hampshire

Democrat		Republican	
Candidate	Votes	Candidate	Votes
Al Gore	76 897 (49.7%)	John McCain	115 606 (48.53%)
Bill Bradley	70 502 (45.59%)	George Bush	72 330 (30.36%)
		Steve Forbes	30 166 (12.66%)

'Super Tuesday' states, March 7 (caucuses in negative)

California	Connecticut	Georgia	Hawaii (D)
Idaho (D)	Maine	Maryland	Massachusetts
Minnesota (R)	Missouri	New York	North Dakota (D)
Ohio	Rhode Island	Vermont	Washington

The general election campaign

The Gore campaign – a leap to the left?

Gore consolidated his nomination by choosing Joe Lieberman as his running mate. Lieberman was widely respected and added political weight to the ticket. As Bush took the Republicans to the centre, some felt that Gore appeared to be taking the Democrats to the left, focusing on poorer working families and raising the suggestion that a vote for Gore might be a vote for the old-style Democratic big government welfare programmes. This may have had the effect of alienating those independent – floating – voters whose support Clinton had cultivated in the previous two elections. Gore was also disadvantaged by the fact that the main third party candidate – Nader – appeared to be taking more of his votes from Gore than from Bush.

The Bush campaign – a broad church

Bush's choice of Cheney as running mate was a key move in addressing concerns that Bush was an intellectual lightweight. In the campaign itself, Bush tried to position the Party more to the centre. Faced by the infighting of earlier campaigns and despite his own conservative views on abortion, Bush was able to bridge the ideological gap between the 'party moderates' and the 'religious right'. The former were appeased by the 'compassionate conservatism' tag that he employed during the campaign and by his apparent acceptance of Dick Cheney's gay daughter, Mary. The latter continued to support him (despite the fact that as the New York Times noted, they got 'more sermons than blood, sweat or policy out of Bush') because he was their only realistic way into the White House.

Congressional elections

2000 also saw congressional elections, with the House and one-third of the Senate up for grabs.

The House of Representatives

The 435 members that make up the 107th Congress elected in 2000 are made up as follows:

Republicans	221
Democrats	212
Independent	2

The Senate

The Senate elections resulted in a balanced Senate. It also saw the election of Hillary Clinton (New York)

Republicans	50
Democrats	50

Between January and June 2001, therefore (before the defection of Senator James Jeffords from Republican to Independent), the Republicans held House, Senate (through the Vice-President's casting vote) and the White House. They had not achieved this since 1952.

The result

In November 2000 the US was plunged into what many saw as a deep constitutional crisis. On November 20, Time Magazine reported that the electoral college stood 262 Gore, 246 Bush with 30 votes still up for grabs (25 from Florida and five from New Mexico); and the winner needing 270.

In weeks that followed the election, the whole process descended into farce with endless in-depth analysis of mechanical voting machines and the merits of the various different types of 'chads'. Different electoral districts within Florida adopted different criteria for undertaking recounts, where they undertook recounts at all. Scarcely a day went by without news of 'new' votes for Gore, closing further the 1784 vote margin in favour of Bush that had existed on November 8, the day after the election. As the wrangling continued, both candidates resorted to the courts culminating in the Supreme Court's decision of December 12 (George W Bush et al. v. Albert Gore JR. et al.) that effectively handed Florida and the presidency to Bush.

22.8 Some key issues and debates

Campaign finance and reform

Where do the candidates get their money from?

1. **personal funds** – most candidates are fairly well off and they therefore spend large amounts of their own money.
2. **individual donations** – telephone donations were a major growth area in the 1990s
3. **donations from interest groups** – business/occupational groups might support a particular candidate (see Ch 24.3)
4. **federal funding** – the federal government provides money for the candidates who can demonstrate a broad-based support – see below

The Campaign Finance Act of 1974

This act was introduced in the wake of the Watergate Affair and, in particular, the corruption associated with the CREEP (Committee for the Re-election of the President) in the 1972 campaign. The Act aimed to limit the spending of candidates and, at the same time, to help ease the financial burden on the candidates themselves.

The Act said that:

In the primaries and caucuses/State Conventions

Each candidate could spend $10 million (index-linked in later years). If a candidate raised at least $100 000 dollars including at least $5000 from 20 different states, then the federal government would provide matching funds. Candidates didn't have to take the money, but it made sense. A limit of $5 million was also placed on public funding for any one candidate during this stage.

In the 'general election' itself

Each candidate could spend $20 million. Matching funds were available (see above). The party itself could collect a further $2.9 million for organisation and, in addition, both parties were given $2 million to pay for their National Conventions. The figure of $20 million was index-linked (i.e. linked to inflation). Reagan and Carter received $29.4 million each in 1980, Bush and Dukakis both spent up to the $47 million limit in 1988, and Clinton and Dole each received $62 million in 1996. The Supreme Court declared the compulsory spending limits unconstitutional (Buckley v. Valeo, 1976) but accepted that **voluntary** spending limits could be a condition of receiving matching funds from the Government. Some candidates, Ros Perot for example, have chosen to ignore the voluntary spending limits even though it has meant waiving millions of dollars in matching funds.

Limits on contributions

The Act placed a limit of $1000 per individual citizen to a single election campaign (primaries and general election are considered separately). No one could spend more than $25 000 in one year supporting candidates, and Political Action Committees (PACs) were limited to contributions of $5000 per candidate.

'Soft money'

In 1979 Congress passed legislation aimed at reviving grass-roots politics. This act allowed money to be collected and spent on measures aimed at increasing voter registration ('registration drives') and turnout ('get out the votes' programmes). Such 'soft money' was not to be covered by the 1974 campaign finance limits. Since 1980, however, the lines between 'soft money' and normal funding have become blurred and a lot of the 'soft money' has ended up going towards candidates' campaigns. This blurring is significant because even in 1992 'soft money' was said to total over $250 million.

Primaries

For	Against
Primaries put power into the hands of ordinary voters rather than the party bosses – the 'fat cats' in their 'smoke-filled rooms'.	The party bosses, or at least experienced politicians, are better placed to choose candidates than the public. Primaries often become straightforward beauty contests and the candidates selected are not necessarily the best for the job – simply the lowest common denominator.
Primaries can encourage higher levels of political participation because people feel that they can have a real input into the decision-making process. Some primaries (e.g. Michigan) saw significantly increased turnout in 2000 compared to 1996.	Of the people who are eligible to vote, only about one in five turn out. This shows that people don't take primaries seriously while, at the same time, undermining the legitimacy of the process.
The primaries are physically and mentally demanding. This is good because it mirrors some of the demands that a President will face in office.	The primary season is too long. With the serious preparation for primaries starting the year before the elections, members of the House are in a perpetual state of election preparation. Some candidates do not stand because they can't afford to waste a year or more of their life seeking nomination and then election.
Primaries allow Washington outsiders such as Carter and Clinton to get in on the presidential election act. These individuals might not have been chosen under a system of caucuses.	Though opening up the field is probably a good thing, one should be wary of seeing 'outsiders' as a 'good thing'. Presidents with inside experience of the federal government are much better placed to achieve legislative success.

The electoral college

For	Against
It works effectively and is well understood. The fact that it is an anachronism is no reason to get rid of it.	It was created as a check on the power of the people and is therefore an anachronism.
The winning President can normally claim the support of 50% of the voters because the electoral college promotes a two-horse race.	Sometimes Presidents are elected with less than 50% of the popular vote (George W Bush, for example, won 540 000 votes fewer than Gore in 2000).
It prevents the voices of the smaller states being drowned out.	It statistically over-represents smaller states because each state is rewarded in the electoral college for the fact that it has two Senators.
Most Electors in the college vote as instructed by their states. Many are bound by legal contract. It is little more than a rubber stamp.	There is nothing that can stop Electors from voting for a candidate other than the one they are supposed to vote for. One Elector voted for no-one in 2000 and in 1988 one Democratic ('Dukakis') Elector voted for Lloyd Bentsen.
The college rarely makes any difference to the outcome of the election.	The winner-takes-all system operating in states exaggerates the winning margin in the electoral college.
Unless third party candidates can amass a massive national support they are never going to win anyway even without an electoral college.	The winner-takes-all system makes life hard for third party candidates. Ros Perot, for example, secured 19% of the popular vote in 1992 but gained no electoral college votes.

23.1 Political parties (outline)

Introduction

The Founding Fathers were suspicious of political parties; as George Washington observed, '[Parties] serve to organise faction ... to put in place of the delegated will of the nation, the will of a party.'

The United States is a pluralist society and most of the Founding Fathers would have agreed with Alexander Hamilton when he said that the aim of the Constitution should be to establish a system of government in which 'no alliance of interests could ever gain control of the whole'. The Constitution was designed, therefore, to break up rather than unite political power through its institutionalisation of the separation of powers and of checks and balances. James Madison acknowledged this fact when he wrote in the *The Federalist* that the Constitution had a 'tendency to break and control the violence of faction'.

The emergence of political parties therefore, was something that the Founding Fathers would probably never have envisaged and certainly never intended.

The rise, decline and revival of political parties

Rise

It was the very fact that many Americans had so little in common that made the parties such an attractive proposition. With so much immigration during the early years of the new Constitution, political parties actually gave many Americans:

- *something to belong to*
- *practical help; they offered a safety net for those facing hard times*

As a result, parties quickly took control of the political organisation of many regions and, in particular, cities. As H G Nicholas noted 'It was elemental like gravity, the sun, the stars, the ocean ... One became in Urbana and in Ohio for many years, a Republican just as the Eskimo dons fur clothes'.

This almost total control of certain areas by the party machine became known as **'machine politics'**. Inside these cities the 'machine' creamed off the surplus profit from private enterprise. The 'liberals' hated the 'machine' system, because they craved 'open government'. Local 'machine politics' was not about open meetings, it was about the city **'fat cats'** in the **'smoke-filled rooms'** where the deals were cut.

Though they controlled all of this power, however, the parties were still essentially local institutions: they came together once every four years for the presidential election but 'win or lose, the national party was a bloodless skeleton between the quadrennial Presidential tourneys' (H G Nicholas). Indeed, parties were decentralised not only to a state but also to a city or county level. Brooklyn Democrats' battle cry, 'the tiger shall not cross the bridge', was directed not at their Republican opponents but at their Democratic neighbours across the river in Manhattan.

Decline

Commentators attribute the decline of 'machine politics' to a number of factors:

1. *The expansion and increasing complication of legislation made parties increasingly weak and irrelevant in Congress.*
2. *The role which the parties played in terms of providing some kind of 'welfare provision', was undermined by the introduction of national welfare schemes.*
3. *State initiatives allowed registered voters to by-pass the parties (see Ch 24.4).*
4. *The rise of primaries over caucuses undermined the parties' role in candidate selection.*
5. *Federal 'matching funds' undermined the role of parties in presidential elections.*
6. *The media increasingly by-passed the party in candidate-centred campaigns.*
7. *The increased importance of presidential aides has distanced the President from his party in Congress.*
8. *The rise of the independent or floating voter.*
9. *The increasing influence of pressure groups, particularly through their use of Political Action Committees.*

Revival?

Some of the factors that have led to a decline in the role of political parties are due to changes in the nature of American society and government and are unlikely to be reversed. In one or two areas, however, the parties have attempted to reverse their decline:

1. Campaign finance
Congressional legislation in 1979 saw the emergence of what is termed 'soft money' (See Ch 22.8). This money is not covered by the limits imposed by the 1974 Campaign Finance Act and is supposed to be focused on initiatives reviving grass-roots politics. Since the 1980s, however, the lines between 'soft' and regulated money have become blurred and a lot of the 'soft money' now ends up being spent on candidates' campaigns. This increases party control of candidates.

2. Candidate selection
Parties still have a significant role in influencing the choice of presidential candidates. For example, around 20% of Democratic Convention delegates are so-called super delegates – elected politicians sent to the Convention because of their position rather than as a result of primaries.

3. Improvements in party organisation
Both parties have made efforts to strengthen their national organisations. The National Committees of each party are now more permanent organisations with offices in Washington DC, rather than simply quadrennial election-organising committees.

23.2 Democrats and Republicans

Structure and organisation

```
CHAIR
   |
NATIONAL COMMITTEE
   |
STATE COMMITTEE
   |
COUNTY COMMITTEE
   |
WARD COMMITTEES
AND PRECINCTS
```

The chairperson
Each party has a 'chair' who chairs the meetings of the national committee. The chairperson acts as a spokesperson for the national party and oversees the day-to-day running of the party.

The national committees
Each party has a national committee elected by the previous national Party Convention; the Republican National Committee (RNC) and the Democratic National Committee (DNC). They organise the election effort and the parties' national Convention in presidential election years. Though the national committees meet twice a year and have permanent offices in Washington DC, they have only a limited role outside the quadrennial party conventions that they organise.

State party organisations
Organisations differ from state to state as regulated by state laws. State parties have a state general committee which co-ordinates the parties' state activities. The committee is chaired by a state party chairperson. The state party committee organises the state party convention and organises the selection of candidates for state office.

County committees
County committees are important because acting at a local level they exercise a good deal of patronage over local party jobs. Delegates from the various county committees make up the state general committee.

Wards and precincts
There are around 180 000 precincts or voting districts. They are normally organised by a precinct chairperson (or captain) and tend to focus on activities such as local fundraising and mobilising the vote on polling day. Ward committees are at the next level up, representing a number of precincts.

Ideology and outlook

General
US political parties have to be broad churches in order to be elected. The result is a situation in which the two parties often appear to have more entrenched differences within them than between them.

Critics have often picked up on this feature of American politics:

Ogden Nash, for example, wrote *'Some politicians are Republican, some Democratic and their feud is dramatic, but except for the name they are identically the same'*

D W Brogan famously said that the two major parties were *'like two empty bottles, both empty but bearing different labels.'*

The Democrats
For most of the twentieth century the Party had the broadest possible range of support, being popular: in the South amongst those who still resented the Republicans' historic role in the Civil War and the subsequent abolition of slavery, with the 'common man' (perhaps a legacy of the New Deal Democratic Party of the 1930s), and amongst ethnic minorities.

The reality is, as outlined on the previous page, that the word 'Democrat' means very little without the addition of a qualifying prefix ('liberal', 'conservative' etc.). Clinton was able to maintain a broad base of support for the Party by appealing to independent voters who would normally be fearful of the Democrats' reputation for big government welfare programmes and higher taxation. In the 2000 election, some of Gore's speeches were too left wing for these groups.

The Republicans
Traditionally, the Republicans have been seen as the more conservative of the two parties. Both Reagan (in 1980 and 1984) and Bush senior (1988) ran on platforms promising low personal taxation. During the 1980s the Party also became associated with the 'New Right' and right wing evangelical groups such as Jerry Falwell's 'Moral Majority' (with their anti-abortion and anti-gay beliefs).

In the 2000 presidential election, however, George W Bush adopted a more inclusive approach in an attempt to broaden the appeal of the Party and get it back into government. He adopted the phrase 'compassionate conservatism' and pushed more extreme members of the Party (the anti-abortionist Henry Hyde, for example) to the fringes of the Party Convention.

23.3 The two-party system and third party candidacy

Introduction to the party system

There have been two major political parties in the US from the time of Jefferson, though the names have changed over the years: Democrats, Whigs, Republicans, Democratic Republicans, or the Federalists. This is partly the result of a natural need for a clear choice and partly due to factors such as:

1. the electoral system
2. issues and debates that have polarised American opinion through time, such as

   the issue of ratifying the Constitution;
   the interests of industrial/financial North v. the agricultural South;
   anti-slavery v. pro-slavery;
   (after the New Deal) the Democrats representing the 'common man', the Republicans representing 'business'.

Major third party results

Year	Candidates		% vote	ECVs
1968	G Wallace	American Ind.	13	46
1980	J Anderson	National Unity	7	0
1992	R Perot	Independent	19	0
1996	R Perot	Reform	9	0

Third parties in Congress

House

Bernie Saunders	1993–	Socialist
Virgil Coode	2000–	Independent

Senate

James Jeffords	2001–	Independent

Third party candidates

The United States does not have permanent national third parties capable of achieving significant shares of the popular vote in elections. This is due to a number of factors including:

the difficulty in securing funding, the first past the post electoral system, the difficulty in getting one's name onto the ballot, the lack of media coverage, public ignorance or lack of awareness.

This does not, however, mean that third party presidential challenges are not worthy of note. They can:

(a) Affect the result of the election

*(i) by depriving the major parties of votes. In Florida in 2000, for example, Ralph Nader secured 87 974 votes on the **first** count while the **original** margin between Bush and Gore was only 1784 votes. Nader voters would have been unlikely to vote for Bush had their man not stood.*
(ii) by winning electoral college votes (ECVs), stopping a major party achieving 270.

(b) Get some of their policies into the programmes of the main parties

Perot, for example, put financial management and the deficit onto the agenda.

Is the US really a two-party system?

Yes

1. The last President elected from outside of the two main parties was Martin Fillmore (Whig) in 1850.
2. All but three of the members of current Congress (two House members and one Senator) belong to one of the two major parties.
3. The combined Republican and Democrat vote in presidential elections invariably exceeds 80% and is often over 90% (99% in 1984 and 1988).
4. Of the 50 state governors, 48 are Democrats or Republicans.

No

1. Clearly, the competition between the two parties is not everywhere: there are still states which always support one party.
2. Some authors have gone as far as to say that rather than a two-party system, the United States in fact has **51 party systems**, each unique: one system of parties on a national level in the federal government and another wholly unique party system in each and every one of the 50 states of the Union.
3. Both parties are really broad churches and include within their folds an enormous diversity of attitude and opinion: the words 'Democrat' and 'Republican' disguise a massive range of ideas.
4. Writers such as James McGregor Burns have suggested more complicated models. In McGregor Burn's construct Republicans from rural areas really have more in common with Democrats from rural areas than they do with their urban Republican 'brothers'. Democrats from urban areas, in contrast, might align with Republicans from districts facing similar social problems trying to force through policies that will help these areas. Others have used terms such as 'liberal Democrats', 'conservative Democrats', 'moderate' and 'conservative Republicans' (see also Ch 23.2) and identified these different shades as being located in particular geographic areas.

Breaking down the party labels

Western **'Liberal Democrats'** and **'Moderate Republicans'** in States such as California.

'Presidential Democrats' or **'Liberal Democrats'** From the North Eastern states **'Presidential Republicans'** or **'Moderate Republicans'** From East suburban districts. States such NY and Massachusetts.

'Congressional Republicans'/'Conservative Republicans' and **'Congressional Democrats'/'Conservative Democrats'** from rural areas. More conservative and suspicious of 'big government'. e.g. Southern Democrats or Republican farmers. States such as Alabama and Louisiana.

24.1 Definitions and classification

Pressure groups in the US

Definitions and context
As we observed in the UK section of the book, pressure groups are groups of like-minded individuals who campaign for their own interests and/or to achieve goals or pursue common causes.

The heterogeneous (or multi-variant) society and the proliferation of pressure groups
The United States is a heterogeneous society – that is to say it is massively varied in terms of population (ethnicity, religion, culture etc.), geographically, climatically and economically. There are, in fact, so many different interests that parties cannot possibly hope to encompass all interests effectively. In this context, pressure groups flourish and proliferate.

Points of leverage
The structure of the US Government both reflects this diversity and reinforces it. As Alexander Hamilton noted, the Constitution aimed to establish a system of government in which 'no alliance of interests could ever gain control of the whole'. Such a fragmentation of power was achieved through:

1. *the separation of powers between legislative, executive and judicial branches;*
2. *establishing checks and balances; and*
3. *identifying the division between federal and state governments.*

This fragmentation of power presents pressure groups with numerous points of leverage: they can exert pressure at federal or state level; on any or all of the branches of government.

Classifying pressure groups
The obvious question to ask here is 'can we use the same typologies for classifying US pressure groups that we employed when classifying groups in the UK?'

Can we apply the sectional/cause typology to our study of US pressure groups?
There is no reason why we cannot apply the sectional/cause classification model to US pressure groups.

Sectional groups
(represent the interests of a particular section of society)
For example, the *American Medical Association*, the *American Bar Association*, the *AFL-CIO*

Cause groups
(campaign for a particular cause or objective)

Sectional cause groups (protect a section of society beyond their membership: they do not stand to benefit individually)
For example, anti-abortion groups would argue that they were campaigning for the rights of the unborn.

Attitude cause groups (aim to change people's attitudes on a particular issue)
For example, *Friends of the Earth.*

Political cause groups (aim to achieve certain political goals)
For example, the *American Civil Liberties Union (ACLU)*

Does the insider/outsider typology work here?
The insider/outsider typology assumes that there is a clear focus for policy-making – a certain centralisation of power around the core executive. This is not *as* true in the US as it is in the UK. The fragmentation of power and the federal/state division in the US creates a situation in which it is possible to be 'inside' or 'outside' on a number of different levels in a number of different contexts. A group might, for example, be very much 'inside' Congress, frustrating the legislative plans of the President, or 'inside the White House' influencing the agenda. On those issues where the state controls policy, pressure groups might focus all of their efforts on one or more branches of the state government. Some groups are, however, clearly 'inside' the policy-making loop in Washington (see right).

Case study – the collapse of Enron (2002)
The collapse of the energy-trading firm Enron and the ensuing scandal revealed the extent of inside influence afforded to some groups in Washington. Enron had made campaign contributions to 71 out of 100 Senators as well as 188 out of 435 House members. It had made phone calls to at least six key members of the Bush team in the run-up to the collapse. Five others had received cash from the company (some as directors or consultants) and four had met with Enron executives. According to *The Guardian*, Cheney had been involved in six such meetings in the year before the collapse.

Other ways of classifying groups
Some US specialists have advanced other typologies Robert McKeever, for example, divides groups into eight types:

Business/trade	Agriculture	Unions	Professional
Single issue	Ideological	Group rights	Public interest

24.2 Methods

Pressure group methods in the US context

US pressure groups share many of their methods and tactics with their UK counterparts. As we have seen, however, a number of factors affect the range of methods adopted by groups in the US. For example:

1. the US Constitution, through the separation of powers and checks and balances, serves to divide up power. This gives pressure groups many potential points of leverage;
2. the US system is federal. For many pressure groups, therefore, they can achieve their objectives at state level because the states retain control over so many aspects of government. The sheer scale of the US also encourages the proliferation of local groups

Pressure group tactics

Influencing the legislative process directly

Pressure groups are massively involved in the work of Congress. Most will:
- *testify at the committee hearing stage, where appropriate;*
- *lobby Congressmen directly, highlighting the impact of certain measures on the voters in the Congressmen's states or encouraging log-rolling for 'pork'.*

Some anti-abortion groups have also used publicity stunts such as sending Congressmen life-size plastic foetuses.

Negating legislative efforts

It is often easier to stop things happening in Congress than to force them through. Pressure groups have numerous opportunities to apply pressure for a bill to be killed or pigeon-holed during its passage through the legislature. A single Senator can talk a measure out of time if they engage in filibustering.

At state level

If the aims of a group are confined to a state or are achievable at state level through a number of state-based campaigns, the group might focus their attention on state governments rather than the federal government. The use of initiatives and referendums in some states (see Ch 24.4) also allow groups to initiate legislation or pass final judgement on it. These mechanisms have been particularly popular amongst groups campaigning for lower taxes.

Influencing the legislative process indirectly through elections

Pressure groups are massively involved in providing finance for congressional election campaigns. For example:

The collapse of the Enron energy-trading firm led to criticisms of Congress. According to *The Guardian*, 71 of the 100 Senators and 188 of the 435 House Members had received campaign contributions from the company (Enron spent $5.8 million on federal election campaigns over 12 years). The same Congress had blocked President Clinton's attempts to close financial loopholes that were allowing companies like Enron to conceal the scale of their debts. Such apparent conflicts of interest have encouraged House members such as Republican Christopher Shays and the Democrat Marty Meehan to sponsor a tougher Campaign Finance Bill, though at the time of writing Bush remains reluctant to lend it his support.

Influencing the executive

In the last page we looked at the links between Enron and the Bush Administration. Pressure groups can also get inside executive agencies and independent regulatory commissions, with the effect of limiting the effectiveness of regulation in the areas that concern the group.

Influencing political parties

As we have seen, political parties are not as central to the whole policy-making process as they are in Britain. That said, many pressure groups have worked within parties with a view to getting their policies onto the parties' approved election platform. Within the Republican Party, for example, the 'pro-life' Christian Right groups were able to maintain the Party's 'pro-life' credentials throughout the 1980s and 1990s – though George W Bush sought to marginalise such elements in the 2000 Convention for fear of alienating independent voters. The Democrats, in contrast, have become the home for 'pro-choice' groups and have had a platform commitment to abortion rights since the 1992 Convention. The extent to which this really matters once the candidates are elected is, however, questionable. After all, neither Reagan nor Bush made any real attempts to act decisively on the abortion issue.

Embarking on legal action

Groups are often invited to brief the courts before formal arguments are heard. This allows them to put their case in areas where they have a legitimate interest. These so-called 'amicus curiae' briefings are also important for the courts because groups can often provide specialist knowledge or a different perspective. Some groups also become involved in their own legal actions in pursuit of their aims. In the case of Reno v. American Civil Liberties Union (1997) for example, the Supreme Court struck down two provisions of the 1996 Communications Decency Act, which sought to protect minors from harmful material available on the internet. The Court maintained that these sections violated the First Amendment protection of freedom of speech (7:2).

Mobilising public pressure

Public campaigns

The constant demands of re-election make Congressmen extremely receptive to popular campaigns. Petitions or letter-writing campaigns (where groups encourage people to literally bury elected representatives and officials with mail-sacks full of support for the group's goal) are especially popular with groups. Acts of civil disobedience and direct action (see right), sometimes violent, have also been evident in the last 40 years.

Direct action

Picketing of abortion clinics, for example, became commonplace during the 1980s and continues. The intimidatory effect of such picketing has been heightened by the upsurge in related bomb attacks against buildings and violence against staff at such facilities. In 1994, for example, Paul Hill (the leader of the Defensive Action League) used a shotgun to kill Dr John Britton and his bodyguard (James Herman Barrett) outside a clinic in Pensacola, Florida. In 1994 there was a total of four murders and eight attempted murders. In October 1998 Buffalo-based obstetrician Dr Barnett Slepian was murdered, by a sniper who shot him through his kitchen window.

24.3 Political Action Committees

What are Political Action Committees?

Political Action Committees (PACs) are organisations that collect and channel money to candidates running for political office. The expansion in PACs took place following the campaign finance reform of the early 1970s, particularly after the 1974 Campaign Finance Act. This reform prevented unions, corporations and trade associations from making campaign contributions directly to candidates. PACs, therefore, became the middlemen; collecting together contributions from such groups as well as other individuals and then channelling the monies towards the candidates that might best serve the interests of the contributors.

Numbers of Political Action Committees 1974 and 1997–2000

The table below shows the total number of political action committees operating in each year according to the Federal Election Commission.

1974	608
1997	3884
1998	3798
1999	3835
2000	4499

PAC funding of federal candidates 1991–2000

The table below shows the amounts contributed in millions of dollars. Again, all figures are from the Federal Election Commission.

	99–00	97–98	95–96	93–94
All candidates	$247.9	$206.8	$203.9	$179.6
Senate	$51.9	$48.1	$45.6	$47.2
House	$193.4	$158.7	$155.8	$132.4

% of total going to incumbents and challengers

	99–00	97–98	95–96	93–94
Incumbents	75%	78%	67%	72%
Challengers	11%	10%	15%	10%
Vacant seats	14%	12%	18%	18%

% going to candidates from each party

Senate	99–00	97–98	95–96	93–94
Democrat	39%	43%	36%	51%
Republican	61%	57%	64%	49%
House				
Democrat	51%	49%	50%	67%
Republican	49%	51%	50%	33%

Top ten PACs by total contributions to candidates (1999–2000)

The table below shows the top ten PACs by total contributions to candidate campaigns.

Name	Total amount
Realtors	$3 423 441
Association of Trial Lawyers of America	$2 656 000
American Federation of State and County Municipal Employees – People Qualified	$2 590 074
The National Automobile Dealers Association	$2 498 700
Independent Voter Action	$2 494 450

Top five PACs by receipts (1999–2000)

The table below shows the top five PACs by receipts (i.e. monies raised)

Name	Receipts
National Rifle Association	$17 881 886
Emily's List	$14 576 209
Independent Voter Education	$9 114 221
American Federation of State County and Municipal Employees – People Qualified.	$8 501 822
UAW Voluntary Community Action Programme	$6 757 923

How does the US public feel about Political Action Committee activity?

According to a Harris Poll (May 16, 2001) a large majority of Americans feel that big companies and PACs have too much influence.

'Big companies have too much power and influence in Washington'	86%
'PACs have too much power and influence in Washington'	83%
'Small business has too little power and influence in Washington'	88%
'Public opinion has too little power and influence in Washington'	73%

24.4 Direct democracy

Introduction

Many US states employ mechanisms that allow for a degree of direct democracy. Some states, Washington for example (see right), have amended their state constitutions to allow citizens the right to initiate legislation. Others prefer to allow public consultation only on measures proposed or passed by the state legislature. Three such mechanisms are dealt with on this page: referendums, initiatives, and recalls.

Referendums

A referendum is a popular vote on a measure passed or proposed by a legislature (as opposed to a measure proposed by the people). Though regulations vary from state to state, referendums generally take place where:

- the legislature decides to put a measure or policy to a public vote;
- the legislature is required by law to put certain measures to a public vote; or
- the people have the right to force a referendum on a law passed by the legislature (known as a petition referendum).

Initiatives

Initiatives differ from referendums in that they allow voters to propose (initiate) laws themselves. They operate – in some form or another – in 24 states. The normal procedure is as follows:

1. Those proposing the law must produce a petition carrying the support of a predetermined percentage of the population (normally 5–15%).
2. If it gains enough support, the issue will be placed on the ballot automatically (in some states) or via the legislature (in others).
3. Registered voters in the state then get the chance to vote on the proposal.
4. The measure fails or becomes law.

Recalls

A recall is a procedure that allows registered voters in a state to remove an elected official from office before the end of their term where there is evidence of corruption, negligence or, in some cases, incompetence. Around one-quarter of US states offer this power to voters, though in practice such recalls are often difficult to execute.

Case studies

Washington State

Washington was one of the first states to allow initiatives and referendums. In 1912 voters approved an amendment to the state constitution that guaranteed the right of voters to initiate legislation:

'The first power reserved by the people is the initiative.'
Article II, Section 1(a), Washington State Constitution.

Measure	Filed	Balloted	Passed
Initiatives (of all types)	1035	143	74
Referendums (referred by legislature)	49	47	38
Referendums (referred by petition of voters)	49	32	4

California's Proposition 13

California has long been associated with direct democracy. When they went to the polls in 1988, for example, Californians were not only electing a president but also having a say on decisions as wide-ranging as car insurance and water conservation. More controversial were California's 1994 Proposition 18, cutting off state-funded public services to those classified as illegal immigrants and its 1996 Proposition 209 effectively banning affirmative action.

Most famous of all, however, was Proposition 13 (the Jarvis–Gann initiative) passed by Californian voters in 1978. This measure cut property taxes by almost two-thirds and forced the state government into spending its surplus in order to protect vital services.

Initiatives in 2000

When they went to the polls in November 2000, voters in many states had the opportunity to have their say on a range of initiatives as well as who should become the next President, House member, Senator, state politician or official. *Time Magazine* (November 20, 2000) reported the results of these votes.

Background checks at gun shows?

These votes came in the wake of the Columbine school killings. The measure would allow checks to be made on those buying weapons.

State	Yes	No
Colorado	70%	30%
Oregon	60%	40%

Ban gay marriage?

State	Yes	No
Nebraska	70%	30%
Nevada	70%	30%

Legalise cannabis (marijuana)?

Several states had already allowed cannabis use for medical use. This initiative went further still.

State	Yes	No
Alaska	39%	61%
Colorado	54%	46%
Nevada	65%	35%

School vouchers?

This scheme would see parents given vouchers for private schools in the face of a perceived deterioration in state-sector education provision.

State	Yes	No
California	29%	71%
Michigan	31%	69%

24.5 Arguments for and against pressure groups

A r g u m e n t s   f o r
1. Pressure groups occur naturally under any system of government. People have a natural desire to unite in protection of their own interests or in advancing a particular cause.
2. Pressure groups are particularly necessary in the US because America is a heterogeneous society with a massive range of views and interests. It would be impossible for any political party to represent the full range of opinion effectively. This is what pluralism is about.
3. Pressure groups allow a greater degree of public participation in the political process, particularly between elections when governments can become complacent.
4. Groups play an essential role in moderating the views of their more extreme members. Without such groups, individuals with extreme views might never have their views challenged and moderated.
5. Groups play a vital role in educating the general public. Many necessary changes have been brought about as a result of public pressure resulting from the activities of pressure groups in raising awareness of issues.
6. Groups provide valuable information to governments. Governments must have access to the best possible information on which to base policy. Pressure groups are often in a position to provide detailed information on specific issues because they tend to be specialised. Many groups also have significant research programmes.
7. Groups can hold the government accountable. They can act as watchdogs, monitoring the impact of policies and bringing public pressure to bear where governments fail to live up to their promises or their obligations under the law.
8. Minority views, often drowned out within political parties or in Congress, can be articulated within pressure groups. People with such views are, therefore, allowed to 'let off steam' without becoming disaffected and adopting very extreme methods.

A r g u m e n t s   a g a i n s t
1. Some groups are far more powerful than others are. We should really be talking about elites theory rather than pluralist theory.
2. Many groups representing poorer people to compete with groups representing business interests. As US political consultant Raymond Strother noted, 'poor people don't often have rich friends'.
3. Human resources are also an issue. Groups tend to be more successful where they have articulate, educated leading members. Many have argued that this tends to favour groups run by the middle classes over those set up by the working class.
4. Groups often have an effect on government that is disproportionate to their size or to the merit of their cause. By using direct action, even illegal tactics, groups can defeat the efforts of popularly-elected governments and change policy. This has been apparent over abortion where anti-abortion groups have used intimidation at clinics and have deliberately jammed free-phone lines in order to shut abortion facilities down de facto.
5. Some groups have worryingly close contacts with government. In the case of Enron, for example, leading members of the federal executive had either worked for the company as consultants or had received monies from the company. Many more politicians and officials take positions as consultants after they leave office. This raises the question of how even-handedly they can act whilst in office.
6. In the US, many business interests often have too cosy a relationship with the independent regulatory commissions that are supposed to be objectively assessing their compliance with the various laws and regulations.

Appendix I   The US Bill of Rights

Context

The first ten Amendments to the US Constitution (ratified in 1791) are referred to as the Bill of Rights. Their addition to the Constitution was, for some states, a condition of their agreeing to the Constitution itself. What follows is the full text of these ten amendments. You should pay particular attention to Amendments I (see also Ch 15.5) II, V, VIII and X (all highlighted).

AMENDMENT I

Congress shall make no law respecting an establishment of religion, or prohibiting the free exercise thereof; or abridging the freedom of speech, or of the press, or the right of the people peaceably to assemble, and to petition the Government for a redress of grievances.

AMENDMENT II

A well regulated Militia, being necessary to the security of a free State, the right of the people to keep and bear Arms, shall not be infringed.

AMENDMENT III

No Soldier shall, in time of peace be quartered in any house, without the consent of the Owner, nor in time of war, but in a manner to be prescribed by law.

AMENDMENT IV

The right of the people to be secure in their persons, houses, papers, and effects, against unreasonable searches and seizures, shall not be violated, and no Warrants shall issue, but upon probable cause, supported by Oath or affirmation, and particularly describing the place to be searched, and the persons or things to be seized.

AMENDMENT V

No person shall be held to answer for a capital, or otherwise infamous crime, unless on a presentment or indictment of a Grand Jury, except in cases arising in the land or naval forces, or in the Militia, when in actual service in time of War or public danger; nor shall any person be subject for the same offence to be twice put in jeopardy of life or limb, nor shall be compelled in any criminal case to be a witness against himself, nor be deprived of life, liberty, or property, without due process of law; nor shall private property be taken for public use without just compensation.

AMENDMENT VI

In all criminal prosecutions, the accused shall enjoy the right to a speedy and public trial, by an impartial jury of the State and district wherein the crime shall have been committed, which district shall have been previously ascertained by law, and to be informed of the nature and cause of the accusation; to be confronted with the witnesses against him; to have compulsory process for obtaining witnesses in his favor, and to have the Assistance of Counsel for his defence.

AMENDMENT VII

In Suits at common law, where the value in controversy shall exceed twenty dollars, the right of trial by jury shall be preserved, and no fact tried by a jury shall be otherwise re-examined in any Court of the United States, than according to the rules of the common law.

AMENDMENT VIII

Excessive bail shall not be required, nor excessive fines imposed, nor cruel and unusual punishments inflicted.

AMENDMENT IX

The enumeration in the Constitution, of certain rights, shall not be construed to deny or disparage others retained by the people.

APMENDMENT X

The powers not delegated to the United States by the Constitution, nor prohibited by it to the States, are reserved to the States respectively, or to the people.

Appendix II Key individuals

U K

Key Government figures

Prime Minister	*Tony Blair*
Deputy Prime Minister with responsibility for Local Government and the Regions	*John Prescott*

Other Cabinet members

Chancellor of the Exchequer	*Gordon Brown*
Leader of the Commons	*Robin Cook*
Lord Chancellor	*Lord Irvine*
Foreign Secretary	*Jack Straw*
Home Secretary	*David Blunkett*
Secretary for Environment, Food and Rural Affairs	*Margaret Beckett*
International Development Secretary	*Clare Short*
Work and Pensions Secretary	*Andrew Smith*
Secretary for Transport	*Alistair Darling*
Health Secretary	*Alan Milburn*
Northern Ireland Secretary	*Dr John Reid*
Welsh Secretary	*Paul Murphy*
Defence Secretary	*Geoffrey Hoon*
Chief Secretary to the Treasury	*Paul Boateng*
Scottish Secretary	*Helen Liddell*
Leader of the Lords	*Lord Williams*
Trade and Industry Secretary	*Patricia Hewitt*
Education and Skills Secretary	*Estelle Morris*
Culture, Media and Sport Secretary	*Tessa Jowell*
Chief Whip	*Hilary Armstrong*
Minister without Portfolio and Party Chair	*Charles Clarke*

Some other key figures

Minister for the Cabinet Office	*Lord Macdonald*
Director of Communications and Strategy	*Alastair Campbell*
Chief of Staff	*Jonathon Powell*
Director of Government Relations	*Sally Morgan*
Head of Policy Directorate	*Jeremy Heywood*

Opposition

Leader of the Opposition	*Iain Duncan Smith*
Deputy and Shadow Foreign Secretary	*Michael Ancram*

Other Shadow Cabinet members

Shadow Chancellor	*Michael Howard*
Party Chairman	*David Davis*
Shadow Home Secretary	*Oliver Letwin*
Shadow Leader in the Lords	*Lord Strathclyde*
Shadow Defence Secretary	*Bernard Jenkin*
Shadow Work and Pensions Secretary	*David Willetts*
Shadow Health Secretary	*Dr Liam Fox*
Shadow Environment, Food and Rural Affairs Secretary	*Peter Ainsworth*
Shadow Culture, Media and Sport Secretary	*Tim Yeo*
Shadow Transport, Local Government and the Regions Secretary	*Theresa May*
Shadow Northern Ireland Secretary	*Quentin Davies*
Shadow Leader of the Commons	*Eric Forth*
Shadow Trade and Industry Secretary	*John Whittingdale*
Shadow Education and Skills Secretary	*Damian Green*
Shadow Cabinet Office Minister	*Tim Collins*
Shadow Chief Secretary to the Treasury	*John Bercow*
Shadow Scottish Secretary	*Jacqui Lait*
Shadow Welsh Secretary	*Nigel Evans*
Shadow International Development Secretary	*Caroline Spelman*
	Eric Pickles
Shadow Transport Minister	
Shadow Minister for Agriculture and Fisheries	*David Lidington*
Shadow Work Minister	*James Clappison*
Opposition Chief Whip	*David Maclean*

Opposition Chief Whip in the Lords	*Lord Cope of Berkeley*

Speaker of the House of Commons

Michael Martin

U S

Executive

President	*George W Bush*
Vice President	*Richard B Cheney*

Other Cabinet Members

President's Chief of Staff	*Andrew H Cord Jr.*
Environmental Protection Agency	*Christie Todd Whitman*
Office of Homeland Security	*Tom Ridge*
Office of Management and Budget Director	*Mitchell E Daniels Jr.*
Office of National Drug Control Policy	*John Walters*
United States Trade Representative	*Robert B Zoellick*
Secretary of Agriculture	*Ann M Veneman*
Secretary of Interior	*Gale Norton*
Secretary of Commerce	*Don Evans*
Department of Justice	*John Ashcroft*
Secretary of Defense	*Donald Rumsfeld*
Secretary of Labor	*Elaine Chao*
Secretary of Education	*Rod Paige*
Secretary of State	*Colin Powell*
Secretary of Energy	*Spencer Abraham*
Secretary of Transportation	*Norman Mineta*
Secretary of Health and Human Services	*Tommy Thompson*
Secretary of Treasury	*Paul O'Neill*
Secretary of Housing and Urban Development	*Mel Martinez*
Secretary of Veterans Affairs	*Anthony Principi*

Some other key figures

Counsellor to the President	*Karen Hughes*
Press Secretary	*Ari Fleischer*
White House Communications Director	*Dan Bartlett*
Senior Policy Advisor	*Karl Rove*
National Security Advisor	*Condoleezza Rice*
Director of the CIA	*George J Tenet*
Director of the FBI	*Robert Mueller III*

Congress

(1) House of Representatives

Speaker	*John Dennis Hastert*
House Majority Leader	*Dick Armey*
House Minority Leader	*Richard A Gephardt*

(2) Senate

President Pro Tempore	*Robert C Byrd*
Senate Majority Leader	*Thomas A Daschle*
Senate Minority Leader	*Trent Lott*

Supreme Court

Chief Justice	*William H Rehnquist*
Associate Justices	*John Paul Stevens*
	Sandra Day O'Connor
	Antonin Scalia
	Anthony Kennedy
	David Souter
	Clarence Thomas
	Ruth Bader Ginsburg
	Stephen Breyer

Appendix III   Guide to websites

Introduction

This list is by no means exhaustive, but it provides a good starting point for students of UK and US politics.

UK politics sites

Media

(1) Newspapers

The Guardian	www.guardian.co.uk/
The Telegraph	www.telegraph.co.uk/
The Times	www.thetimes.co.uk/
The Independent	www.independent.co.uk/

(2) Magazines

The Economist	www.economist.com/
The Spectator	www.spectator.co.uk/
Private Eye	www.private-eye.co.uk/

(3) Television News

BBC	www.bbc.co.uk/news/
ITN	www.itn.co.uk/

Government

The one-stop site	www.ukonline.gov.uk/
Parliament	www.parliament.uk/
Ombudsman	www.ombudsman.org.uk/
Prime Minister	www.pm.gov.uk/
No. 10	www.number-10.gov.uk/
Cabinet Office	www.cabinet-office.gov.uk/

Political parties

Labour	www.labour.org.uk/
LibDem	www.libdems.org.uk/
Conservative	www.conservatives.com/
SNP	www.snp.org/
Plaid Cymru	www.plaidcymru2001.com/
Green	www.greenparty.org.uk/

Pressure groups

Loads to choose from, for example ...

Greenpeace UK	www.greenpeace.org.uk/
Countryside Alliance	www.countryside-alliance.org/

Something more unusual ...

Surfers Against Sewage	www.sas.org.uk/

Census material

www.statistics.gov.uk/census2001/default.asp/

US politics sites

Media

(1) Newspapers

USA Today	www.usatoday.com/
The Washington Post	www.washingtonpost.com/
The Washington Times	www.washtimes.com/
The New York Times	www.nytimes.com/

(2) Magazines

Time Magazine	www.time.com/
Newsweek Magazine	www.newsweek.com/

(3) Television News

ABC	www.abcnews.com/
CNN	www.cnn.com/

Government

The one-stop site	www.firstgov.gov/
The executive	www.whitehouse.gov/
The legislature	www.congress.gov/
	www.thomas.loc.gov/
For Supreme Court	www.uscourts.gov/
	http://supct.law.cornell.edu/supct/

Political parties

The Democratic Party	www.democrats.org/
The Republican Party	www.rnc.org/
The Green Party USA	www.greenparty.org/
The Reform Party	www.reformparty.org/

Pressure groups

Again, loads to choose from, for example ...

AFL-CIO (union)	www.alfcio.org/
ACLU (civil liberties)	www.aclu.org/

Something more unusual ...

Trout Unlimited	www.tu.org/

Census material

www.census.gov

State initiatives and referendums

try Washington State	www.secstate.wa.gov/inits/

Good search engines: **www.google.co.uk**   **www.yahoo.co.uk**   **www.webcrawler.com**

Please note that website addresses can change, and that neither the author nor the publisher can be responsible for the contents of any of the websites listed.

Glossary

Accountability	To have to answer for one's actions and conduct. For example, MPs are accountable to voters and ministers are accountable to Parliament.
Affirmative action	Or 'positive discrimination'. Policies that favour minorities in an effort to reverse past (historic) discrimination.
Agenda-setting	A role often attributed to the media. Determining the focus for policy by focusing on certain issues and to the exclusion of others.
Amicus curiae	Commonly used term in the US courts where groups with an interest in policy can file 'amicus curiae' ('friends of the court') briefs to put their case before legal argument is heard by the court.
Anonymity	One of the three principles upon which the British civil service is traditionally said to be based: civil servants are not public figures because they are not accountable for policies. See 'Neutrality' and 'Permanence'.
Appellate jurisdiction	The area over which a court can consider or review a case on appeal from a lower court.
A priori [reasoning]	Literally meaning 'prior to experience'. Where knowledge does not 'depend for its authority upon the evidence of experience' P K Moser (ed.) *A Priori Knowledge* (Oxford, 1987). In other words, where reasoning is not based upon an examination of the evidence, but on ideas or an ideological framework that precede it.
Balancing the ticket	In the US. The practice of choosing a vice-presidential candidate from a different ethnic, religious or geographical background than the presidential candidate, in order to broaden the appeal of the ticket.
Band-wagon effect	Where favourable opinion poll ratings result in even more voters backing the party or candidate that appears to be 'winning'.
Bicameral	Having two chambers (e.g. Congress = House and Senate)
Bill of Rights	In the US, referring to the first ten amendments to the Constitution. In the UK, a measure passed in 1689 placing some restrictions on the power of the monarch, identifying some key parliamentary powers and certain limited individual rights.
Bipartisanship	Where two parties co-operate on particular issues (bipartisan coalitions).
Boomerang effect	Where favourable opinion poll ratings result in some supporters of the party that is ahead becoming complacent and not voting and/or more of the losing party's supporters making an effort to get out and vote and/or people voting for the party that is behind out of sympathy. The result is that the gap between the parties identified by the poll closes.
Broadsheets	The larger more substantial daily and Sunday newspapers (*The Guardian, The Times, The Telegraph, The Independent, The Financial Times, The Observer*).
Cabinet	The committee of leading members of the government (most of whom are heads of departments). In the US, traditionally more administrative; in the UK, traditionally more important in decision-making.
Calendar	Normally refers to the timetable of legislation awaiting action in the US Congress.
Caucus	In the US. A meeting of party members convened to select candidates or decide strategy.
Cause groups (Promotional groups)	Pressure groups that aim to promote a particular cause or set of ideas.
Certiorari	A writ of certiorari from a court instructs a lower court to make details of its decision available for review in a higher court, in order that the decision can be 'made certain'.
Checks and balances	Where each branch of government exercises controls over the other branches and is, in turn, controlled by them.
Cloture	A cloture (closure) motion sets a time limit on a debate, effectively ending it. In the US such motions can be employed to end filibusters.
Coalition	Where two or more parties combine to form a government.
Coat-tails effect	Where candidates from the same party as a popular presidential candidate are also swept into power on the crest of their popularity.
Codified constitution	Where the various rules under which a country is governed are drawn together in a single constitutional document that is both explicit and systematic.
Collective responsibility	The principle that Cabinet ministers must publicly support decisions taken collectively in Cabinet, or resign and make their criticisms from the back benches.
Common law	Law which is part of custom. Law built upon precedent (case law) established by judges.
Community Charge	Or 'Poll Tax'. The local tax on every resident adult, brought in to replace the rates in 1990. See also 'Council Tax'.
Concurrent powers	Powers held by federal and state governments jointly (e.g. the power to tax).
Conference committee	A committee consisting of House members and Senators, brought together with a view to reconciling the differences between the House and Senate versions of a bill.
Consensus politics	Where there is broad cross-party agreement on the necessary direction of policy.
Constitution	The fundamental rules governing the organisation of a state – particularly the distribution of powers between different state institutions and between the state and the people.

Core executive	The decision-making centre in British politics. Focused on the Prime Minister, Cabinet, top civil servants, Cabinet Office and the Prime Minister's Office.
Corporatism	Where economic interests (business and labour) are brought together formally within structures that allow them to jointly develop public policy. See also 'Tripartism'.
Council Tax	The property-based local tax brought in to replace the Community Charge in 1993. See also 'Community Charge'.
Cross-benchers	Members of the legislature (some Lords, for example) who are not aligned to a particular party.
Democratic deficit	Most commonly used in relation to the EU. Where key institutions (the Council of Ministers or the Commission, for example) are not directly accountable to citizens but wield enormous power over them.
Devolution	The delegation of power from central government to regional or local parliaments, assemblies or councils.
Divided government	Most commonly in the US. Where one party controls the White House and another controls part or all of congress. See also 'Gridlock'.
Due process	The constitutional right of US citizens to be protected from arbitrary government action.
Elective dictatorship (sometimes called Electoral Dictatorship)	A phrase commonly associated with Lord Hailsham, referring to the way in which, once elected, the head of the majority party in the Commons can do pretty well as they see fit until the next election.
EMU	European Monetary Union. The process leading to the introduction of the Euro.
Enumerated powers	Those powers explicitly granted to particular institutions, or assigned to federal or state governments, by the US Constitution.
Environmentalism	A political ideology that puts ideas such as sustainability and care for the environment at the centre of policy-making.
Europhiles	Those who are sympathetic towards closer European integration.
Europhobes	Those who oppose closer European integration, in some case calling for withdrawal from the EU.
Executive	One of the three branches of government. The executive makes government decisions and executes policy rather than legislating or adjudicating. See also 'Legislature' and 'Judiciary'.
Executive agencies	Semi-autonomous bodies charged with administering some aspects of government policy.
Executive agreement	In US politics. An agreement between the President and a foreign power that has the weight of a treaty without the need for Senate ratification.
Executive privilege	The right of a President to keep communications between himself and his advisors secret.
Fat cats	Wealthy party contributors or local power-brokers who once controlled the government of many US cities.
Filibuster	Where a politician (particularly a US Senator) talks at length, using up the available time on the floor and preventing a bill from being passed. 'Talking a bill to death.'
First past the post	Or 'simple plurality' system. An electoral system where a candidate need only secure the support of one voter more than their nearest rival in order to win.
Floating voters	Voters who exhibit low levels of party identification and are therefore liable to switch support between parties during the election campaign or between elections. Also called independent voters.
Founding Fathers	The representatives from the various states who gathered in Philadelphia in 1787 and drafted the US Constitution.
Franchise	The right to vote, as determined by various acts of parliament in Britain and state regulations and constitutional provisions in the US.
Freedom of information	The right of individuals to access government information and records. Enshrined by the Freedom of Information Act in the US, less clearly identified in Britain – even when the new British Freedom of Information Act finally comes into force.
Gender gap	A gap between the support given to certain candidates by women and the support given to the same range of candidates by men. Broadly speaking, the view that women have traditionally been more likely than men to vote Democrat in the US and Conservative in Britain.
Gerrymandering	The practice of moving electoral boundaries with a view to giving a party electoral advantage (for example, by excluding the supporters of an opposing party from a particular electoral district).
GOP	The Grand Old Party or Republican Party (founded in 1856).
Gridlock	Most commonly where a US President from one party is prevented form pursuing his policies by a Congress controlled partly or entirely by another party.
Honeymoon period	The period just following his inauguration, when a US President is normally given the benefit of the doubt by Congress, the public and the media.
Hundred days	A period during which a new President's administration is often judged as it attempts to push through its policies while support remains strong.
Ideology	A coherent system of ideas, beliefs and values applied to the organisation of politics.
Implied powers	In the US Constitution, those powers that Congress needs in order to carry out the roles given to it (enumerated) in the Constitution. Mostly emanating from the 'necessary and proper clause'.
Impeachment	Where the US House of Representatives formally accuses a member of the executive or the judiciary of misconduct. This normally leads to a trial that can in turn lead to the individual being removed from office.

Impoundment	The practice by which the President refuses to spend funds appropriated by Congress. Congress tried to limit this through the 1974 Budget Control and Impoundment Act.
Incumbent	The person already holding a particular office.
Independent regulatory commissions	In the US. Bodies set up by the government and charged with regulating predetermined areas of policy. For example, the Securities and Exchange Commission set up in 1934.
Independent voters	See 'Floating voters'.
Initiative	Where a predetermined number of electors sign a petition that puts a question on a ballot paper proposing new legislation. In short, a form of direct democracy allowing registered voters the right to initiate legislation.
Insider groups	Pressure groups that work very closely with politicians and top civil servants either at a local or a national level.
Interest groups (Sectional or Protectional Groups)	Pressure groups that represent the interests of a particular economic or occupational section of society. **NB: In the US the phrases 'interest groups' and 'pressure groups' are often used interchangeably.**
Item veto	The ability of an executive to strike out particular sections of a bill, whilst allowing the rest to become law. Sometimes called a 'line-item veto'.
Judicial review	In the US. The practice by which the courts can declare the actions of other branches of government (at state or federal government level) unconstitutional.
Judiciary	The branch of government concerned with enforcing or adjudicating the laws where disputes arise.
Junior ministers	In the UK. Ministers of state and parliamentary under-secretaries.
Keynesianism	An economic theory based upon the ideas of J M Keynes, essentially involving a mixed economy with some government intervention.
Kitchen cabinet	A small group of advisers that Presidents or Prime Ministers might draw around them. Term probably dates from US President Andrew Jackson's administration in the mid-nineteenth century.
Lame duck	A politician (normally a President) who has lost the election but remains in office – without real authority – until his successor is inaugurated.
Law	A rule or set or rules enforced by the courts.
Legislature	The law-making branch of government.
Legitimisation	The process of making something legitimate; for example, legitimising a policy by holding a referendum.
Liberal democracy	The western style of democracy incorporating free and fair elections and a belief in the importance of core rights and responsibilities.
Lobbyist	An individual who works on behalf of a pressure group and who aims to influence the legislative process.
Log-rolling	Where members of the legislature (normally in the US) trade support with one another to gain the passage of measures that will benefit them or their constituencies.
Mandarins	The very few senior civil servants who have a meaningful role in policy formulation through their regular meetings with ministers.
(Electoral) Mandate	The right of an elected government to carry into law those policies that formed the basis of its manifesto in the preceding election.
Manifesto	A document most commonly produced at the time of an election outlining the platform (i.e. the policies) on which that party is standing.
Michels' iron law	Michels' iron law of oligarchy holds that popular mass movements cannot not be truly democratic because they will always be controlled by a small guiding elite (an oligarchy).
Ministerial responsibility	The view that ministers are responsible for all that goes on in their departments regardless of their part in it and that they should resign where major infractions of procedure take place (so-called 'role responsibility'). Also, that there are certain codes of personal behaviour that ministers should observe while they remain in office (so-called 'personal responsibility').
Ministers	The 90 or so most senior government figures (Prime Minister, Cabinet, ministers of state and parliamentary under-secretaries).
Monetarism	An economic policy advocating minimal government intervention, beyond controlling money supply.
Neo-liberalism	Often associated with the New Right. A belief that the free market is the vehicle best suited to achieving sustainable economic growth and most able to provide for individual needs.
Neutrality	Or impartiality. One of the three principles upon which the British Civil Service is traditionally said to be based. The idea that civil servants should not allow their personal political beliefs to enter into their work, and that they should be able to serve a government of any political persuasion. See 'Anonymity' and 'Permanence'.
New Right	Politicians in the US and in Britain who adopted neo-liberal monetarist policies and, in the US especially, conservative social positions (anti-abortion, anti-gay etc.).
Next Steps	The name commonly used for the Ibbs Report (1988), which advocated the setting up of numerous executive agencies in order to improve efficiency (agencification).
Ombudsman	A 'people's friend' who investigates complaints of maladministration or injustice. In Britain, most commonly referring to the Parliamentary Commissioner for Administration.

Outsider groups	Pressure groups who do not have easy access to ministers and top civil servants. Often kept outside because of what they represent or the tactics that they adopt, but might also choose to be outside for ideological reasons.
PACs	In the US. Political Action Committees are organisations that channel funds from corporations and groups such as unions to candidates in elections.
Parliament Act	In 1911 the Parliament Act replaced the Lords' right to veto (kill) legislation with the power to delay bills for two years. At the same time, the Lords were effectively prevented from amending, vetoing or delaying money (e.g. tax) bills. The Parliament Act of 1949 reduced the power of delay to one parliamentary session.
Party	A political party is a grouping of people who share similar views and come together to seek power – most often by seeking election to political office.
Peak groups	Peak (or umbrella) organisations co-ordinate the efforts of a number of groups with common interests. For example, the TUC draws together various individual unions.
Permanence	One of the three principles upon which the British Civil Service is traditionally said to be based; civil servants remain in position regardless of the results of elections, often serving parties of different political persuasions. See 'Anonymity' and 'Neutrality'.
Pigeon-holing	In US politics. The process by which bills are essentially shelved and allowed to die, normally in committee.
Platform	In US politics. The policies upon which candidates stand in elections. Most commonly referring to the policies advanced by presidential candidates and formalised at their party's nominating convention.
Pluralism	Where power is fragmented and decisions are arrived through the open competition of groups representing different interests.
Pocket veto	In US Politics. Where a president can kill a bill by pocketing it, as long as the congressional session ends before the ten-day deadline for the President to sign or veto the bill passes.
Poll Tax	See 'Community Charge'.
Pork-barrelling	Where Congressmen add riders (amendments) to appropriations bills that secure funding for projects benefiting their constituents; thereby aiding their chances of re-election.
Precedent	Where a past decision or court judgement is taken as a guide for a one that is current.
Pressure groups	Groups with a shared interest or a common goal that seek to influence policy without normally wishing to become the government through elections.
Primary	An election held prior to the main (general) election in the US for the purpose of selecting a party's candidate for the main event.
Prime Minister	The head of the executive branch in the British government who presides over the Cabinet.
Prime-ministerial government	Advanced by politicians such as Richard Crossman and Tony Benn. A model of executive government that sees the Prime Minister as supremely powerful (presidential, even) and the Cabinet as increasingly irrelevant.
Private member's bill	A bill advanced by a backbencher, normally without government backing.
Privatisation	The process by which nationalised industries, services and assets are returned to the private sector.
Proportional representation	A collective term for electoral systems that seek to apportion seats to political parties in near proportion to votes won (either nationally or regionally).
Protectional or Protectionist groups	See 'Interest groups'.
Quangos	Quasi-autonomous non-governmental organisations. Created in order to allow certain services a greater degree of independence and impartiality. Sometimes criticised for a lack of accountability. Examples of such organisations include the Commission for Racial Equality (CRE)
Recall	A device by which registered voters in some US states can initiate a public vote with a view to removing an elected officer or politician from office over matters such as corruption or negligence.
Referendum	A government-initiated popular vote authorising or legitimising a predetermined course of action.
Reinforcement theory	The belief that the media, rather than changing minds, simply reinforces opinions that individuals already have.
Reserved powers	In US politics. The powers retained by the states under the Tenth Amendment to the Constitution.
Rider	An amendment to a bill that has nothing to do with the primary purpose of the original bill. Most commonly associated with 'pork-barrelling' (see above).
Royal prerogative	Powers held by the monarch but now, largely through convention, exercised by the Prime Minister. For example, the power to sign treaties.
Salisbury Doctrine	This doctrine dates from 1945 and is named after the then Conservative leader in the Lords, Lord Salisbury. The Salisbury Doctrine put in place the principle that the (unelected) Lords should not oppose government bills at second reading where the (elected) government had a clear mandate (through its manifesto commitments) to pass such measures. The doctrine acknowledged the potential problems caused by the inbuilt Conservative majority in the Lords at that time.
Sectional groups	See 'Interest groups'.
Select committees	Since 1979, UK departmental select committees have had the role of scrutinising the work of the various Government departments. Other non-departmental select committees are given a particular focus. The UK

Public Accounts Committee, for example, has the role of ensuring value for money in Government. In the US, select committees are normally set up to conduct specific investigations outside of the scope of existing standing committees.

Seniority system	In US politics. The system by which the top positions (particularly in congressional committees) were given to the individuals with the longest continuous length of service.
Separation of powers	The principle, advanced by writers such as Montesquieu, that the three branches of government (executive, legislature, judiciary) should be separated so as to avoid tyranny.
Simple plurality	See 'first past the post'.
Smoke-filled rooms	The rooms in which secret meetings were held to choose candidates and direct party policy. See also 'Fat cats'.
Soft money	Money which often ends up with candidates but is not regulated under the 1974 Campaign Finance Act because it is supposedly targeted at helping party organisation, voter registration drives and improving voter turnout on the day.
Sovereignty	The legitimate and exclusive right to exercise power within a given area.
Split-ticket voting	Where candidates vote for a variety of candidates from different parties for different offices. For example, a voter might favour a Republican President but a Democrat as a Senator.
Standing committees	In the UK, standing committees are formed to undertake detailed consideration of a bill after its second reading. In the US there are 34 standing committees (17 in the House, 17 in the Senate). They also have the role of working on specific areas of legislation.
State	The collective term for the formal institutions and bodies that exercise sovereign power within a given territory.
Statute law	A law passed by Parliament.
Subsidiarity	The principle that all decisions should be taken at the lowest possible tier of government. This principle was enshrined in the Maastricht Treaty.
Swing	The movement of voters' support (normally measured as a percentage) from one party to another.
Tabloids	Smaller format national daily and Sunday newspapers. For example, *The Sun*, *The Mirror* and the *News of the World*.
Tactical voting	Where an individual votes for a candidate who is not their preferred choice because the candidate they are voting for has a more realistic chance of defeating the candidate that they favour least.
Term limits	A legal restriction preventing the holder of an elected office from serving more than a pre-determined number of terms in office.
Think-tank	An organisation formed to develop public policy proposals and lobby for their incorporation into the Government's programme.
Ticket	In US politics. The collective term for a party's presidential and vice-presidential candidate.
Tribunals	Quasi-judicial bodies that aim to resolve conflicts between individuals or between individuals and public bodies without the need for lengthy and costly litigation.
Tripartism	A looser arrangement than corporatism. Where business interests, unions and government come together for consultation, particularly in areas where policy is of common concern.
Ultra vires	The doctrine by which public bodies (local authorities, for example) can only do that which they are authorised to do by Parliament. All else is beyond their authority.
Unitary state	A state where sovereignty resides with the central government.
Veto	In US politics. The power of the President to block legislation passed by Congress. Congress, in turn, can override the veto with a two-thirds majority in each chamber (House and Senate).
(Electoral) Volatility	Where the electorate is unpredictable and large numbers of voters make up their minds late in the election campaign and may change their minds during the campaign itself.
Wasps	Often used in discussion of US politics. Referring to White Anglo Saxon Protestants.
Welfare state	Where basic human needs are met by the state through tax revenues as opposed to individuals paying less tax and taking out private insurance to cover any needs that might arise.
Whips	Members of the legislature who are appointed by their party to ensure that other members of the party are aware of and vote in line with the party's position on key policies.
Write-in candidate	In the US. Where supporters of candidates whose names do not appear on the ballot can 'write in' the names of their favoured candidate in spaces provided.

Index

Bold type indicates main entries. Glossary pages are not included.